The Potato

How the Humble Spud
Rescued the Western World

The Potato

*How the
Humble Spud
Rescued the
Western World*

LARRY ZUCKERMAN

 FABER & FABER : BOSTON & LONDON

First published in the United States in 1998 by
Faber and Faber, Inc., 53 Shore Road, Winchester, MA 01890

Copyright © 1998 by Larry Zuckerman

Library of Congress Cataloging-in-Publication Data

Zuckerman, Larry.
    The potato : how the humble spud rescued
    the western world / Larry Zuckerman.
        p. cm.
    Includes bibliographical references (p.   ).
    ISBN 0-571-19951-8 (cloth)
    1. Potatoes—History.   2. Potatoes—Social aspects.
    3. Plants and history.   I. Title.
SB211.P8Z83 1998
641.3'521—dc21
                                                97-49107
                                                CIP

Sources for maps: Ireland, England, and France: Earle Wilbur
Dow, *Atlas of European History* (New York: Henry Holt & Co.,
1907). United States: Dixon Ryan Fox, *Harper's Atlas of
American History* (New York, London: Harper & Brothers,
1920). All maps courtesy of Map Collection and Cartographic
Information Services, University of Washington Libraries.

Jacket design by Ha Nguyen
Book design by Will Powers
Typesetting by Stanton Publication Services, Inc.
Illustration by Patricia Curtan
Printed in the United States of America

Contents

For Helene, who likes the ways I serve potatoes

Acknowledgments

Throughout my researching, writing, and preparing this book for publication, many people have put their knowledge and resources at my disposal for the asking. First on the list are the librarians at the University of Washington, who graciously granted me access to the materials I wanted, no matter how rare, and helped me get the most from them. They have earned my undying gratitude. Without them, this book would never have been written.

Whatever other sources I needed, the interlibrary loan staff of the Seattle Public Library hunted down, and so reliably that I came to see them as magicians who knew how to pull hard-to-find rabbits out of hats. To these untiring searchers, and to the many libraries unknown to me that loaned me books, go my thanks.

Dr. J. G. Hawkes, Professor Emeritus of the University of Birmingham, generously shared his expertise on the South American potato. William H. McNeill, Professor Emeritus of the University of Chicago, kindly read the manuscript and offered valuable suggestions. So did Professor Joseph Amato of Southwest State University, Minnesota, whose enthusiasm and advice warmed me deeply. To these three, whose comments have gone far to improve this book—but who are not responsible for any errors or interpretations I have made—I owe a large debt.

My editor at Faber & Faber, Claire Kelleher, has shown such wizardry with my words that I could swear she was watching me when I wrote them. To her, and to the staff at Faber & Faber, go my thanks.

Finally, I must thank Ed Knappman, my agent, who decided to take a chance on an unknown author. Without him, these pages would not now be in print; and without his wisdom and patience, the task of putting them there would have been much harder.

Introduction

I have always thought that the art of subsistence
should be the most serious occupation of man . . .
ANTOINE AUGUSTIN PARMENTIER

WHY THE POTATO?
I must have answered this question a hundred times since I began this book. In a way I don't mind, because explaining my ideas tells me how they sound. Besides, the *why* implies that my listener is intrigued, which means we have something in common.

The smile that accompanies the question, though, is another matter. That smile coaxes me to drop my pretenses and say what I'm really working on, that this potato thing can't possibly be serious. If it's history, the subject must be so dull that I'm afraid to say what it is. Or if I am writing about potatoes, I must be doing it as a stunt. As a historical subject, aren't potatoes a joke?

Actually, they're not. I admit that a title like *How the Humble Spud Rescued the Western World* invites laughter, but that's part of my story. Over the past four centuries, Western societies have feared, mistrusted, disdained, and laughed at the potato. Even today, we deride it, as in the phrases *couch potato* or *potato head*. The tuber is a homely thing to us, ordinary and beneath notice, similar to what the Spanish thought when they brought it home from

Peru in 1570. Yet from the late eighteenth century on, when the potato rose to power, it resolved or made more manageable so many problems of time, space, labor, land, fuel, and income that, without it, daily existence would have been unrecognizable. Consequently, describing how it achieved such influence reveals how Western domestic and social life functioned. On a grand scale, the potato affected population explosions and famines; on a small one, housework and the length people grew their thumbnails.

Starting with the Spanish Conquest and concentrating on the period 1770–1914, this book explains how the tuber outlasted two centuries of prejudice to become a social force in France, England, Ireland, and the United States. In panorama, the narrative sketches how people in these societies lived and died; at ground level, it shows how gardens, kitchens, and workplaces molded the outcome. To cite one example, Irish land laws forced the peasantry to treat the potato like investment capital, with disastrous results during the Great Famine of 1845–49. But without other, less obvious considerations—such as home design, pig raising, and use of the spade—that devastating equation might not have come to be.

Through the potato's eyes, therefore, the historian can see social dramas whose details unfold in unusual ways. Whether the scene is epic or private, whether the action revolves around the potato, or the tuber is a supporting player, its vantage shows how history played out. Moreover, how people saw the potato reflects how societies work, theirs and ours. Victorian attitudes toward Irish poverty sound like those voiced in present-day debates on welfare reform, while what nineteenth-century American women told their diaries about housework applies to today's arguments over gender roles. Less has changed than we think.

When I started my research, none of this had occurred to me. I was intending to follow a traditional approach, to trace the potato's sway over great events. Then, in Paris, I saw a statue that inspired me to consider another direction. The statue depicts Antoine Augustin Parmentier, a late eighteenth-century pharmacist and agriculturist. It's in the métro station that bears his name, which means electric carriages rumble and whine past a monument honoring a man from a horse-drawn age.

The Paris métro offers a few surprises in decor, but Parmentier's memorial is particularly unusual. I didn't expect to find, in a white-tiled tunnel agleam with light bulbs, a marble gentleman wearing knee breeches and a powdered wig. At first, I explained away this oddity by saying that urban monuments often contrast with their surroundings, but still, that didn't account for what the gentleman was doing. He was holding a basket of potatoes under his left arm and offering one to another man. To judge by the second man's rolled-up shirtsleeves and a tool held in one hand, he must be a farmer. His free hand was reaching for the potato, but dubiously. He kept his arms close to his body, and his face looked suspicious. It was as if he knew the lumpy thing wouldn't grow and wondered why this man was bothering him.

I was inclined to agree. Nothing grew in that concrete maze several stories below street level. The tacky mural behind the two statues—brown fields, blue sky, white birds—only underlined the point. Without intending to, the authorities who put up the monument had made their hero out to be a crank.

How perfect: It's just what Parmentier's contemporaries thought. In preaching the potato gospel, which he did for forty years, he fought constantly against the ridicule that faced his tuberous protégé: It was poisonous, unfit for human food, a social pariah. He argued, often in vain, that these beliefs had terrible consequences. Because the French peasantry trusted nothing but grain (wheat above all) and the bread and porridge that came from it, when grain failed, famine struck. The eighteenth century alone witnessed sixteen general outbreaks.

Looking at the farmer with the rolled-up sleeves, I wanted to know what would lead entire populations to risk starvation rather than grow a vegetable. Of course, those people later relented, sometimes within a generation. French provinces where the potato was virtually unknown ten or twenty years before the Revolution were supplying the nation within a decade or two after it. But I wanted to know how that happened, too, and how the turnabout affected daily life. Parmentier and his singular vocation intrigued me, but the dubious farmer engaged me even more, as did the woman or women who cooked for him. Food choices help define people, to themselves and others, and aren't made lightly. If millions of Europeans abandoned tradition for the potato at about the same time, they must have had compelling and perhaps similar reasons.

To find out what those reasons were, I delved into memoirs and public documents about farmers, travelers, factory workers, housewives—anybody who might have eaten, grown, or cooked the potato, or watched others doing it. This was a lot like ransacking haystacks for the proverbial needle. Not everybody thinks that what they or someone else eats is worth discussing. But if haystacks don't conceal needles, comparing the hay can be worthwhile. It led me to consider kitchens, especially what fuel people burned and what utensils they had. The house surrounding the kitchen was therefore worth knowing about, which in turn reflected standard of living. That included wages, which had to do with occupations. If farming was the occupation, then the potato's influence followed from land-tenure laws and agricultural habits. And so on.

These issues cross many disciplines and involve aspects of existence that, at first glance, seem to have little or nothing to do with a vegetable. Nevertheless, they're related. Marriage customs, attitudes toward poverty and the poor, mortality rates, the length of factory shifts, land hunger—these are only some of life's facets that the potato story uncovers. Consequently, though a few well-known historical figures like Parmentier appear in these pages, most of the characters are represented by the other statue in the métro memorial.

Little firsthand writing survives about these people, far less than about the wealthy or powerful. Much comes from curious onlookers, which puts a spin on the reporting. That should remind the historian, if nothing else does, that it's impossible to reduce life to one universal experience. Writing social history is like standing atop a mountain and trying to capture the valley in a single snapshot. However breathtaking the picture, it must be incomplete or unclear, not to say distorted. In displaying my snapshot, I realize that public surveys are skewed, and that not every farmer who could write a diary, did. Then, too, those who didn't might have been more accurate observers. Nevertheless, I think that my picture reveals patterns. Whether another trip up the mountain will show them in a different light, time will tell.

A word about the scope of this book. Four countries is a narrow definition of the Western world, and since most of the narrative takes place in Ireland before 1850 and in England until 1914, my emphasis is narrower still. I could have chosen a longer time frame—the potato played a crucial role in the world wars, for example—but the social ideas and changes that are my focus appeared well before then. To have continued would have risked repetition and, in the case of Ireland and the Great Famine, an anticlimax. Similarly, I could have applied my ideas to the Low Countries, Poland, Russia, Scandinavia, and the German-speaking lands, where the potato again competed with grain, except often with rye, not wheat. But in writing this book, I wished to expound a theory, not prove it in every instance. If someone else takes it up regarding places I've omitted, I'll be pleased.

Besides, perhaps the most important part of research is knowing when to stop. I take my cue from the late Redcliffe N. Salaman, whose classic *History and Social Influence of the Potato* gave me much to think about. Having studied the potato for forty years, Salaman remarked that he had left more questions unsolved than anyone had ever thought existed. He hadn't planned to spend forty years on the potato; neither do I. As he said, people question your sanity if you devote your life to "so banal a subject."

My readers, I hope, will come away recognizing that the potato is anything but banal. If they believe in my sanity too, so much the better.

The Potato

How the Humble Spud
Rescued the Western World

1 Treasure of the Andes

... a scarcely innocent underground stem
of one of a tribe set aside for evil.
JOHN RUSKIN

JUST BEFORE THE FIRST WORLD WAR, an American explorer traveling in Peru witnessed an ancient agricultural ceremony. The celebrants were Quecha Indians, descendants of the Incas. The place was a hillside potato field near La Raya, a town 14,500 feet above sea level. Day had just dawned, and the air was bitter cold.

The field had been marked into squares, separated by furrows fifteen feet apart. A long line of men stood by, waiting, their ponchos removed to free their limbs. Each man held a long-handled spade to which footrests had been lashed. Facing each pair of men was a woman or girl who remained fully covered, as the explorer imagined that modesty required. At a signal, the men shouted and leaped forward in unison, driving their spades into the soil. Once these "plows" had broken the turf, the women and girls turned the loose clods over by hand, and the men worked their way across the marked field.

The American explorer noted that though plowing was "hard and painful" work, the community effort made the task seem joyous. Everyone pitched in, and those who couldn't keep up were teased. This spirit impressed the explorer, yet something puzzled him. The Peruvian landowner supervising the work wore European clothes and was, he remarked, "evidently a man of means and intelligence." A railroad even ran through the neighborhood. Nevertheless, Western progress hadn't changed agricultural life at La Raya. The explorer saw no modern tools and was told that the Indians would use only those their ancestors had possessed. He guessed, then, that this kind of plowing went back before the Spanish Conquest.

He couldn't have known what an understatement that was. Some scientists now believe that wild potatoes grew on the Chilean coast thirteen thousand years ago, an era before any human agriculture. The profusion of wild species on the altiplano, as the central Andean highlands are called, suggests that the plant traveled upland soon afterward. Granted, *soon* is a relative term in a thirteen-millennium span, and humans didn't cultivate the new plant right away, but its age as a domesticate is still very impressive. No later than seven thousand years ago, Andean peoples farmed potatoes, possibly on the northern Bolivian altiplano between Lakes Titicaca and Poopó. Seven thousand years predates the oldest known cities in Mesopotamia. The Inca empire, if it existed today, would be about seven hundred.

A Spanish woodcut from the late sixteenth or early seventeenth century shows the Incas plowing in much the way the American explorer saw. In the woodcut scene, work has stopped for a refreshment break. While the laborers lean on their spades or crouch on the ground, a woman brings them *chicha*, or corn beer. The seventeenth-century Jesuit missionary Bernabe Cobo described plowing as a festive occasion, like a wedding, with people chanting rhythmically to the rising and falling *tacllas*, the spades with footrests. No doubt the *chicha* satisfied parched throats and lent force to the singing, which, Cobo said, could usually be heard a couple of miles away. But however antique these traditions seemed to the Spanish—or to the twentieth-century scientist—their true age must be far greater. Even if the Incas designed the first *taclla*, they couldn't have been the first Andean highland people to plow like that. The spade is ideally suited to the altiplano's topography, which suggests the potato has been raised that way for thousands of years.

What the Spanish also didn't realize when they ran across the potato, no later than 1537 but likely four years earlier, was what tremendous wealth and power they had found. They aren't entirely to blame, because two centuries passed before the West exploited the potato's gifts to any significant extent, and nearly two more centuries elapsed before science could even explain what some of them were. Nevertheless, the Spanish should have paid more attention, because proof of the tuber's remarkable character was all around them.

First, anything that lives on the altiplano, windswept valleys and plateaus that lie at least twelve thousand feet above sea level, has to be hardy and tenacious. This is no less true for plants than for humans. The thin atmosphere lets the daytime sun radiate unimpeded but provides no insulation at night, causing radical temperature swings (highs of perhaps 62°F, lows of freezing or less) within a twenty-four-hour period. Not only does this constantly interrupt a plant's physiological processes, it means that frost may occur in any season, the likelihood increasing with higher altitude. Half the year, little or no useful precipitation falls, and a shifting weather pattern may bring local drought for a year or more. Under such conditions, wheat, corn, and barley stand almost no chance of reaching maturity. Few trees grow, and most vegetation is close-lying and dwarflike.

But the potato thrives. Its starchy tubers feed the plant during all but the most severe frosts, and during droughts up to seven and a half months. The hardiest species can cope with life at fifteen thousand feet, probably a world record for food crops. The potato grows in even the poorest soils and in every conceivable habitat, a precious benefit on the altiplano, where soils are thin and lack nutrients more common at lower altitudes. The domesticated potato also has more wild relatives, 230, than any other cultivated plant, which allowed the early highland peoples to select varieties that fit local conditions. Similarly, since the mid–nineteenth century, Western plant breeders have profited from this array by introducing disease- and pest-resistant South American strains into European and North American stock.

For good reason, the potato was the center of the altiplano diet. Arable land was scarce, generally arranged in narrow terraces from which farmers had to coax high yields without plows or draft animals. The potato met that need by bearing many tubers to a plant, tended only by a spade and human hands. Keeping and cooking food were also difficult, because fuel was even scarcer than land, and frost could ruin anything in storage. Potatoes, containing about 80 percent water, were particularly susceptible, but the highland peoples turned that to advantage. They let part of the harvest freeze overnight and squeezed the water out to obtain a freeze-dried preparation called *chuño*. Today, we think of fast-food potatoes as french fries, but *chuño*, whose recipe is at least several thousand years old, softened rapidly in boiling water and was quickly ready to eat. Unused, *chuño* stored in a sealed room for up to ten years, excellent insurance against famine. In addition, once on the table, the tuber gave superb value. Science now knows that the potato supplies all vital nutrients—including, in its fresh form, vitamin C—except calcium and vitamins A and D. One acre's worth provides more than ten people with their annual energy and protein needs, something that can't be said of corn, wheat, rice, or soybeans.

This was what the Spanish brought home around 1570, waiting more than thirty years after they first happened on it. At that, the potato probably crossed the Atlantic as an afterthought, a curio stuffed in a pocket. Three years later, it began its European career, feeding patients in a Seville hospital. But had the Spanish only known it, the curio offered a map to Europe's future, because in time, the potato would leave much the same mark as it had in the Andes. It would yield a huge amount of food on little arable land and in thin soils, a boon to land-hungry peasants and a safeguard against famine. Since a spade was the only tool necessary, wage-laborers and even urban workers would raise potatoes in their gardens. (Even the spades would sometimes look like the *taclla*, and the planting beds resemble those at La Raya.) With milk or dairy products to furnish calcium and vitamins A and D, the potato would anchor a nutritionally complete diet that many Europeans would have lacked otherwise. The tuber would also prevent scurvy, benefiting populations that had little or no access to fruit. Finally, the potato would supply cheap, quick meals requiring little fuel or equipment—fast food again—qualities that accommodated lower-class kitchens especially.

However, in European eyes, many of these advantages were the potato's undoing, because it became known as food for the poor. In this case, the Conquistadores were partly to blame, though not because of their general reputation as loot-hungry brigands, blind to anything but overt wealth. Blind they were, but it's hard to imagine anyone in 1570 predicting that the world's annual potato harvest, today valued at more than $100 billion, would be a much richer haul than all the gold and silver the Spanish could take from South America. The very idea would have made any European laugh, even in the late eighteenth century, when the tuber's potential became more apparent. Rather, the Spanish appraisal of the potato wasn't a missed investment as much as it was social prejudice. They decided that if their new world underlings relied on the tuber, especially to replace bread, it must be inferior.

The prejudice most often emerged indirectly, because, though the new world's Spanish chroniclers rarely mentioned the potato, they usually did so to praise it. One called potatoes "a very good food," whose insides were like boiled chestnuts; another said they were "floury roots of good flavour." Only Bernabe Cobo, who thought the Peruvians would eat anything if it didn't hurt them, including "a thousand different kinds of repulsive vermin," dissented. He called potatoes one of several "very ordinary" foods that replaced bread—except when Spanish colonial women prepared them, and "the most delicious fritters" resulted.

Despite the potato's proven qualities, the general view was that it belonged to the conquered peoples, and they could keep it. Pedro de Cieza de

Leon, the most perceptive and sensitive Spanish observer, whose *Chronicle of Peru* (1553) was widely read, wrote how people "would go hungry if it were not for these dried potatoes," meaning *chuño*. Cieza approved of how the Inca state had collected *chuño* as tribute to secure itself against famine. Yet all his countrymen did with that knowledge was to use it against their subjects. When the Spanish discovered the fabulously rich Potosí silver lode in 1545, their merchants bought up *chuño* and resold it to the miners, who were little more than slaves. Cieza said many Spaniards made fortunes that way and went home prosperous men. One wonders whether they would have dared exploit a Spanish staple so brutally, but the substance of their actions and the timing reflect a certain contempt. Cieza was writing seventeen years before the potato reached Spain, which means that the merchants had no thought to bring the secret of their wealth back with them. *Chuño* was slaves' rations, and both it and the vegetable it came from were unfit for export.

Which explains why, seven decades after the Spanish saw their first potato and three after it had crossed the ocean, one chronicler of colonial life could call it "a delicacy to the Indians and a dainty dish even for the Spaniards." Not only was it newsworthy that the two peoples could share the same food, the comment implies that in Spain, the potato was still exotic and of doubtful worth. Almost thirty years later, a different historian recorded a similar remark. If Spanish readers needed to be repeatedly reminded that the tuber was good food, little had changed in nearly a century since the explorers stumbled on it.

A blanket disdain for indigenous foods doesn't explain the delay, because Spain was avid to adopt a different new world root. The sweet potato, a vine in the morning glory family, returned to Spain right away with Columbus, after his landfall at Haiti. From 1493 on, Spanish ships bound for Europe from Haiti and other points west carried sweet potatoes in their holds. A variety found in Darien (Panama) was brought to Hispaniola in 1508 and within eight years, Spain. King Ferdinand and Queen Isabella may have liked them enough to have had them planted in their court gardens. Their son-in-law, Henry VIII of England, liked them too, but for a reason they would have deplored: Supposedly, he thought the plant was an aphrodisiac.

If Henry believed that, he wasn't the only European who did, because the myth lasted far longer than his stormy marriages. The "venerous roots" from Spain supplied English banquets decades after the king's death, a fashion that Shakespeare's pen noted before the sixteenth century was out. In *The Merry Wives of Windsor*, Sir John Falstaff, thinking he is about to bed two women at once, cries, "Let the sky rain potatoes"—and the date the play was written makes clear he's referring to the sweet kind.

Europe, and Spain in particular, chose the sweet potato over the Andean for social reasons. First, the all-important question of origin favored the sweet potato. It came from the lush Caribbean islands and the Central American isthmus, whereas the altiplano was a rude place whose barrenness aroused comment from every Spanish chronicler. The Spanish range most like it, the Pyrenees, has always been a poor region. Then, too, the sweet potato was a rich person's food because Spain was the only country whose climate supported its cultivation. Rareness and expense, besides that quality Henry VIII appreciated, lent it chic. Also, "the most delicate root that may be eaten," as the sixteenth-century English mariner and slave trader John Hawkins called it, suited European taste. Sweet novelties like vanilla and chocolate were just then coming into vogue. Cooks built meals around "sundry outlandish confections, altogether seasoned with sugar"—tarts, gingerbread, marzipan, jellies, conserves, and the like. Henry ate his sweet potatoes in heavily spiced and sugared pies, a fashion that survived at least until the 1680s.

The Andean potato had no patrons, no advocates, and no special powers (though its rival's occult reputation rubbed off on it through confusion). Rather, the Andean tuber reached Europe with a fateful verdict against it: *Only the wretched eat this root.* But if the Spanish handed down this judgment, other societies accepted and enlarged on it. Vestiges remain today. In 1991 the United States ranked fourth among the world's potato producers, and for many Americans, dinner isn't dinner without spuds. Yet ethnic jokes about potato-eating peoples remain current, as do mocking phrases like *couch potato* or *potato head*, and such expressions aren't unique to English. The French say that a sluggard has "potato blood," or that someone with two left feet "dances like a sack of potatoes." Such jokes are much tamer than references to slaves or amazement that upper and lower classes could share the same food. Nevertheless, the commentary comes from a common source, and its beginnings are four centuries old.

By 1600, after spending three decades in Europe, the potato had entered Spain, Italy, Austria, Belgium, Holland, France, Switzerland, England, Germany, and most likely Portugal and Ireland. But that impressive-sounding itinerary is deceptive, because in none of these eleven places had the wandering tuber found a true home. It was strictly a garden crop, unworthy of field cultivation alongside grains. Almost the only people who grew it were botanists, often not even in their own gardens, but those of their noble or wealthy patrons. Had these scientists not shared the tuber among themselves, it would have crossed fewer borders and left its imprint even later than it did. How ironic that a vegetable destined to mold and sustain lower-class life owed its initial presence to privileged caretakers. But where the botanists saw an intriguing plant, the people who needed it most, Europe's hungry peasantries, saw evil and refused to touch it.

This uncommon hatred began with the plant itself. As botanists described it, the potato of 1600 was a beautiful but savage-looking thing about the size of a small bush. Its grooved, thick, slightly hairy stems grew anywhere from two or three feet tall to twice that height and shot out profuse foliage of pale green leaves. Within three months of spring planting, the branches split into two pedicels apiece, each supporting a few flowers that released a rich perfume. The blossoms, a striking bluish purple with crimson stamens, formed angular, five-sided stars about an inch across. As the plant matured, the flowers gave way to clusters of ridged, green berries, which turned either black or white and contained many flat, round seeds.

Meanwhile, mysterious workings were happening below ground. The main root had branched into a whitish network to which long, thick fibers were attached. By autumn, the fibers had sprouted tubers, sometimes fifty or more to a plant, but the biggest weighed no more than an ounce or two. All had rough skins, red or yellowish, and pitted with deepset eyes. The smallest were mere nodules. They had a thin white covering and looked as if they hadn't ripened. But large or small, the tubers possessed a strange power: If replanted, they sprouted.

To the layperson, all this was terrifying. For one thing, every other edible plant reproduced by means of seeds, not grotesque, misshapen tubers. Surely, the devil crafted that magic. Then there were the stems, which looked like the tomato's; the flowers, which took after the eggplant's; and the berries, which resembled the mandrake's and the deadly nightshade's. That composite sketch accused the potato of diabolic associations, and in 1596, the Swiss botanist Gaspard Bauhin confirmed them by naming it *Solanum tuberosum*. *Solanum* is the eggplant genus—Bauhin was classifying by structure—but it was also a frightening word. It belongs to the family Solanaceae, the nightshades, whose members include, besides the tomato, eggplant, and sweet pepper, the deadly nightshade, mandrake, tobacco, and henbane. The name *Solanum* is believed to derive from the Latin *solamen*, or "quieting." If so, the meaning was apt. The potato's more infamous siblings were poisons, narcotics, and witches' spells.

The mandrake was all three. Its forked root recalled a human shape and so accorded it mysterious powers, including the ability to help women conceive. The idea is at least as old as the book of Genesis, which recounts how Rachel asks Leah for mandrake roots to cure her barrenness. By the seventeenth century, the mandrake still had uses in women's medicine, reputedly hastening menstruation and expelling a stillborn child. But the plant was most renowned as a dangerous soporific. Shakespeare has Iago rank it among "the drowsy syrups of the world"; the herbalists agreed.

As for henbane and the deadly nightshade (or belladonna), they were noted poisons. Some people smoked henbane instead of tobacco, a substitution that made them giddy or put them in a stupor "but to little profit." Henbane and the deadly nightshade did find use in ointments. But the English herbalist John Parkinson, among many, pleaded for "heede and care" so that "children and others" wouldn't eat nightshade berries, "least you shall see the lamentable effects it worketh." What was more, the nightshade grew as tall as the potato, and other resemblances were well known. Most people didn't buy or read herbals, but that simply meant that if it took a trained eye to distinguish between the two plants, a prudent person would avoid both.

Ironically, modern science has shown that Europeans were right to approach the tuber with caution. Potatoes, like at least 350 Solanaceae, produce steroidal alkaloids whose properties affect members of every major taxonomic group from microbes to humans. The effect can cut two ways, a fact that medicine has exploited, in China as well as the West. Even henbane and the deadly nightshade have their uses, yielding hyoscyamine, from which the antispasmodic atropine is derived. How steroidal alkaloids behave in nature is only partly understood, but they seem to repel predators, a trait that geneticists are trying to harness. Nicotine, for instance, may deter certain insects from eating tobacco leaves. Solanine, the potato's alkaloid, may protect tubers and foliage.

However, solanine is also toxic to humans. Healthy tubers cause no harm, but eating enough damaged or diseased potatoes can make a person ill. Because solanine concentrates in potato skins, careful peeling and trimming are generally all that even a greenish tuber, one that has been exposed to too much sunlight, needs.* Nevertheless, the hesitation to consume the

---

* The University of California's *Berkeley Wellness Letter* advises buying undamaged tubers, storing them in a cool, dark place, and using them within two or three weeks. Trim spots or blemishes, the newsletter says, gouge out sprouts, and peel a greenish skin. (Other peels are nutritious and best left intact.) A soft or well-sprouted tuber shouldn't be eaten, nor should a cooked potato that tastes bitter.

nightshade potato wasn't wholly misplaced. It has even been suggested that in eighteenth-century France, where certain kinds were said to taste bitter, solanine was the cause.

But if seventeenth-century Europeans followed any kind of logic in fearing the potato, they abandoned it in judging other nightshades. The tomato caused hesitation, but neither the eggplant nor the sweet pepper conjured up special terrors. Tobacco, arguably the most noxious nightshade that wasn't an outright poison, reached Europe about the time the potato did but won favor almost immediately. It, too, grew purplish blue flowers like the belladonna's, and its harsh character was obvious. "'Tis one of Natures Extreams," remarked Thomas Tryon in *The Way to Health* in 1691. He added that only continual use could "destroy its poysonous Qualities" or inure anyone to them. Other English herbalists praised tobacco as an expectorant or, in liquid preparation, as a way of killing parasites and head lice. It also, so experts said, cured deafness if placed in the ears, and eased headaches, toothaches, and kidney stones.

Perhaps tobacco escaped the nightshade curse because smoking and taking snuff were expensive leisure activities, and potatoes were cheap and lower class. Still, even after harder truths about tobacco were generally acknowledged, no sermons or medical advice could harm its reputation. Conversely, no publicity campaign or medical testimony could coax people to eat potatoes.

The tuber even suffered from comparison with the wicked weed. As late as 1869, the eminent art critic and social theorist John Ruskin called the potato the "scarcely innocent underground stem of one of a tribe set aside for evil." His dislike centered on tobacco, the "worst natural curse of modern civilization" because it encouraged idleness. Many Victorians held that sin against the potato, but Ruskin, known otherwise for progressive views, never got that far. The tuber offended him merely for its corrupt siblings.

Doubtless unwittingly, Ruskin singled out what had plagued the potato since its European debut. The "underground stem" was, in plain language, a root, and in sixteenth- and seventeenth-century Europe, root vegetables were scarcely innocent. They were said to prompt women to menstruate or lactate, and men to produce sperm. Not every herbalist ascribed the same properties to each root, though almost all said that roots provoked lust. The radish, the onion, the leek, the skirret (which resembled the carrot), the turnip, the parsnip, and the sweet potato were all given this ability. This explains why Henry VIII's taste for sweet potatoes wasn't just a royal whim.

Roots also upset the body, sending it into imbalance and therefore causing illness. The onion and leek, for instance, drew strong cautions. When Tryon said that onions sent poisonous fumes to the head, his warning was only one of a kind. Mid-seventeenth-century herbalists cautioned that pregnant women might give birth to lunatics if they ate too much "vaporous food," meaning onions or beans, or that the child might have a poor memory. Among the general population, such food was said to cause headaches and dull the senses. This was because the plants polluted the body. They increased the "evil blood," as did garlic, which would "offend the Brain" if used with indiscretion.

This was significant, because fevers and infectious diseases were thought to result from inflamed blood. If roots corrupted blood, it was only logical to say that they spread infectious disease. And around 1620 a rumor arose, reported of France, in England, and probably elsewhere, that potatoes caused leprosy. Why people fastened on "leprosy," a term the seventeenth century used for various skin diseases, is a mystery, unless the rough-skinned tuber evoked their symptoms. But even herbalists who reasoned that way about appearance and disease asserted that plants would cure the ailments or afflicted body parts they resembled, not cause the trouble. Besides, other roots prompted no such rumors—surely not the sweet potato, food of the rich.

All plagues have lower-class associations, but leprosy has always elicited something particularly untouchable or base, as the meaning of *leper* in common usage suggests. Whether the seventeenth century thought the vegetable suited the disease or the disease suited the vegetable didn't matter. The potato, tainted by affiliation, was fast becoming a leper itself. Accordingly, for more than two centuries, Europeans who adopted it were making a class statement about themselves, despite—and at times because of—the social and economic advantages they gained from it.

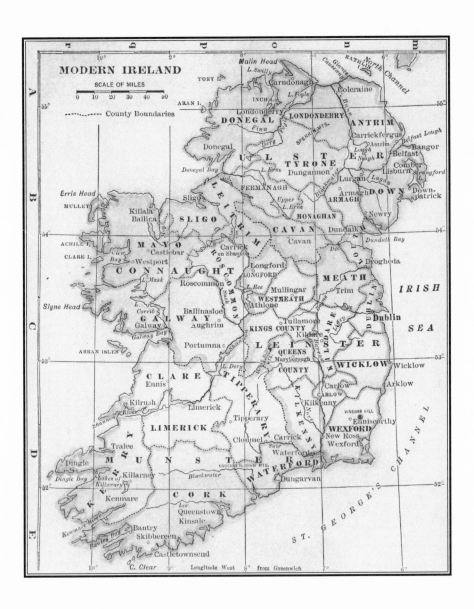

MODERN IRELAND

SCALE OF MILES

0   10   20   30   40   50

--------- County Boundaries

2   The Solace of Miserable Mortals

Sauce of the poor man—a little potato with the big one.
IRISH SAYING

No European nation has had a longer, more intimate partnership with the potato than Ireland. The first Europeans to accept it as a field crop in the seventeenth century, the Irish were also the first to embrace it as a staple, in the eighteenth. The potato emerged in Ireland partly because it suited the soil, climate, and living conditions remarkably well, though that was also somewhat true of other countries at later times. But what set Ireland apart was the way the peasantry seized on the potato as a safeguard, however meager, against the tandem social plagues of unemployment, poverty, overpopulation, and land hunger. By 1780 those afflictions had helped push the tuber to dominance.

But the dominance did not result purely from the need to survive. Rather, the potato was universally liked. Why that should have happened among people reputed to be superstitious has never been explained. After all, they were willing to trust their eyes when their European neighbors were not. Again, this trust probably arose in Ireland because the evidence of the potato's soundness and fit was so overwhelming. But whatever the reason, rich and poor alike willingly ate praties, as they called them, without the shame or fear that made the tuber a pariah elsewhere.

Nevertheless, even in Ireland, it became a social marker of sorts. Those who could afford to put other things on their tables looked down on those who couldn't. The "sauce of the poor man," went a saying, is "a little potato [eaten] with the big one."

It was these Irish, the generations of poor whose only sauce was potatoes, who symbolized Ireland to the world. The traveler Philip Luckombe wrote in 1780 that in his native England even "the meanest cottager is better fed, better lodged, and better dressed, than the most opulent farmers" in Ireland. He added that the poor Irish enjoyed nothing like "what our peasants reckon the comforts of life," knowing "no luxury but in deep potation of aqua vitae [alcohol]." However gross the comparison, it fit what the eighteenth century expected of the poor, particularly of the Irish. It was also assumed that the poor had many children, one expectation the Irish lived up to. Visiting the country in the mid-1770s, the English agriculturist Arthur Young said even "the most inattentive observer" could see the population was large. Young, sympathetic to the Irish, found nothing wrong with that. Other Englishmen thought differently, whether from hatred of Ireland's Catholicism or the threat of a large, unfriendly population, or because of fears of poor people in general.

The potato was therefore implicated in both Ireland's poverty and its population explosion. This was easy to say because, for many Irish, the pratie held the balance between sustenance and starvation. Even beyond that thin margin, the tuber pervaded social and domestic life until it defined them. With time it affected everything from housekeeping to attitudes toward marriage to the length people grew their thumbnails. Outsiders who saw this unheard-of bond to a vegetable wrote as if the potato *were* Ireland, and that to appraise the country without appraising its chief food was impossible. They were right.

No one knows how the potato reached Ireland. Legend says that in the 1590s, Sir Walter Raleigh brought it to an estate he owned at Youghal, county Cork. The story goes that he gave tubers to his gardener, who planted them without knowing what they were, and who mistakenly ate the berries from the stalks, not realizing where the edible part was. If so, Raleigh had gotten these tubers in England, where botanists had received them around 1590, but not from South America. (Unfortunately, the romantic tale that either he or Sir Francis Drake or both introduced the potato to Europe is a fable born of the Elizabethan imagination. Yet the story keeps reappearing; in 1991 *Newsweek* reported the Drake legend as fact.) But there is no proof Raleigh brought potatoes to Ireland, and an unknown Spanish sailor may have been responsible instead.

In any case, the potato first surfaced as a field crop in the 1640s in county Wicklow, ironically thanks to English immigrants who liked the way it suited the Irish climate. The new plant won favor but not instant preference. Oats remained the staple, both in Gaelic Ireland and in the so-called Anglo-Norman areas, most of whose inhabitants traced their ancestry to Britain. The Gaelic Irish typically ate oats as porridge, but they sometimes mixed the grain with butter and roasted it on the hearth. Butter and dairying figured heavily in Irish life. Butter, whey, and curds made up the summer diet, before the oat harvest in autumn. Come autumn, the Gaelic Irish buried tubs of butter to tide them over the winter and early spring, months when their cows couldn't graze. This practice lasted centuries. As late as 1802 in county Tyrone's remotest corners, a proverb went that you lived on buttermilk in summer, the butter in winter.

The oat-butter diet's major weakness had to do with winter scarcity. If the autumn oat harvest fell short, the Irish had little else on which to survive the lean months. However, with another food in the larder to last the winter, life would be more secure. The potato was such a food, which was probably why it graduated from garden to field in the first place. Evidence suggests that several times during the 1660s and 1670s, the potato had already become a backup during shortages, affording famine relief in certain places where grain harvests had failed.

In other countries and even in parts of Ireland, farmers saw no need for the potato as a fallback. One reason was bread, the traditional dietary mainstay. Gaelic Ireland ate little bread, a habit that began to change only toward the end of the seventeenth century, and even then, not greatly. Where the purest wheaten bread inspired fierce loyalty in England and France, in Anglo-Norman Ireland, wheat held no special power; Irish bread was usually made of oats or mixed cereals. Even by 1809 wheaten bread was scarce in Ireland's northern counties, having appeared only lately, and only in wealthier homes. (The famed Irish soda bread became common only after the mid–nineteenth century.) Still, bread was bread, and Anglo-Norman reliance on it prevented the potato from taking hold more quickly. So did peas and beans, which ripened early and kept well when dried. Bere, or winter barley, was important too, because it matured in July before any other cereal did, or potatoes, for that matter.

However, Ireland's physical and social environment was so primed for the potato, and the tuber offered so many blessings, that it couldn't stay in the background forever. The wet climate, for one, was greatly responsible. This sounds odd, given that the plant came from the altiplano, but potatoes thrive on rain, of which Ireland gets plenty. The west receives sixty inches yearly, the southwest coast as much as eighty, most coming during winter and autumn. But the air can be moist in any season, as visitors have learned to their dismay, with wet leather refusing to dry and "waterproof cloaks" being somewhat less than advertised. Fittingly, the Irish language has specific words to describe dew, kinds of drizzle, medium rain, heavy rain, downpour, pelting rain, wet weather, and wet weather that may cause flooding.

The water-loving potato not only benefited from the climate but withstood it when other crops didn't. Eighteenth-century food shortages often resulted from intense rain, more likely to injure grain stalks growing aboveground than tubers beneath. The same kind of protection helped during seventeenth-century revolts and invasions, or eighteenth-century brigandage. Where grain and livestock made easy pillaging, potatoes were harder to destroy.

For reasons undiscovered until the present century, the weather also safeguarded the potato's health. Despite the lethal blight that brought on the Great Famine of 1845–49, Ireland's habitat shielded the potato. The country's first serious, sustained outbreak of potato disease—"taint," or dry rot—didn't occur until the 1830s. Before then, the most talked-about European potato disease was "curl," a scourge that arrived from North America around 1764. Curl is a viral malady that distorts and stunts foliage and tubers, reducing yields by 75 percent or more and causing the surviving tubers to dwarf. None of this takes place, however, without the help of the aphid that carries the virus, and there the Irish climate intervenes. Rain and strong prevailing winds—the Irish language has many words for those too—keep the pest at bay. As a result, when curl began ravaging England in the 1770s and threatened to end potato cultivation there, Ireland escaped mostly untouched.

Ireland's habitat favors the potato in other ways too. In western Ireland particularly, thanks to the Gulf Stream, winter and spring are mild for a northern latitude. An early nineteenth-century writer noted how snow rarely occurred, and frost only three or four times a winter, seldom for long stretches. Only once every ten or twelve years, he said, did a river freeze over. Irish summers are usually cool and moderate, perfect potato weather, with July temperatures averaging 53°F, except in the southeast, where they are 60°F. August is as warm as July, while September, the month of the autumnal equinox, is as mild as June, the time of the summer solstice. Consequently, the growing season is long, steadily mild, and late. By contrast, Aroostook County, Maine, is five degrees latitude south of Cork, yet the potato-growing season is only seventy-five days. Farmers sometimes have to bulldoze the snow off their fields before spring planting.

As it happened, Ireland's mildness particularly favored the early European potato, which grew foliage and flowers aplenty when daylight was long but no tubers until daylight shortened to twelve hours. The altiplano, lying between the equator and the Tropic of Capricorn, regularly provided such days, but northern Europe didn't. That was why contemporary botanists described such a florid, wild-looking plant; it spent the summer bursting with branches but didn't get down to business until late autumn. Spain, Italy, and southern France also provided mild, frost-free autumns, but the potato attracted little support there.

Over the centuries, the European plant evolved to permit earlier harvests, but the true early bearers belonged to a different, long-day subspecies. Northern Europe could have used long-day cultivars (a cultivar is a variety originating as a domesticate), but breeders didn't oblige until the 1850s. Consequently, when the tuber reached northern Europe, Ireland was the nation best suited to it. By the 1680s, the only other places to see it leave the garden were Flanders, the German Palatinate, the eastern French provinces of Franche-Comté and Vosges, and, possibly, parts of northwest England.

However, if the Irish climate seldom turned as cold as Maine's, fuel considerations were nevertheless important, in themselves and concerning the potato's role in the kitchen. The pervasive damp was nasty enough to make staying warm a prime creature comfort, probably the one the Irish ranked second, after a full stomach. Since fuel was plentiful and cheap, whereas cloth and money to buy it were scarce, Irish peasants preferred to keep a constant fire burning and skimp on clothes. The custom drew comment in both the eighteenth and nineteenth centuries. With characteristic reasoning, Young praised the Irish for taking greater pains to feed their children than clothe them, the happy opposite, he said, of English practice. But an unnamed author writing in the prestigious *Edinburgh Review* in 1822 turned this argument upside down. The Irish were "content to vegetate in rags and wretchedness," this writer said, "provided they are able to obtain a sufficient supply of potatoes." That was the view most outsiders had. Even government examiners, normally an impassive group, raised their eyebrows when confronting evidence of a ragged population. A government panel in 1836 asked Galway witnesses what the yearly expenditure was on clothes, only to be told "it would be fairer to ask what was the *five yearly* expenditure on clothes." The examiners supplied the italics.

Ireland was lucky to have a cheap, plentiful fuel supply, because there was hardly any wood. Starting in the early seventeenth century, Irish forests had been cut down and sold to make casks. Trade was brisk and profits high, but the destruction denuded the countryside. Young said the want of trees gave Ireland a "naked, bleak dreary view." Some seventy years later, another observer guessed there were "probably thousands of women and children on the western coast" who had never seen "a shrub more than four feet high." His remark implied that men had a better chance of seeing them because they traveled elsewhere looking for work. Lending credence to that was the story of the eight-year-old daughter of a coastal county Mayo hotelkeeper. When the girl visited a nearby inland town, she saw trees along the road and feared they would fall on her.

Coal was less common in Ireland than England, though during the eighteenth century, it began to appear in Irish towns. In 1752 people called Kilkenny "a marvelous place" because it had "fire without smoke" (coal) and "water without mud" (paved streets). Irish coal imports rose sharply toward the end of the century, a mark of growing affluence. But most Irish couldn't afford coal and wouldn't have had the equipment to burn it. Instead, they dug peat, known as turf, from the many bogs peculiar to the country. Turf is a moss that withers and turns to pulp. The turf-gatherer dug it with a spade, then cut it and spread it out to dry. A nineteenth-century Irish diarist thought the finest turf was that "kneaded by the feet and then made into sods with the hands by women." Whether that recipe yielded the best fuel or not, high-quality turf kindled easily and gave a bright, clean flame. It burned without tending and, unlike coal, remained lit even if moved or disturbed.

Consequently, cutting turf was an important chore for Irish peasants, said to be as vital as harvesting grain. The right to gather it figured in negotiations to rent land. Happy was the tenant whose lease included this right, especially if the leaseholder didn't demand a bribe to secure it. However, just because turf was abundant didn't mean it always answered the peasants' needs. Heavy rains might wet it so that it couldn't dry, and when that happened, the cottager was in trouble. Two notable instances of this occurred in the nineteenth century. In 1839 southwestern Ireland was drenched severely, and turf wouldn't kindle. A German traveler reported that Cape Clear villagers drew lots to see whose house would be pulled down to supply fuel for the rest. But even this desperate sacrifice went awry, he said. With more people huddled around fewer hearths, typhus quickly spread. In 1848, the height of the Great Famine, a county Wicklow landowner's wife told her diary that heavy summer rains had kept turf from drying. She wondered what people would do during the winter, which promised to be hard.

Even dry turf could be a nasty beast, one that took poorly to domestication. Low-quality turf in particular created an unpleasant smell and stung the eyes, though that might have been less noticeable with better ventilation. Good ventilation, however, was precisely what the peasants' cabins didn't have. "It is true," Young wrote, "they have not always chimneys to their cabbins, the door serving for that and window too: if their eyes are not affected with the smoke, it may be an advantage in warmth." Up to the Great Famine, other writers said much the same, and their eyes *were* affected. When the Poor Inquiry reported on peasant living conditions in 1836, it repeatedly noted how dark, cramped, damp, and smoky the cabins were. The sole difference from Young's day was that windows were more common. But even there, the inquiry found, progress was mixed. When the glass broke, the hole was plugged up, not repaired.

The cabins, the survey said, were usually one room, twelve feet by thirteen or so, or, if two rooms, as large as twelve by twenty-one. The walls were most often mud or clay, with the roofs thatched with sod, reeds, straw, potato stalks, or a combination of these. The roofs often leaked, making the dirt floors muddy and forcing the inhabitants to move their beds during heavy rains. Kitchens were rudimentary. Many cabins had the turf fire on the ground against a wall. When chimneys existed, they were usually wickerwork, not stone, though occasionally clay or mud daubed on wooden frames, a singular construction that many writers commented on. Frequently, however, cabins had only a hole in the roof. Smoke left through the door, which meant acrid fumes "attacked the eyes, and were intolerable to those who were unaccustomed to it." Even where there was a flue, the lack of an external chimney kept the smoke from exiting properly. An observer who saw Ireland six years before the Poor Inquiry said that the smoke escaped through every crack and opening, giving the impression the cabin was on fire. His first impulse, he said, was to raise the alarm. But he cheerfully admitted that as an Englishman he was quick to panic at such things.

More than one visitor pointed out that they, the newcomers, were the ones likely to suffer. Even so, that doesn't mean the Irish were completely insensible to their own comfort. Young thought that some of the women's complexions resembled "smoked ham," a poignant comment on people celebrated for their beauty. And the Irish were conscious of the smoke to some extent, because they assumed strangers couldn't tolerate it. Luckombe wrote that when he entered peasants' cabins in county Tipperary, he was offered a low stool—the only one in the house—so that he would be sitting below the gathering cloud of fumes. The children, meanwhile, nestled around the fire almost naked, toes in the ashes. Other observers told similar stories.

But how hardened the Irish were or weren't is beside the point. Rather, having traded fresh air for warmth, and living under conditions in which complex cooking was a chore, the Irish were bound to think the potato presented advantages. In other words, fuel and household considerations help explain why the tuber found its niche in Ireland. Preparation was simpler than that of oats: no threshing, no drying, no long-bubbling cauldron to stir for porridge or griddle to mind, as with oatcakes. A meal of potatoes needed only digging, washing, and either boiling or, less often, roasting in embers. Peeling took place at the dinner table. Cooking required almost no tending, so therefore no faceful of smoke. Not that the Irish adopted the potato because they suddenly decided that they hated their hearth fires. After all, they had prepared other foods before the tuber came and did so afterward. However, anything that became a staple had to be simple, especially if it were to compete.

Simplicity, and the fuel that allowed it, also yielded a social advantage: A child could roast potatoes safely without an adult's help. Young reported that "children eat potatoes all day long, even those of a year old will be roasting them." He may have exaggerated the youthfulness of these chefs, but clearly the Irish had realized the virtues of quick snacks that children got for themselves. Such snacks demanded no utensils or culinary skill and satisfied hunger without the child having to wait for organized meals. Young, knowing that many of his readers disdained the Irish and would think their family life barbaric, saw fit to extract a moral. He said that giving the children the run of the larder was more open-handed than the English practice of keeping the bread and meat locked away.

However, the social benefit the Irish obtained from quick, easy meals was in part drawn from necessity. Peasant cabins, at least those of poor cottagers, were sparsely equipped. Typical furnishings included a pot for boiling potatoes, a rude table, several three-legged stools, a knife, several plates, and a spoon. An American woman who saw Ireland in 1844 believed that cooking and eating habits had not "varied for two centuries." They depended, she said, on a turf fire, a wooden stool, a pot, and a griddle. She had practical experience on this point, too. While in county Kerry, she was dismayed to find that the inn where she was staying couldn't prepare the cocoa she had brought. The only pots the inn possessed were a large kettle for potatoes and a small one for tea. Maybe she was luckier than she knew, because among the peasantry, a large kettle served many uses. It not only boiled the potatoes, it was a washbasin, a barricade to keep animals out of the cabin, a dish from which children and pigs ate, a wastecan, and "alternately a vessel of honour and dishonour." Some people emptied the kettle once the potatoes were boiled and inverted it to use as a table.

The dearth of furniture, kitchen equipment, and eating utensils among Ireland's poor made the tuber a godsend. If cottagers had these furnishings, so much the better, but if they didn't, the potato diet didn't require their purchase. That allowed the household budget to stretch farther, helpful to a tenant-farming peasantry that seldom saw currency. Or, as some writers said, it let households exist. Of course, there were social undertones. Travelers noticed, sometimes with a shudder, that the poorer Irish sat on dirt floors and ate with their fingers. But the custom of eating with the hands, a habit that has long helped color the potato as low class, differed little from peasant manners elsewhere. It wasn't as if utensils were common. The knife was eighteenth-century Europe's principal dining implement. French peasants carried one everywhere, even to eat at someone else's home. Forks were new, having reached royal households only as the sixteenth century ended and then gradually filtering down the social scale. Two hundred years later, forks remained rare in such places as America, northeastern France, and southern Germany.

The tools inside the house were only part of the picture, however. Just as important, if not more, was the absence of one in the field: the plow. The plow had always underlined social rank on the land, because only the nobility, wealthy landowners, or better-off farmers could afford one. In late eighteenth-century Ireland, even an inexpensive model might cost forty shillings, or what a cottager paid in yearly rent. As a result, most farmers went without—and a half-century later, they were still without. The Poor Inquiry heard from witnesses who said "there are not six ploughs in the barony" of Murrisk, county Mayo. Cottagers in two county Leitrim baronies reportedly had none. A county Cork landowner wrote in 1880 that when he inherited his estate forty years before, there were things called plows on it. Only they were iron-tipped logs, incapable of turning a furrow, and looked like pictures of implements the ancient Romans used.

The lack of plows, especially the clumsy, wooden prototype, wasn't necessarily a drawback. Ireland had the spade, a cheaper, easily fashioned, and adaptable tool. Many varieties existed. A common kind was the loy, which had a narrow handle five feet long, and a blade whose top right-hand edge protruded to form a footrest, much like the Andean *taclla*. The Irish spade could cut, turn over ground, or strip sod away, which made it useful for preparing fields for planting. The long blade and footrest permitted deep digging, and the back of the blade broke up clods. The blade's curved shape allowed solid objects such as potatoes to be lifted undamaged and deftly set aside. Its sharp edge severed roots, scraped away weeds, and chopped up hard soil.

Moreover, even if Irish tenant farmers had possessed plows, like the Andean highland dwellers, they lacked the horses to pull them. A horse was an even more distinctive mark of rank in Ireland than a plow, because it offered refined pleasures like hunting and visiting neighbors in a carriage. The poor, of course, had other worries. What money they could spare to buy livestock was better spent on pigs, cows, or chickens. Milk and eggs fetched precious cash, and selling the animals helped pay the rent. Those tenant farmers who kept horses generally had only one, so that plowing by a team, the ideal, was impossible. A visitor to county Tyrone in 1822 noticed that horses were so rare, any tenant farmer who wished to borrow one had a long wait.

Men with spades were always available, however. Unemployment was Ireland's chronic ill, visible in the crowds of hopeful laborers that gathered on large estates and in towns and cities. Paid work was so scarce that hundreds of men might walk ten or twenty miles on a rumor they would find it. Wherever they assembled, boys sometimes hid among them, standing on stones to appear taller, trying to fool the foremen. Every spring, workers from Connacht, a poor western province, traveled eastward, looking to earn cash and board as extra hands for haymaking and the harvest. By the mid–eighteenth century, some Irish were making their springtime migration to England, where wages were higher, and returning in autumn with the money they had saved.

To fit their meager resources—spades and the workers to wield them— Irish farmers had developed a method of cultivation. The method was the so-called lazy bed, also called ridge planting, forms of which date back to ancient and medieval times. Each ridge was a rectangular plot, separated from its neighbors by a shallow trench, to create raised planting beds. For potato culture, the beds were five feet to nine feet wide, depending on local custom, and the trenches a foot and a half to three feet wide. Using a spade, the farmer turned over the soil and applied lime and fertilizer, the latter usually animal dung, or, near the coast, seaweed. With a spade or a dibble, an iron-tipped rod called a *stiveen*, the farmer then dropped the seed potatoes into the bed. Ten workers could turn over an acre's worth of beds in one day; forty might spend a day sowing the acre.

For an effort involving so many hands, *lazy bed* is an odd name. One historian thinks the term derives from the French verb *laisser*, "to leave" or "to let," as in *laissez-faire*. If so, perhaps the connection came about because neither the lazy bed nor its chief resident, the potato, require much care after planting. In any event, to those who disliked spade culture for scientific or social reasons, the lazy bed gave further evidence of sloppy husbandry. By the nineteenth century, critics were saying it mocked honest labor. That a farmer might plant, leave matters to nature, yet harvest sufficient food—and what odious food—was too much to stand. No wonder the phrase *lazy bed* came to evoke that most terrible Victorian sin, indolence. Ironically, the gentlemen who frowned when they said it probably had no inkling the words might be related to the name of their guiding star, laissez-faire economics.

Like any method, the lazy bed had careless practitioners, and Irish agriculture was backward in some ways. Nevertheless, even a few critics who preferred the plow conceded that the lazy bed was useful. The raised beds allowed drainage, vital in Ireland's climate, and cheaply. Underground drainage, a more efficient but costly alternative, didn't appear until the second half of the eighteenth century. Some areas didn't receive it until the late nineteenth or early twentieth centuries. Furthermore, the lazy bed had looser soil than plowed land, providing a nourishing environment for crop roots. To some degree, the beds also protected the seeds from frost or human destruction. In addition, the landscape didn't always permit plowing, as on hillsides or near bogs. However, the weightiest argument, so to speak, lay with the potato. In 1836 the Poor Inquiry learned that, depending on the type of potato, soil, and the region, per-acre yields averaged 6.5 to 8.5 tons, sometimes more.

Simple arithmetic shows what that meant. Edward Wakefield, who spent the years 1809 to 1811 traveling through Ireland, calculated that each member of a potato-eating family consumed, on average, 5.5 pounds daily. He believed the amount varied with the season, soil, and how the family cooked their potatoes. Nevertheless, at the 5.5 figure, one acre's worth would feed six people for a year (5.5 x 6 x 365 = 12,045 pounds, or about six tons). Wakefield further cited the case of a farmer who, on a single hectare (2.47 acres), fattened four bullocks and eighteen pigs, produced seed tubers for four acres, and fed his family of twenty. No doubt this family ate other food as well, because the number of animals implies a prosperous household (the sort Wakefield would have interviewed most comfortably anyway). Nevertheless, the example does illustrate the huge advantage the potato gave the land-poor Irish peasant.

The figure of 5.5 pounds per day also suggests a remarkable fact about the Irish dinner table. Wakefield's arithmetic model family of six included young children who couldn't eat as much. The man of the house, the laborer, probably consumed the difference, which put his daily intake at eight to ten pounds. Visitors shook their heads, amazed at such a repetitive and, they thought, gross diet. Such food could not, they said, give a laborer the fuel to work hard. Even Wakefield, sympathetic to the peasantry in some ways, thought that relying so heavily on "vegetable food" was debilitating. He longed to see "the mass of the people in Ireland enjoying a comfortable meal of good beef fed upon the pastures of the country." As Luckombe had pointed out thirty years before and as Wakefield well knew, the Irish peasantry seldom ate meat.

Luckombe's contemporary Arthur Young dissented. He asked how the potato could be "unwholesome food" if the poor Irish who lived on it were robust, attractive, vigorous people with many children. "I will not assert," Young wrote, "that potatoes are a better food than bread and cheese," the supposed English staple. He insisted, however, that a full belly of one was "much better than half a bellyfull of the other." The statement enraged his countrymen, because he was suggesting the Irish poor ate better than their English counterparts. Further, he allowed that Irish milk was superior to the small beer, gin, or tea the English drank. This comparison drew less attention, but it was vital. If the Irish family had a cow or access to dairy products, their diet included the calcium and vitamin A the potato lacked. It was only when they couldn't get enough milk, butter, or other source of vitamin A that their diet failed them.

This isn't to pretend that five or six pounds of praties made exciting daily fare, especially if the kitchen wanted tools or the cook imagination. The potato is a versatile vegetable, but having only a lone kettle sharply reduces the chance of making culinary magic with it. Therefore, it says something that a cultivar called the Irish Apple, introduced in the 1770s, caught on quickly and brought high prices. The Apple was famous for, among other things, its mealy consistency when boiled. So boiled the potatoes were, with peels on, the poorer folk scraping them off with a thumbnail kept long for the purpose. Sometimes the Irish fried their praties in butter, perhaps having boiled them first, the latter treatment producing a sort of potato cake.

The rich served their potatoes boiled with skins on, and had them brought to the table several times during a meal, fresh and hot.

There were variations, if rare, even in what the poor ate. One was colcannon, or cale-cannon, turnips or cabbage mashed up with potatoes and stewed. (A northern version, popular in county Armagh, substituted beans for the turnips and cabbage.) *Colcannon* entered English usage in 1774, but the dish may be older. What is more certain is that colcannon was a treat—few cottagers grew turnips or cabbages. That didn't stop it from becoming a delicacy, however, because the peasants reportedly liked to steal the missing ingredients now and then. When Irish immigrants came to the United States, they introduced colcannon to American cuisine. A Philadelphia cookbook published in 1850 gave a recipe for the dish, meant to accompany corned beef, salt pork, or bacon.

Another delicacy was cobbledy, potatoes with milk, salted butter, salt, pepper, and onions. In 1834, a traveler happened on this dish in county Donegal, the first time in Ireland he'd ever eaten potatoes that weren't boiled in their skins. The cook mashed them, added a pint of boiled onions, mashed the mixture, put in a quart of milk and a lump of butter, and stirred until the whole was like cream. The result, the traveler reported, was "by no means despicable in the sight of a hungry man."

A decade before the Great Famine, cobbledy perhaps seemed remarkable because the plain boiled potato had come to dominate the Irish diet. It was thought to be, as a leading nineteenth-century English cookbook implied, an Irish specialty. Irish domestic life in that era, when nearly half the country lived on potatoes, made it hard to imagine when the tuber did not rule. That time wasn't so far in the past, however. The eighteenth century had begun with the potato in a purely supporting role, a position that didn't change anywhere in Ireland for forty years. During those four decades, oats or bread remained the center of the Irish diet. Potatoes were winter food or hardship fare. By the 1740s, only in Munster, the province where the tuber might have first reached Ireland, was it anyone's staple, and then only of the poorest people. According to some accounts, even pigs did not eat them, living instead on grain, beechmast, or garbage.

The potato's importance was visible and growing, though. Perhaps nothing showed this more clearly than what happened when calamity struck. The famine of 1728–29, which killed thousands, came about because the oat crop failed, and potatoes alone could not make up the difference. It was this famine that prompted Jonathan Swift to write his classic pamphlet, "A Modest Proposal." Swift's essay is best known for its absurd premise—get rid of the Irish poor by eating their children—his metaphor for what he thought Britain was doing to Ireland. Symbolism aside, though, Swift's starting point was factual. He noted that signs of poverty appeared in Dublin and the countryside, on streets and in homes. He said that everywhere one saw "beggars of the female sex, followed by three, four, or six children, all in rags and importuning every passenger for an alms." Swift added that this situation would not soon improve, because employment was rare and "money a thing unknown." Further, he fixed Ireland's population at 1.5 million. Historians suspect the true figure was perhaps twice that. But his warning was ominous enough and would be repeated in other forms, if in those less critical of Britain.

A much more severe famine occurred in 1740–41, when an unusually cold winter froze the potatoes in storage (they were kept outside, in pits), and the oat crop failed. Starvation and disease wiped out entire villages, and bodies lay on the roads. The countrywide toll might have reached two hundred thousand to four hundred thousand, or some 10 percent or more of the population. It was eighteenth-century Ireland's worst disaster. Nothing like it happened again until the Great Famine.

The two eighteenth-century famines underlined problems in the farm calendar. Irish oats ripened in October, later than in lowland Scotland, England, or France, whereas potatoes were ready in September, and early bearers in August. If the oats failed, the potatoes had to last through the winter and summer until the next crop. Whether that happened depended not only on the size of the harvest but its keeping quality, because Ireland's dampness spoiled most potatoes after eight months or so. When the Irish Apple appeared in the 1770s, it offered a unique virtue: It kept longer. Young heard that the Apple lasted two years, though that was either a tall tale or a singularly lucky occurrence. In any case, the Apple had to grow before it filled anyone's storage pit. If the crop failed, unless reserves picked up the slack, there would be two hard months before the oat harvest, and another six before the next potato planting. Therefore, neither oats nor potatoes alone promised security, though the potato might deliver it if nothing went wrong.

As the eighteenth century progressed, that was the risk more Irish were taking. For example, in 1752, a clergyman visiting county Mayo saw peasants living on oat cakes, potatoes, and buttermilk. Twenty-five years later, Young found there that the potato and milk was the diet of the poor. The luckier ones had small amounts of herring, cockles, and oatmeal too. Young also observed about an estate in county Meath that potato culture had "increased 20 fold within 20 years." Some historians think this judgment applies to much of Ireland, and it may, but Young did find districts in which the potato was as common several decades before his tour as during it. The tuber's importance also varied by region, with the south depending on it earlier and more completely than the north. However, it's probably safe to say the potato first became the country's chief staple by 1780, while noting that the process was gradual and that some places had succumbed sooner.

This doesn't mean that by 1780 the potato had crowded out everything else from field and table. Oats were still part of the diet, particularly in the north, where stirabout, or thick porridge, remained a staple. Wheat cultivation and flour milling became more widespread toward the century's end, especially in the eastern counties, though much of the flour was exported to England. Meat appeared on some Irish farm tables, though usually such farms were at least forty or fifty acres, a sizable holding then. Consequently, the potato wasn't every Irish person's food, first, last, and always. Nevertheless, Luckombe could aptly observe in 1780 that the "common Irish" subsisted on potatoes and milk year round, "without tasting either bread or meat, except perhaps at Christmas once or twice."

The growing reliance on the potato fit into the changing agricultural economy, particularly when it came to the pig. As eighteenth-century Europe's major exporter of beef and butter, Ireland had long furnished animal products for sale abroad. Until the last third of the century, however, pork occupied a minor place commercially. Beef had an advantage because, after 1735, common practice exempted grazing land from church tithes. Cattle grazing was also the most gentlemanly way to farm, more respectable than tillage. Moreover, Irish pork was then of inferior quality. The typical Irish pig was long-legged, high-backed, and bony, noted for huge, heavy ears and the slowness with which it fattened. Gradually, encouraged by high export prices, breeders raised meatier hogs. Farmers large and small began producing more pig food—grain, potatoes, and milk whey—and the pigs that consumed it. Pork exports rose eightfold in the last three decades of the century, and not only the provision merchants benefited. By the mid-1770s, potential profits had enticed most cottagers to keep pigs.

To the cottager or small tenant farmer, cows offered more advantages. They furnished milk and butter for the table and for sale, and they need not be slaughtered. However, keeping pigs also made sense, and the two animals together provided even more security. The pig could live on milk and potatoes, just as its owners did, and its dung helped fertilize the lazy beds. If there were no cow, for want of pasture land or money, the pig ate potatoes and the peels the family threw away. Better-off farmers might keep several pigs and slaughter one for themselves, salting the meat for use during the winter. Poorer farmers refrained from killing their pigs, or any other animals, for home consumption because the cash they fetched was too precious to forgo.

As with any notable aspect of domestic life, the way the Irish raised their livestock had a social sidelight. More than one traveler was surprised to meet a pig—or chicken, duck, or cow—dwelling with its owners inside the cabin. Inquiries often prompted a reply such as: "And sure, haven't they a right, for don't they pay the rent?" The animals also kept the place warmer. Still, some visitors weren't used to cohabitation, like the clergyman who rose from bed at an inn to see pigs watching him. But there was nothing to worry about, and he knew it. Irish hogs behaved docilely, like pets. They lay down on command and needed only the lightest tether to keep them from wandering. Naturally, however, reports of indoor livestock colored views of Irish poverty. That wasn't entirely fair, because certain English and French farmers lived with their animals and continued to do so past the mid-nineteenth century. Perceptive travelers in Ireland came to realize that a cabin where a pig resided was more prosperous than one that had none. They welcomed the sight, even if the beast compromised hygiene and challenged their sensibilities.

Sensibilities aside, eighteenth-century Ireland *was* mostly poor. Some historians have argued that visitors' writings about Connacht and other poor areas have created the false impression that all Ireland suffered untold misery. Many places, these historians point out, enjoyed prosperity, especially in the century's final decades. Dublin and Cork were improving cities, and the eastern counties particularly were profiting from the boom in farm exports. Canals and roads were built, and small mining operations started. This isn't to deny that Connacht and other areas were dirt-poor, or that appalling squalor often begged on substance's doorstep. One reason this conflicting picture existed was that Irish affluence was fragile. It was liable to give way under pressure from famine, an economic ill wind, or from two eternal troubles, land hunger and unemployment.

Emigration offered a potential, if risky, remedy. In the eighteenth century, emigration happened on a smaller scale than the next century's more famous exodus, but the movement was significant nonetheless. Those who left Ireland weren't the penniless or desperate, but people who had the money to cross the ocean and the drive to make it pay. One wave of emigrants that attracted notice sailed in the summer of 1727, when, it was said, three thousand left in that time alone. The flow subsided in the 1730s, as Ireland rebounded from the famine of 1728-29, but it resumed in the decades following 1740-41. During the 1760s twenty thousand emigrants left from Ulster seaports, most bound for North America, on ships that returned with flax destined for the linen looms. The departures caused uneasy discussions in Britain's Parliament.

There was reason for concern, because Ireland was losing skilled workers. Ironically, they were the Ulster linen weavers for whom the flax was imported. But weaving was an erratic trade, and when a sharp downturn came in the early 1770s, thirty thousand people left Ulster seaports in four years, again most to North America. The outflow prompted Young to remark that "when the linen trade was low, the *passenger trade* was always high." Not all the passengers were skilled, however, or found ready employment. In 1774 a Scotsman traveling in New York remarked how eager "adventurers from Britain and Ireland" were to earn the high wages colonial employers offered. However, so many ships had landed bearing immigrants—twenty-two within the past year, he was told—that jobs were scarce for them. The stream of emigrants had grown so heavy that had the American Revolution not stopped the outflow, Britain might have tried to restrict it by law.

One reason people left Ireland, and that those who stayed depended more on the potato, was the scarcity of cheap arable land. Many Irish cottagers farmed nothing as large as the hectare that fed a barnful of animals and a huge family of people. Or, if they did, that hectare was divided among many ridges. Encouraging the division was rundale, a traditional system of tenure that operated throughout much of eighteenth-century Ireland. A rundale community, known as a village, comprised a group of families who, through one or two elders, rented land from a single landlord. The elders split the farmland into parcels, perhaps as many as twenty or thirty, which in turn were broken into fields and further divided into ridges. Only grazing land remained whole. The villagers then drew lots to decide who farmed what ridges, a practice repeated every three or four years so that no land stayed permanently under one tenant. No fences separated one holding from another, only balks, or unplowed strips. Tenants held land in proportion to the rent they paid, but a large holding might be scattered in thirty or forty pieces. Moreover, tenants settled portions of their rental on their adult children, so that individual holdings kept getting smaller.

Rundale functioned well when the population remained stable or increased slowly, and when the village produced enough to be self-sufficient. It also worked when the villagers valued custom and the ties gained through intermarriage more than they disliked the many nuisances the system entailed. These annoyances included the absence of fences, which allowed livestock to trample or eat the crops, and disputes over rights-of-way, which caused many court cases. The most painful drawback, though, had to do with little children, who, almost as soon as they could walk, were made to stand out in all weather, guarding against trespass and herding animals. A county Mayo landowner who ended rundale on his estate was told, "Even the little children will have to bless you." Despite that, his tenants had resisted his efforts.

By the late eighteenth century, roads had opened villages to outside markets, and population pressure sharpened land hunger, making the system obsolete. From 1815 on, landlords did their best to end rundale, so that by 1845, it was common only in county Mayo. Its passing occasioned no remorse among landowners or officials. In 1848 Charles Edward Trevelyan, Britain's permanent head of the Treasury, called rundale "barbarous" because it made "the industrious and thriving responsible for the short-comings of the idle and improvident." Perhaps he thought rundale deserved his indignation because a half-century before, England had cast off a similar arrangement with less fuss, the way a modern, improving nation should.

The population that crowded out rundale expanded very fast. Historians generally agree that the increase began in the eighteenth century and continued in the nineteenth, but exactly when it grew, why, or by how much remain subjects of fierce debate. The debate may never end, either, because the first regular national census wasn't taken until 1821, and its reliability is also a matter of debate. Nevertheless, a few judgments are plausible. Ireland seems to have numbered, in round figures, four million people in 1780 and eight million in 1841. Such a rapid doubling would be striking anytime, but the date it began, when the potato achieved dominance, is very intriguing. Was the population explosion linked to the potato's influence?

To some contemporary eyes, the connection wasn't hard to fathom. Given the time-honored view of root vegetables aiding reproduction, it was only natural that people would see Ireland as scientific proof. Ireland wasn't the first country singled out that way; an early seventeenth-century observer had drawn similar conclusions about Wales and the leek. However, with Ireland, the belief appears to have been more widespread and lasted longer. An English farm manual of 1771 said that in western Ireland, where the potato was "almost the only diet of the laboring poor," households commonly harbored six to ten children each. Two decades later an eminent Dublin physician prescribed potatoes for women who were childless, "and an heir has often been the consequence." Even people who didn't consult eminent Dublin physicians believed in the potato's power. A French traveler once asked, "How is it that your countrymen have so many and so healthy children?" Came the answer: "It's the praties, Sir."

More skeptical observers looked to the potato's economic and social influence, not its magical powers. Marriage, particularly early marriage, was thought to drive up the birthrate, and thinkers like Thomas Malthus believed that the cheap potato encouraged marriage. He also thought, as did others, that Irish priests induced their parishioners to marry early because fees for performing weddings provided income. This charge suggests anti-Catholic prejudice, but it may have had some truth to it, because a few Catholic clerics spoke up about the practice and condemned it. However, the Irish seem to have needed little urging to marry. Young said the Irish considered it a misfortune not to have children, who weren't thought a burden. Wakefield added that family feeling was important. He noted that children cared for their aging parents, "a noble trait in the character of the indigent Irish." Thirty years later, William Makepeace Thackeray wrote that "the extreme love of children" was visible everywhere, and no visitor could help being touched by it.

Wakefield saw economic reasons for marriage too. Like Malthus, whom he appears to have read, he cited the cheapness of potatoes. He also thought that children furnished needed labor. But there were other motives. A single male faced social and economic hurdles that a married male did not. Not only did the bachelor have to manage both house and field—and suffer his neighbors' scorn for it—but he might be the poorer for remaining single. Marriage was a commercial bargain. A bride, particularly if she were well off, would bring a dowry in land, livestock, or cash. Even poor young women might have good portions, their families having scrimped to provide them. In addition, staying single gave a man no edge in the job market. Most jobs involved day labor, and a married man could do that work just as easily.

Besides, in several ways, marrying was the only freedom, small though it was, the poor peasant could exercise. Law and custom heavily favored landlords over their tenantry, and with landownership came a social license that was often abused. "A landlord in Ireland," wrote Young, "can scarcely invent an order which a servant laborer or cottar dares to refuse to execute." Ireland wasn't unusual in deferring to landed interests. However, the law further discriminated against the country's Catholic majority, who, by Young's estimate, made up four-fifths of the population. Among the laws and practices that Catholics objected to involved church tithes. Catholics and Protestants alike hated paying them, but Catholics found tithes especially galling, because the money went to the established Protestant church.

Another grievance involved the Penal Laws. These laws denied Catholics the right to buy or bequeath land, or to keep it if a Protestant could lay claim to it. In addition, Catholics couldn't teach school, vote, attend Dublin University, become lawyers or freely apprentice themselves to a trade, carry arms, or lend money in a mortgage. Some Penal Laws went unenforced or had loopholes, as when Protestants "claimed" Catholic property, then secretly returned it. Even so, the laws had broad effects, not least the predictable resentment and tension. And, rather than encourage conversion, their intent, they inspired subversion. This could be political, as with so-called hedge schools, rural Catholic schools in which teachers might preach seditious lessons. Or it could be economic, as with underground moneylenders who evaded the rule on mortgages. In the open economy, fewer choices existed. The Penal Laws effectively excluded Catholics from landowning and from all professions except the Continental armies, the church, and medicine. Some of the laws were repealed or relaxed in the 1780s and 1790s, but full legal equality wasn't granted until the Catholic Emancipation Act of 1829.

Some Irish fought back. During the early 1760s secret societies arose to protest excessive tithes and punish dishonest tithe collectors. The secret societies were "lawless ruffians," Luckombe wrote, "called White-boys. They are ignorant peasants, who do not chuse to pay tythes or taxes . . . they stroll about the country, firing houses and barns, burying people alive in the ground, cutting their noses and ears off, and committing other barbarities on their persons." He was exaggerating, but less the barbarities than the motive. The Whiteboys didn't demand abolishment of tithes, only that they be fairly levied. Before 1800, most counties outside Ulster had seen Whiteboy activity, with varying degrees of violence or the threat of it.

Other Catholics turned to trade. They became eighteenth-century Ireland's merchants and conducted most of the country's business at home and abroad. Besides middlemen—tenants who sublet their holdings, of whom few contemporaries had anything kind to say—the merchants were

Catholic Ireland's middle class. However, to what extent they, or the prosperity that produced them, influenced the vast majority of Irish is an open question. The merchants were town and city dwellers, and Ireland was mostly rural. Even by 1800, after the towns had expanded, rural Ireland sustained 94 percent of the population. It was the land that counted, the land that Catholics couldn't legally buy or inherit. What did economic growth mean to most peasants beyond the ability to keep more than one pig, or a cow besides the pig?

If Irish peasants couldn't aspire to the middle class, the best they could hope for was land tenantry, which meant either subsistence or, with luck, a cut above it. No wonder they seized on marriage with such conviction: At least it offered the prospect of companionship and family happiness. Several writers remarked that the poor Irish married because they had nothing to lose. "The only solace these miserable mortals have," Luckombe wrote of county Tipperary, "is in matrimony, accordingly they all marry young." Most girls, he said, were mothers at sixteen. As might be expected, Malthus agreed with this assessment and developed it. He spoke of "the humiliated Catholic, with no rank in society to support," who found subsistence "without much difficulty" and "overspread the land with his descendants."

No doubt the Irish impulse to marry was strong, but contemporary observers misinterpreted how far the Irish carried it and how it affected population growth. This was partly because particular cases led to false assumptions, and no census data existed to correct them. For instance, like Luckombe, Wakefield referred to marriages between girls of fourteen and fifteen and boys only a year or two older, in county Kerry. Later writers reported hearing of similar practices, which reinforced the idea that they were general. Since it was an article of faith that early marriage increased the population, observers readily believed that adolescent marriage was only an extreme example of a widespread Irish custom. Today, however, many historians disagree. They have argued that though the Irish propensity to marry may have increased the population, marriage didn't occur as early in life as contemporaries thought, and that adolescent marriages were almost certainly exceptions. Further, scientific opinion is by no means uniform on what effect early marriage has on population increase.

Ascribing contemporaries' views to faulty arithmetic or observation leaves a question unanswered, however: Did they see what wasn't there because they were looking for it? Eighteenth- and nineteenth-century thinkers explained the difference between rich and poor in moral terms. That outlook greatly affected the potato's reputation and that of the people who relied on it, a theme that recurs throughout this narrative. Regarding Ireland, the notion went that imprudent marriage was immoral, because it condemned the couple and their unborn children to poverty, making them wretched and burdening society. Significantly, in revising his famous treatise on population, Malthus added "moral restraint" to the list of otherwise apocalyptic influences that checked population growth. The idea had wide authority, both among people who read political economy, as economics was then called, and those who didn't. The unnamed author in the *Edinburgh Review* thought the "most expedient and proper method" of controlling Ireland's surplus population would be to forbid building cabins on anything less than five to ten acres of land. Do that, he argued, and there would be no cheap potatoes, and therefore, no imprudent marriage. A county Wicklow landowner's wife expressed a similar desire to stop a poor couple she knew from marrying. "The idea of such a pair of incapables marrying without a home, without employment; it is really a moral sin, though they none of them comprehend its enormity."

Accordingly, Ireland's population and how it got to be so large weren't neutral issues. This was taking up where Swift had left off, except at face value, dangerous to do with arguments whose purest expression comes from a satirist. If Ireland was a nation of beggars in 1729, that it still was one eighty years later meant that conditions hadn't changed and needed to.

Since surplus population was poverty's presumed mother, then whatever caused the population to grow must also be at fault. Therefore, the potato couldn't be just a vegetable; it had to be immoral, economically crippling, and encouraging the vices that went with (or caused) poverty. Even those who had a measure of compassion for Ireland mentioned the tuber in the same breath as social ills for which it couldn't possibly be responsible. Luckombe, for one, believed the Irish would deserve to rank "with the most respectable societies in Europe" if they had more and better food, the Penal Laws were removed, and the people harnessed "the native spirit of enterprize, which now lies torpid within them."

Almost thirty years later, Malthus argued the same cause. It should be said that he favored the potato, thought it a useful hedge against famine, and believed English farmers should grow more of it. Where he opposed it was as a principal staple, and of course that meant Ireland was in trouble. If trends continued, he said, Ireland would number 20 million people by 1900. Malthus generally had hard words for the poor, and he later attacked the Irish, but here he was campaigning for Catholic emancipation. He wrote that justice, if not common sense, demanded that Britain treat Ireland better, if only to avoid having 20 million enemies on its doorstep.

The idea of 20 million Irish was unsettling. Neither the eighteenth nor nineteenth centuries knew what to do with the moral, sexual essence of the poverty/population issue (and today's welfare reform debates suggest we don't, either). It seemed as if Ireland's population was outstripping even the cheapest food supply, while the peasantry recklessly married and had children whenever they could find an acre on which to grow that food. What could anyone do about that except preach? That the sermons sounded smug and condescending in certain well-to-do mouths doesn't mean the observations behind them were completely groundless. However, the critics missed the point. The potato wasn't the villain. The real source of Irish poverty was laws and practices surrounding land tenure. Perhaps it was more comforting to imagine suppressing the potato than turning landed society upside down. No doubt, too, it was simpler to say that the human qualities the potato allegedly encouraged—laziness, ignorance, hopelessness, and childlike dependence—were at fault, and not the system in which they existed or its architects.

ENGLAND AND WALES
SINCE
THE FIFTEENTH CENTURY

SCALE OF MILES

ENVIRONS OF
LONDON

3 The Better Sort of People

*God may send a man good meat, but the devil may
send an evil cook to destroy it.*
SIXTEENTH-CENTURY ENGLISH PROVERB

As IF THE RUMORS linking the potato to leprosy weren't enough, to the English during the late sixteenth and early seventeenth centuries, the tuber had a crippling defect: It was a vegetable. Among the nobility and well-to-do, who set the era's culinary trends and from whom comes most evidence of daily habits, pleasures of the flesh meant exactly that. The English never met a joint of meat they didn't like. Fruit was always welcome, the sweeter the better, but vegetables occupied a lower rank, as their prominence during Lent implies. Covent Garden, London's famous produce market, opened only in 1670.

Even the word *meat* was synonymous with food. "God may send a man good meat, but the devil may send an evil cook to destroy it," went one sixteenth-century proverb. The devil was kept busy, apparently. In English cuisine, greens meant herbs, more often than not, and herbs meant seasoning for "pottage," juices from stewed meat mixed with oatmeal. Around 1580, the chronicler William Harrison remarked that the English were only slowly revising their opinion that "herbs, fruits and roots" were fit for "hogs and savage beasts." The year 1615 saw what were reportedly the first vegetable recipes to appear in print: a few salads, "some only to finish out the table, and some both for use and adornment." A sample menu from a cookbook published in 1681 suggested a summer feast, admittedly "extraordinary," of fourteen courses. They included but two vegetable dishes, one being "potato" pie—most probably sweet potato—and that one contained beef marrow.

Ten years later, the herbalist Thomas Tryon wrote that in other European countries, a pound of meat "with Herbs and Roots" would feed four or five people. This was healthier, he said, than the "dangerous and noxious custom" in England of eating a pound or two of "Fat Flesh" with "scarcely a bit of bread." Yet even Tryon, who defended vegetarianism, warned against the evils inherent in salads, ranking lettuce as dangerous as onions. Well into the nineteenth century, English writers were saying that cold salads needed pepper to warm the blood, or that they "contain little nourishment, and are not much to be recommended."

The English passion for a meat-and-potatoes dinner was yet unheard of, because the tuber was neither familiar nor desirable. The backyard, said one authority, was the first place to gather provisions, while Harrison warned about seeking food from abroad, "as if nature had ordained all for the belly." The wealthy ignored that advice, but when they garnished their meat, they chose only the better kind of vegetables. Artichokes, new when the potato reached Spain, quickly became "one of the most excellent Fruits of the Kitchen Garden." Asparagus, of slightly longer reputation, was favored for its taste and because it was said to benefit the bladder. The poor didn't eat such fashionable vegetables, but the cheaper roots—onions, leeks, parsnips, and the like. The botanist John Parkinson observed in 1656 that however "much esteemed" turnips were, most wound up on poor peoples' tables. Or, he might have added, in animals' stalls. A late sixteenth-century import from Holland, the turnip had, by Parkinson's day, earned use as fodder in the east and south.

There was a hierarchy among roots. Tryon argued that some were "more familiar to our Natures" than others, depending on how close they grew to the surface and when they matured. Plants harvested in late autumn were good neither "for Food or Physick," and roots raised in cold countries were less healthy than those from warm ones. Deep-growing roots were even worse. Not only did potatoes grow more deeply than, say, leeks or onions, they weren't even attached to the foliage. Pulling up a leek involved touching a stalk aboveground; harvesting a potato meant digging below. This put the potato in a different realm—to the pious or superstitious, an unearthly one, paradoxically. Further, when Tryon warned about late-maturing roots in cold climates, no better example existed than the short-day potato growing in Europe's northern latitudes.

Consequently, though England's educated classes might have raised the potato in their gardens and disregarded the myths about nightshades and plagues, they still viewed the tuber as if it bore a stamp of vulgarity. This feeling surfaced even as they argued for the potato's wider use. For instance, in 1662, a thoughtful Somersetshire gentleman wrote the newly chartered Royal Society to suggest that potatoes might protect England from famine. The society, whose business was (and is) advising the government on scientific matters, agreed. It urged its landowning members to plant the tuber and to persuade their friends to do the same. It also resolved to recommend potatoes to the nation.

Along the same lines, in 1664 one John Forster wrote a pamphlet claiming that the tuber furnished "a sure and easy remedy" for food shortages. With wheat flour added, he said, the potato made good bread, and at half the cost of pure grain. Further, he predicted that if the tuber were planted commonly in England and Wales, it would work an economic miracle. Ten thousand men who could not feed their families would soon become prosperous citizens worth thirty pounds a year each. To interest King Charles II,

Forster offered that His Majesty might sell rights to grow and market potatoes, and thus collect revenue. Charles, though needing money, did
not adopt the idea, missing his chance to license the world's first potato
franchises.

Food history supplies myriad instances in which the upper classes set a
trend that the lower classes copied, but the potato hadn't followed that
path and never would. These two public efforts on the potato's behalf, England's first, go far to explain why. In praising the potato, the philanthropists handled it from a careful distance, as if using tongs. The social
message was clear. Commenting on the Royal Society's resolutions, one
member wrote another that "vulgar potadoes" could indeed combat
famine. He knew because he had seen that happen among "the better sort
of yeomanry and tradesmen." Of course, he belonged to neither class. Similarly, John Evelyn, the society's gardening expert, told his diary what the
tuber was good for. It would, he confided, help the poor or even one's own
household during a bad year "when there are many servants" who needed
to be fed.

Nowhere did these men say that they or their friends enjoyed eating or
growing the potato. That omission, and the gulf they implied between
themselves and the supposed root eaters, merely underlined the potato's
character as food for desperate or inferior people. Such were the sort
thought to inhabit a hated neighboring island, so there was no question
where that logic led. In 1688 an anti-Irish London mob put the matter precisely when it brandished sticks with potatoes stuck on the end.

Small wonder that when the eighteenth century arrived, the tuber carried a social stigma in England. The wealthy continued to raise it in their
gardens, while the poor avoided it. Experts continued to scratch their heads
and say that a valuable resource was going unused—by someone else. The
author of a 1726 gardening manual noted "how much Profit" potatoes
brought to families who grew them and wondered why the "poorer parts of

our Country" failed to take heed. In a way, this remark said that those who couldn't afford respectable food, bread and meat, should stop being fussy. Or, in other words, that popular prejudice was a luxury to which the poor had no right. The poor resented this so much that even as the century ended, some risked starvation rather than give up what they considered to be their birthright. Others took to violence.

One might suppose that the poor also resented being told to poison themselves with a vile nightshade. If so, however, that resentment doesn't show up among commonly voiced objections. Moreover, by the mid–eighteenth century, English science was challenging the nightshade superstition. Talk of deadly roots had faded somewhat, as the English had begun to think that certain solanaceous plants were harmless after all. For instance, an herbal published in 1756 pronounced a long-overdue verdict when it absolved the potato, the tomato, and the eggplant of wrongdoing. Such thinking could only help a nation whose moral arbiters called bread and meat the only proper foods.

However, the physician who wrote the herbal, John Hill, did not joyously welcome these three vegetables to the English table. Hill only stressed that they weren't poisonous as once thought and noted that some people actually ate them. In particular he cited the tomato, which, he said, English gardeners grew for its beauty, though in foreign lands the "love apple" found its way into soups and salads. To inform those who might wish to follow this odd custom, Hill judged the tomato "innocent" but remarked that it had "little nourishment in it." He had acquitted the nightshades but left intact the national suspicion of vegetables.

If eyewitness impressions are accurate, this suspicion was fairly unusual. Meat continued to rule England the way it did nowhere else. Daniel Defoe, touring his native country in 1725, was amazed by the quantity of meat in London's Leadenhall Market. It seems he wasn't the only one to think so, for he quoted a Spanish ambassador as having said the market sold as much meat in one month "as would suffice all Spain for a Year." Like the Spanish, the French followed the sparing Continental way with meat, as Tobias Smollett observed during the mid-1760s. Smollett, who disliked everything French, spent time in Boulogne, whose bourgeoisie he called misers, in part because they ate so little flesh. They lived, the novelist said scornfully, mostly on shellfish, porridge, and salads—and, it appears, neglected to invite him to dine. As for the French poor, he opined that they had dry, rough faces because they ate meat even less often. Smollett was echoing the widely held view that meat eating reflected social class and nationality. Meat eating and disdain for vegetables were customs that helped define how the English saw themselves.

Had Smollett met Pehr Kalm, a Swede who visited England in 1748, they might have had a lively discussion. Moving among the well-heeled in and around London, Kalm was surprised that every Englishman who was "his own master" ate meat daily. No other people, Kalm ventured, knew how to roast a joint like the English, which he thought lucky because their culinary art did "not extend much beyond roast beef and plum pudding." Nevertheless, he saw English people garnishing meat with boiled potatoes and turnips. These vegetables were served with melted butter, sometimes sharing the meat plate. As for salads, cooks exiled lettuce or cucumber to separate plates, because not all diners liked green vegetables, or if they did, not always the same ones.

That Kalm noticed potatoes on midcentury London tables meant little concerning England at large. Such up-to-date habits had yet to affect rural life. Farmers neither ate potatoes nor fed them to their livestock. Some even disapproved of turnips—still. Defoe heard of objections to Suffolk cattle because farmers gave them turnips; purists thought the beef would "taste of the Root." Defoe disagreed, but only because experience showed there was "no Reason for this Fancy." Throughout the century, root crops as fodder remained a disputed issue. Thirty years after Defoe's tour, a farm writer complained, "Potatoes are good for none but swine and those they won't fatten." If this charge had any practical basis, it may have been that Irish pork, known to be potato-fed, was then inferior to the English product. However, that couldn't have been the whole story. In the mid-1790s, while England was importing boatloads of Irish pork, experts implicitly accepted that potato fodder was a lesser alternative to grain. One agricultural inspector, hearing that a farmer had tried potatoes successfully, called the experiment "an interesting subject for inquiry." For his time, that was a warm endorsement.

Therefore, as the century approached its last quarter, potato cultivation was anything but general in England. Which, as some writers pointed out, was a financial bonanza missed: High yields offered a good return per acre. In 1770 Arthur Young chided his country's lack of enthusiasm for a "most useful vegetable" and guessed that three-quarters of England's counties could benefit from growing it. No doubt more farmers would have done so had the English consumer led the way, but that argument is chicken-and-egg. In any case, when Britain's Board of Agriculture and Internal Improvement commissioned county-by-county farming surveys, those from 1794 showed that potatoes seldom appeared in main rotations or as secondary crops. And even when they did, farmers didn't always take advantage. For example, Middlesex, known for dairying, grew potatoes in two of eight districts. The county's leading milk buyer was London, whose population (almost 900,000) made it the kingdom's largest market, and whose nearby location allowed short freight hauls, reducing costs and the risk of spoilage. For similar reasons—cheap freight, high population—London should have been a tempting market for Middlesex potato growers. Yet the Board of Agriculture report mentioned no trade in them. It seems farmers preferred to feed them to their livestock.

Sometimes, the board surveys found, land practices worked against potato growing. In two counties farm leases forbade potato culture except for home use. This was probably because the tuber required lots of manure, a key resource that eighteenth-century farmers didn't always exploit properly. Landlords worried that their tenants would fertilize one field to excess and skimp on others, letting the land become overworked. Connected to that fear was the controversial belief that wheat couldn't follow potatoes on the same acreage. The board investigators' views reflected the split within reigning opinion. One agreed that potatoes depleted the soil; another thought they enriched it so that better wheat grew the next year. If expert opinion varied so sharply, no wonder landowners, few of whom had studied farming as a serious subject, took a conservative stance.

Nevertheless, the eighteenth century saw the potato nose its way into English life. For that to have happened suggests that powerful forces propelled it, and that they arose quickly, given how steadily England had shunned the tuber. Oddly, the push likely came not from the farms but the cities, a pattern that sets England apart from Ireland and France, and probably all Europe. English conditions paralleled those elsewhere—bread as the potato's enemy, population growth as its friend—but even these played out differently. This was the England of the industrial revolution, where life's pace was quickening. A summer's journey from Edinburgh to London, roughly four hundred miles, took ten days in 1754, four days in 1776, and three in 1786. That tempo was reflected in the landscape, as rural yielded to urban. Such changes helped the potato break through, and when the transformation continued in the nineteenth century, gathering momentum, the tuber truly came into its own. However, its future role probably emerged in outline around 1770, even as Arthur Young was grumbling that not enough farmers grew it.

England was in the midst of a remarkable population surge. As with Ireland, no exact figures exist, because the first census wasn't recorded until afterward, in England's case, 1801. Even so, estimates are revealing. They say that the country numbered about 5 million people in 1700, 5.7 million in 1750, and 8.7 million in 1800. Consequently, eighteenth-century England grew by 72 percent overall, but by half during the second fifty years alone. Just as significant, however, England's population was clustering in cities. London was burgeoning, and so were industrial towns like Manchester and Liverpool. These two counted some eighty thousand inhabitants each in 1800, having quadrupled in a half-century. Moreover, urban crowding was a fact that England knew but other nations didn't. In 1800 Britain, Belgium, and the Netherlands were the only western European countries with a tenth of their populations living in towns of ten thousand or more.

Population growth and concentration meant that England needed more food delivered to central places. That was no easy job. Passengers may have spent less time traveling between major cities, but neither humans nor cargo moved efficiently or safely. The country's unpaved turnpikes were dreadful, sometimes "nearly in a state of Nature," as one appalled observer wrote of West Dorsetshire in 1796. Frequent, careless use only made the roads worse. Freight wagons were "frightfully large, with very high wheels," and "loaded with an astonishing weight." They cut deep ruts, which filled with rainwater and became muck, making later passage difficult if not impossible. When horses threw their riders, the victims sometimes suffocated in "mud and filth." So went, reportedly, a coroner's ruling on such a case in 1769.

Food transport was, therefore, a time-consuming, expensive, and involved business. That was the good news, because the eighteenth century had it easy compared with previous times. In 1725 Daniel Defoe marveled at the turnpikes—the ones later observers found so awful—which, he said, had done wonders for the table. London mutton was now cheaper in the winter, because herders no longer had to sell their flocks come autumn, before the roads to the metropolis became impassable. Equally impressive was the effect on fishing. Defoe waxed ecstatic because fresh herring that once took six days to reach Birmingham and fetched a high price now made the journey in only two.

Though potatoes are bulky and costly to ship, England's transport hardships indirectly benefited the tuber. As the population clustered, the task of raising crops had shifted onto a smaller set of shoulders. More people were buying food from shops, while proportionally fewer were producing it. Because rural populations had moved and fewer people were depending solely on the land for employment, supply and demand were less likely than before to balance within a given region. This was especially critical for the potato's chief enemy, wheat, whose cultivation depended on certain soils that might exist far from an area's best markets. Potatoes, though they couldn't replace wheat—perish the thought—presented several advantages. They grew in almost any soil and could be sold locally, eliminating long freight hauls. Further, potatoes needed no milling, saving not only expense but spoilage—once wheat is ground, the crushed kernels release an oil that easily turns rancid.

The region that took the greatest advantage was the northwest, principally the counties of Lancashire and Cheshire. There, boasted one writer in 1795, people had discovered how wonderful the "inestimable root" was when the rest of benighted England still thought it a mere garden crop. This was no empty bragging, either, because Lancashire's damp, mild climate, deep soils, and small-farm land tenure had favored the potato's wide use early, perhaps by 1680. Supporting that claim, a well-known Lancashire dish, lobscouse, dates from around 1700. It combined potatoes, meat, onions, and strong seasonings, and might have been the first English recipe that did not dress the tuber like a sweet potato. With hardtack added, lobscouse was sailors' fare, a use well known in Lancashire because of its several ports, the chief one being Liverpool. So closely, in fact, did the dish become associated with sailors that by the 1880s, *lobscouser* was a nickname for seaman.

However, it wasn't the sea that made Lancashire and Cheshire farmers England's chief potato growers. It was Manchester and Liverpool, the two biggest markets. Farmers benefited not only because these cities were large and growing rapidly, but because the communications that served them were improving. This change was badly needed. In 1770, according to one observer, the typical Lancashire road had ruts four feet deep awash with mud, even in summer. Repair meant rolling large stones into the ruts, which suggests that carriage passengers got a thorough jolting. Moving freight on these roads would have been a nightmare, so roadside pack-horse trails called causeys, or causeways, served that purpose. But such antiquities wouldn't do for a modern manufacturing and mining region, so, around midcentury, the industrial interests built canals to link the cities to natural waterways. That helped a lot, because one horse could tow a canal barge, which held up to thirty tons of cargo. A wagon, however, carried only six tons—legally, that is—and required a team of horses.

The canal builders had planned to haul bargefuls of coal, but the farmers realized that other lumpy objects, edible ones, could also travel that way. Water connected the Cheshire district of Frodsham, which reputedly grew more and better potatoes than "any parish in the kingdom," to both Manchester and Liverpool. Frodsham, it was said, sent these cities 4,500 tons of spuds annually, an amazing output for the time. They managed this partly with a superb yield, 13.5 tons per acre, and because they wintered their seed tubers in a warm spot, encouraging them to sprout by early March. Not only did this put potatoes in city markets a month or more early, it allowed their fields to support a second, autumn crop. The northwest wasn't the only region to try this technique; farmers in Cornwall and outside London did it too. However, it's striking that Cornwall had mines, and London, factories. The presence of industry was beginning to show how profitable the potato could be. It could be said that the potato was the vegetable of the industrial revolution in England and perhaps elsewhere.

The message rang loud and clear when curl struck England in the 1770s. Lancashire, paying for its discerning taste, suffered more than most places. For a time, the tuber's future there seemed in jeopardy, and that couldn't be allowed. Accordingly, curl did what nothing else had, push plant breeders to pay attention to the potato. They failed to develop any immune to curl, but they did increase the number of cultivars, something that Europe badly needed. Moreover, the disease forced people to think about why the potatoes sickened. They decided that the plant stock had "degenerated," an idea with unfortunate moral overtones, but their error steered them in a promising direction. In trying to revive the "degenerate" potato, they sent for seed tubers from Ireland and Scotland, where the disease had caused less damage. This worked for a while, but within several years, the imported varieties sometimes also fell victim. So experts began to suspect what Andean peoples had long known, that using seed pods, not tubers, would create healthier stock.

Why anybody cared about a degenerate plant is a curious question. With tradition and popular feeling running so strongly against the potato, people might have said good riddance. They might have seen curl as an unmixed blessing, perhaps a divine message that the plant was fatally flawed. That this belief existed was clear eighty years later, when the Great Famine evoked loud misgivings about the potato's moral and physical fitness. If the tuber was going to collapse before each terrifying disease that came from who knew where, didn't that prove that trusting it was a tragic, reckless mistake? One wonders what might have happened had curl arrived thirty or forty years earlier, when the potato was much less important. With fewer people to mourn it, perhaps no one would have cared to save it.

However, by the time curl ravaged English fields, the potato was starting to prove itself where it counted, at home. It had, of course, been a domestic champion before, but never in an urban setting. That difference aside, how the potato suited domestic needs has a familiar ring. Witness what a visitor to Birmingham in 1785 said about the city's work habits and pace of life. He remarked, with approval, that home-employed nailmakers rose at three or four in the morning and worked until nine or ten at night, stopping only a few hours at midday. This schedule wasn't unusual for England's home-employed or for shop workers, though it's unlikely they kept it every day. "Saint Monday," a tradition that made Monday either a holiday or a slow or shortened workday, applied in almost all trades and in the mines. Then, too, the demand for goods in a particular trade decided how many hours—or even whether—the home artisan worked. Nevertheless, the standard workday at home or shop was anywhere from twelve to sixteen hours. Factories, which employed a growing percentage of manufacturing workers, enforced the longer schedule. And factory owners did not welcome those who worshiped Saint Monday.

To earn the most income, every member of a family who could work did so, down to young children. (By the way, child labor, though among the industrial revolution's evils, wasn't restricted to factory or home workshop. Farm workers' six- and seven-year-old children toiled long days too.) Such a demanding pace left urban laborers' families with little time or energy to eat, let alone cook. Moreover, it's doubtful they had much equipment to cook with. In 1795, wrote one observer, Manchester's poor lived in "offensive, dark, damp, and incommodious habitations" whose squalor rivaled London's or was even worse. These homes, and even those of better-off workers, surely had none but the crudest kitchens or cooking implements. In particular, working-class houses lacked ovens. For a meal such as Sunday dinner, many urban families hired an oven from a baker or other tradesman, a practice that continued well into the next century.

Lacking ovens, people weren't about to cook anything complex or bake bread, even assuming they had the time and knew how. But these weren't the only obstacles to culinary art. Few people had the fuel. Coal was cheaper in industrial centers than elsewhere, but heating and the simplest cooking quickly absorbed the supply. Also, lower-class housing often lacked proper receptacles for fuel, so it had to be bought by the barrow, not the hundred-weight, which cost more in the long run. As a result, home baking declined. Urban dwellers bought their bread, and their other food was likely to be cheap, quick, and filling. They either bought it prepared or chose what needed little fuss or coal. Potatoes fit all these requirements. Sometimes workers grew them in gardens, as happened in Nottinghamshire until urban expansion swallowed the land. Mostly, however, they bought them. By 1795 potatoes were, Manchester's portrayer said, "a most important aux-iliary to bread in the diet of all classes."

They also served a crucial nutritional purpose, which doctors were just beginning to realize. In the 1770s, Dr. Richard Budd, physician-apothecary at a London orphanage school, noted that when the children ate potatoes, the scurvy that normally existed among them disappeared. When potatoes were scarce, the ailment returned. Since many people couldn't afford fresh fruit, and the urban poor had no access to orchards or farms, potatoes could have offered them cheap vitamin C. No doubt, too, spuds were more palatable than patent medicines like Spilsbury's Anti-Scorbutic Drops, often advertised in newspapers. But, sadly, the nation that worshiped meat and bread had no idea that health might depend on anything else. One thinks of John Hill saying the tomato, a rich source of vitamin C, had no nourishment in it. Or of Tobias Smollett, confirmed carnivore and scorbu-tic sufferer, wondering whether "sea-scurvy" resulted from the excess quan-tity of salt at sea—and he was a retired naval surgeon. Sixteen years after Smollett wrote, an expert reminded the Board of Admiralty that lemons and limes had proven themselves, and that Britain's sailors need not suffer the way they did. Eventually, the navy took heed, but Dr. Budd's observa-tion went unnoticed. The potato's value in combating scurvy was not com-monly accepted until about 1840.

For the poor, the meat part of the bread-and-meat diet was often beyond reach, or reserved for special occasions. Bread was the daily staple. Most eighteenth-century English bread consisted of mixed cereals, especially in the north, but in the urban areas of the south, everyone, even the poor, demanded pure wheaten. Kalm wrote in 1748 that most Englishmen he met, Londoners, didn't know anyone who ate rye bread. They thought rye was cattle feed. Of course, they knew little about the country at large, but it would be hard to overstate the loyalty and respect that wheat commanded. People defended their right to wheaten bread as if their lives depended on it, which, at times, was true. When grain shortages limited the bread supply, the potato became a leading candidate to replace it, which pleased no one.

The English preference for wheaten bread had a sturdy tradition behind it. Sixteenth- and seventeenth-century authorities had praised it to heaven. It was said to comfort the heart and the spirit and to be the "Foundation of all good nourishment." Wheaten bread was what Christ had compared to the "Heavenly and Spiritual Food of the Soul." But its allure wasn't merely spiritual. For centuries, wheaten bread had been a mark of social rank. The gentry ate it, while their servants or less fortunate neighbors consumed bread made from barley or rye or, during shortages, from beans, peas, or oats. When matters were most desperate, even acorns found their way into the loaf.

However, pride wasn't the only reason the eighteenth-century poor preferred wheaten bread. Quality was another. During George II's reign (1727–60), bakers' bread came in two categories, wheaten or household, meaning mixed. By law, bakers had to stamp their loaves with *W* or *H* so that the public could select by grade and know what it was buying. Unfortunately, that didn't stop bakers from adulterating their bread or selling one kind for another, notably to their poorer customers. Nor did the law resolve the social issue of who deserved to eat what, because the rich bought wheaten while the poor often had to content themselves with the lesser household kind. In 1773 George III tried to make the system fairer by adding a middle category, standard wheaten, marked *SW*. Even then, however, standard wheaten sometimes cost more than the poor could readily afford, particularly when the wheat harvests failed and there wasn't enough grain to go around.

As it happened, that cruel condition marked the period from 1793 to 1814. During that stretch, fourteen of twenty-two grain harvests fell short in one way or another. The years 1795–1800 especially saw a string of bad harvests. Frost, cold, and rain repeatedly caused heavy crop losses. Food prices soared. In 1802 beef and mutton cost 70 percent to 100 percent more than they had in 1793. Wages rose too but didn't keep pace, particularly for unskilled work such as agricultural labor. Occupational statistics weren't kept then, but one may guess what agricultural labor meant when, in 1800, 80 percent of the population was rural. As the eighteenth century closed, life was so hard that one historian has argued that in 1795 and 1799–1800, England suffered famine, despite the government's refusal to utter the word. Famine or no, however, it was shocking how the world's richest nation was scrambling to feed itself.

What was more, normally law-abiding people protested, and violently. In April 1795 the *Leicester Herald* reported that six hundred women seized food at the Exeter marketplace and forced its sale at prices they considered reasonable. The paper may have exaggerated the number but not the mood. Miners in Nuneaton also confiscated food and sold it, first having paraded bearing a pole to which they had fixed a bread loaf decked in funeral crepe. Such incidents happened often, and what was even more disturbing, His Majesty's soldiers occasionally joined in. The turmoil carried a particularly frightening meaning in 1795, for similar disturbances had recently thrust France into bloody revolution.

That revolution had brought about war with England, and the conflict was now raging. Given England's cause and France's perceived character, the war underlined, for those who saw things that way, the risks of long-term food shortage. It also made the scarcity that much worse, because England's armed forces absorbed vast quantities of food and animal fodder, and because war spending strained the economy. When harvest prospects for 1795 looked bad, following a poor year in 1794, the government sought ways to guarantee the bread supply. How seriously it judged the situation may be seen in its attempts, fumbling and half-hearted though they were, to dabble in grain subsidies at home and purchases abroad. The effort prompted a famous essay from Edmund Burke, "Thoughts and Details on Scarcity," which defined how a prophet of laissez-faire views such policies. Burke wrote that "an indiscreet tampering" with the markets controlling food supply was most dangerous precisely when people most wanted it. Further, he declared that both government poor relief and market management would bring ruin; the first encouraging dependence, the second stifling competition. He did stress that charity was a Christian duty, but one in which the government had no part.

These opinions would have great long-term importance in how Britain saw the poor. More immediately, they would also color a special philanthropic effort, one that revealed how bleak matters were. For the first time, the English government, aided by upstanding citizens, promoted the potato.

The way they went about it, one would have thought they were discussing a sensitive, very private matter. In late February 1795, the Board of Agriculture released a pamphlet titled "Hints Respecting the Culture and Use of Potatoes" and circulated it in newspapers. Arthur Young was the board's secretary, and no doubt he agreed with the pamphlet's message, but "Hints" dared neither his acerbic wit nor his impatience with backwardness. Rather, the style was nervously diffident. "Hints" even apologized for the way it asked the clergy, without warning and in so public a manner, to help make the potato popular. With utmost tact, the pamphlet addressed only practical matters, and without comment, attempting to avoid thorny social issues. Yes, the tuber could be very profitable—"Hints" calculated the gain—and without ruining the soil for grain. Yes, curl was a problem, but certain cultivars withstood it better than others. The pamphlet's only social nuance infused the advice that on large farms, laborers might plant potatoes "for themselves, in such angles and corners as might otherwise be neglected."

Which was letting the cat out of the bag. Once more, the potato might profit the farmer, who didn't need to eat it, but it would feed his poor hireling, who did. The social distinction of who must eat the lowly root wouldn't go away, no matter how lightly reformers trod around it. In part, this was because "Hints" was intended for landowners, not laborers, a familiar story. At least, however, the Board of Agriculture was promoting the potato as a valid cash crop, not a stopgap until England's larder was better stocked. Accordingly, it lobbied for a modest potato subsidy, an idea the government rejected.

No such radical notion inspired the *Times* (London), which was most concerned with preserving the nation's grain supply, and to that patriotic end spent much ink cheering the tuber. The paper offered recipes to show how potatoes stretched meat dishes and bread, and reported the many official experiments that mixed potato flour with wheaten. Further, the *Times* handed out praise for self-sacrifice, lauding "the most noble example" of a man who ate four loaves of "brown" mixed-cereal bread a week instead of twelve white ones, and who supplemented the bread with potatoes and rice. When the *Times* calculated that wheat would cost fifteen shillings less per sack if everyone used potato flour, "God forbid," the paper declared, "that any one should, on this account, reprobate the use of potatoes in bread."

Many did, however, including the *Times*. Barely four months later, the paper reversed itself, calling potato flour useless and saying barley made better mixed bread. So it did, but that wasn't the problem. Those who had recommended the potato to reduce England's reliance on wheat had seriously misjudged public taste. The London poor, who lived on bread, wanted the best wheaten, shortage or not. In vain, the government and the *Times* extolled Standard Wheaten or the mixed household loaf, saying that outside London, people ate only mixed bread. However, in London the mixed loaves weren't much cheaper than best wheaten, which meant that the patriotic poor saved themselves little. Besides, lacking ovens, they had to buy what the baker sold. Since many bakers wouldn't sell mixed bread, the poor could either look for one who would, a nuisance, or take what was offered, and possibly be cheated either way.

Parliament noted how the poor refused to eat mixed bread, whether of potatoes, oats, or barley. Some members talked of passing laws forbidding bakers to sell wheaten, and petitions demanding such action came in from various places. After all, the king and many families of "rank and fortune" had voluntarily cut back on bread and other foods. However, much as Parliament wished the poor behaved like the rich, no laws insisted on it. Enforcing taste was a dangerous thing. The poor were suffering the most, and forbidding them their only luxury would be unjust and provoke anger. Moreover, food habits were ingrained, part of national pride, and couldn't be legislated away. And even if they could, how could the government intervene in such a private matter?

All this missed the point, however. Those who had advocated the potato failed to consider how they viewed it themselves. They didn't advertise it as a worthy food, only as a substitute for bread. The king did not announce that his household would eat potatoes instead of bread, nor did the *Times* suggest that anyone should. Rather, the *Times* asked its readers to refrain from expensive food—to give up pastry, eat mixed bread only and less of it, serve only one kind of butcher's meat per meal "when circumstances permit," and have fish as often as possible. Of course, the paper said, one had to tell the servants that these measures came not from meanness but from concern for the poor.

And the poor were told a different story: that the potato was their meat, literally. As a philanthropic-minded man wrote the *Times*, charity went wrong when a rich person roasted an ox and distributed the meat to the poor. Rather, the letter-writer said, the poor had to be taught how to cook. Echoing Smollett and Defoe, he pointed out that only in England did a pound of meat mean a pound of food, dinner for one. Everywhere else, that pound of meat fed six people because vegetables went into the pot. To prove it, he provided recipes, each including sizable amounts of potatoes. Along the same lines, officialdom asked workhouses, hospitals, and public charities to rely more on potatoes, rice, and vegetables (though it didn't advise going without meat).

No doubt England needed sermons on the virtue of vegetables, but the preaching went to only the lower classes. Since midcentury if not sooner, the wealthy had enjoyed potatoes with their steak, yet, during the crisis of 1795, they were still not admitting it. That the potato could have passed as respectable is suggested by Hannah Glasse's *Art of Cooking Made Plain and Easy*. In the 1796 edition, Mrs. Glasse's popular guide offered eleven potato recipes, probably more than any English cookbook had up to then. Strangely, almost half included sugar or other sweet ingredients, recalling English cuisine of the century before. One wonders whether potatoes commonly tasted bitter, but that charge was probably truer of French cultivars than English. More likely, English cooks hadn't yet fully appreciated the potato's gifts. Even pan-fried potatoes required sugar, according to Mrs. Glasse.

Nevertheless, lack of appreciation differs from lack of acknowledgment. How curious that no upper-class person stepped forward to praise potatoes from experience, especially with the nation at war and survival, as some thought, at stake. What would such an endorsement have cost? That none was made sent the old message. Potatoes were hardship fare, the food of misery. The agonies of 1795 did, as the Board of Agriculture noted, prompt certain districts to begin growing the potato. But it cannot be true, as his-

torians have sometimes said, that by 1800 most English farmers were raising it. Rather, no doubt everyone expected that once the shortage ended,
potato bread would be a bad memory, and pure wheaten would resume its
rightful throne. When that happy day arrived, someone might still be stuck
with the tuber, but not the better sort of people.

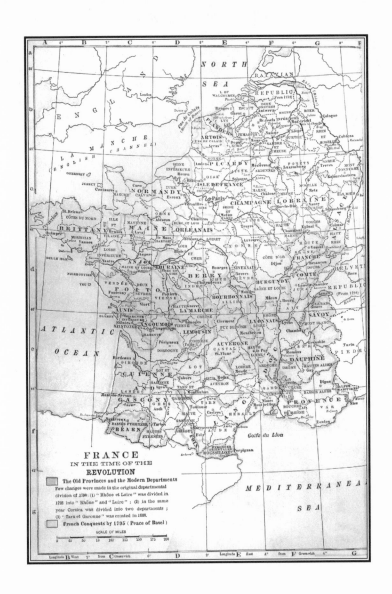

FRANCE
IN THE TIME OF THE
REVOLUTION

The Old Provinces and the Modern Departments
Few changes were made in the original departmental
division of 1790: (1) "Rhône et Loire" was divided in
1793 into "Rhône" and "Loire"; (2) in the same
year Corsica was divided into two departments;
(3) "Tarn et Garonne" was created in 1808.

French Conquests by 1795 (Peace of Basel)

SCALE OF MILES

4 *Vive la pomme de terre*

The potato is rightly reproached for causing gas;
but what are winds to the robust bodily organs
of peasants and laborers?
DENIS DIDEROT

PEASANT AGRICULTURE of seventeenth- and eighteenth-century France was a delicate mechanism. When nothing went wrong, the nation produced enough grain to feed itself, but no more than that; and things often went wrong. Yields varied wildly. Even an ordinary harvest might be twice what its predecessor was, whereas the following year could bring a sharp drop. Then there were extraordinary years. Famine struck France thirteen times in the sixteenth century, eleven in the seventeenth, and sixteen in the eighteenth. And this tally is an estimate, perhaps incomplete, and includes general outbreaks only. It doesn't count local famines that ravaged one area or other almost yearly.

Grain's enemy was less cold weather (though that took its toll) or storms, which damaged crops in localities, than wet summers, which prevented the grain from ripening and caused it to rot. When that happened, those who had grain hoarded it, sometimes as speculators. The short supply drove up the price to the point where the poor could no longer afford it. They searched for bad flour, or flour that was dirty or slightly mildewed, or stretched what they had by mixing in half-germinated seeds, crushed beans, acorns taken from the pigs, cabbage cores, fern roots, leaves, even tree bark. And when these tactics failed—or even when they worked—people starved or died of digestive or other diseases, spread by bad water or human waste.

A solution lay at hand, or, rather, under foot, in a new plant that thrived in wet weather and was hardier than grain. It had been there no later than 1600, when the agriculturist Olivier de Serres had written about it. Sow after the spring thaw, de Serres had advised, during a waning moon, four fingers deep. He had even given the potato a name that was destined to be famous: *cartoufle*, which he got by corrupting the Italian for truffle (*tartufi* or *tartufoli*) or potato (*tartuffo* or *tartuffolo*). In the eighteenth century, *cartoufle* became the German *Kartoffel* and its variants in Russian, Polish, and many other tongues.

Unfortunately, the French were much better at naming the potato than growing it. Eastern France got it around the time de Serres wrote, chiefly along the Swiss and Flemish borders, but its expansion was unwelcome, and it didn't emerge in importance there until the late seventeenth century. When marauding troops destroyed the vineyards in the Saint-Dié Valley in the Vosges during the Thirty Years War (1618–48), farmers who replanted in the tuber provoked general disgust. Opinion held it to be a "vile and gross" plant, like the acorn "destined rather to feed animals than people." The Burgundians, people who were said to have "silk intestines" because they knew good food when they saw it, did tinker with improving potato yields. (They also nicknamed the plant *pomme de terre*.) But the Burgundians were also alleged to be the ones who outlawed it for causing leprosy. Even Paris, magnet for the new, saw the tuber only in 1665.

It wasn't as if the French despised vegetables the way the English did. The upper-class diet did revolve around meat, bread, cheese, pastries, and wine. But salads were more common, containing ingredients like watercress, lettuce, endive, carrots, parsnips, onions, and roasted leeks, though not all had a wide following. Parsnips, like the newly introduced spinach, were Lenten fare. Cucumbers were thought unhealthy. Cabbages and turnips were highly prized, especially in Paris. As in England, asparagus had long won approval, though the eyes were the body part that the plant supposedly benefited, not the bladder.

But that was how a select few lived. The poor enjoyed no such luxuries. Grain was their sustenance, and when it failed, they starved. Consequently, the odds were high that peasants in any locality would know severe hunger once or more each decade and could recall a time when there was nothing to eat but grass. These terrifying ordeals taught the survivors strict frugality and self-denial. Sadly, accepting an alternative to grain was a lesson much longer in coming.

By the mid-eighteenth century, the potato was still so exotic that if agricultural experts referred to it, they used its Latin name and not the homey *pomme de terre*. One of the few authorities who mentioned it in print was de Combles (his first name is unknown), who described it in *School for the Kitchen Garden* (1749). De Combles treated the potato as if rarity were its reputation, which he refuted while saying it was undeserved. Not only the poor or country folk ate the tuber, he said; he knew city sophisticates who loved it. He declined to admit that they suffered a "depravity of taste," implying that others said just that. However, he wouldn't argue with anyone who disliked it, and he thought it was "insipid" and "heavy."

Like his English counterparts, de Combles was mildly praising the potato as food for someone else. Unlike them, though, he was also suggesting that people who prided themselves on their palates might enjoy it without appearing lower-class. Further, he listed many ways in which to cook it, implying that France was starting to take notice. Poorer people, de Combles said, roasted potatoes in the embers and ate them with salt. The better-off ate them sliced thinly, powdered with flour, and fried in butter or oil—the french fry's ancestor. Or the potatoes were boiled, sliced, and fricaseed in butter, with onion. Some people had them in white sauce; others, in wine.

But the best way, de Combles remarked—could he have thought the potato *that* insipid?—was to make a paste with bread crumbs, egg yolks, and herbs. The cook covered the potatoes with it and browned them in butter.

The culinary flair de Combles described apparently sprang up in more than one place, the way creativity does. However, these recipes lacked wide currency. Despite what he said about the tuber's rising popularity, at the time he wrote much of the country had never seen it or had only just done so. The Rhône Valley, where he said he had found it, got it around 1713. But western France didn't grow it until much later, with the coastal provinces accepting it last. In 1769, Irish merchants in the port of La Rochelle were forced to send home for potatoes because they couldn't find any. The region just to the north, the Vendée, barred its doors until 1788. Late as these dates are, even they are misleading, because they say only when the potato first entered a place. Acceptance didn't always follow, nor did it mean every district succumbed. Whatever headway the potato made before the Revolution, it didn't gain wide confidence until around 1815.

The historian Fernand Braudel has ascribed the slow progress partly to the lack of suitable cultivars. No doubt that was an obstacle, because France had only two in 1752, and they couldn't have conformed to all climates and soils. Also, plant breeding was a hit-and-miss affair, hardly the science informed by modern genetics, and often done by amateur gardeners. But amateurs or not, they took care where they got their seeds, preferably from trusted associates, and propagated only specimens that had proved themselves. A classic French gardening book, translated into English in 1691, urged its readers to follow this rule "if you be ambitious to have the best." But where the potato was concerned, no one was ambitious. Long-day cultivars would have required fresh stock from South America, an idea whose time hadn't yet come, but no one, French or English, experimented even with the plants already available. Once they got around to it, the number of cultivars increased rapidly, and even before the Revolution there were at least twelve. More French farmers could have grown potatoes before 1789. Why they didn't speaks to their food traditions and what values they treasured.

The French held to their fear of nightshades longer than the English. Reformers tested this stubborn myth because this was the Enlightenment, but not everyone wished to be enlightened. In 1761 Anne Robert Jacques Turgot, intendant of Limoges, ate potatoes in public and made peasants sit with him so they would see he was unharmed. Turgot wasn't one to shrink from challenges—he later tried to reform Louis XVI's finances—but prejudice didn't budge easily. In 1771 the Faculté de Paris saw fit to publish a paper swearing the potato was innocuous, even useful. Still, many people doubted. Antoine Augustin Parmentier wrote in 1789, after yet another famine, that though the tuber was a nightshade, it wasn't soporific. He knew because he had chemically analyzed it. Parmentier also complained that many people, not just peasants, insisted that it spread disease. The Faculté's effort, he noted, had come about because of an argument in the press. An irate man in Normandy had insisted that the tuber was dangerous because water used to make potato bread turned dark readily, proving that it contained putrefaction. No sane person would eat that.

When poison wasn't an issue, social grace was. Intellectuals said the potato was undignified food, fit only for beasts or people who lived like them. Shockingly, those who espoused this idea included Denis Diderot, a key figure of the Enlightenment. The 1765 edition of his famous *Grande Encyclopédie* noted how some peasants ate the insipid, starchy root for "a good part of the year." It wasn't a "pleasant" food, though abundant, and adequately nourished those who didn't care about anything except sustenance. The *Encyclopédie* also said that the potato caused intestinal gas but opined that this was no drawback for laborers or peasants, whose robust insides could withstand the disturbance better than those of more refined folk.

Perhaps this last comment owed something to Diderot's fixation with his digestion, which the philosopher mentioned in almost all his letters.

Then, too, Diderot later modified his views. A supplement to the *Encyclopédie*, published in 1777, stressed the potato's usefulness. Nevertheless, others warned that it would debase people who ate it. In 1770 a Pyrenean cleric cautioned that if humans adopted what had been animal food, it would lower the standard of living. Even animals had reportedly balked at eating it—cows, it was said, had rejected it at first because they didn't recognize its smell.

They weren't the only ones whose noses were out of joint. A well-known Parisian gourmet voiced outrage in 1783 because potatoes had briefly achieved a certain chic in the capital. He couldn't understand how such vile stuff could have appeared "even on good tables." Potatoes had a doughy taste and were insipid, unhealthy, and indigestible, qualities that had led the finer houses to reject them after that short, horrible fling. Which, he remarked, justly left the tuber to the common people, whose rough palates and sturdy stomachs could be satisfied by everything that eased their hunger. This was precious snobbery, of course, but not that far from what philanthropists had said in the potato's defense. Even a noted agricultural expert who praised the tuber had winced at the taste and called it famine fare.

Probably the potato's biggest hurdle, however, was the French peasant diet. It was a vehicle that ran on two wheels: bread and *bouillie*, or porridge. As an extra starch, the potato was a third wheel, and life had no room for frills. Besides, bread and *bouillie* were made of grain, an honest product of the soil, whose mythic power touched the soul more profoundly than any vegetable. Grain had a long tradition; the Bible extolled it, and its most glorious form, bread, appeared at every meal. Most often, bread contained oats, rye, or barley, and was black, brown, or gray. White wheaten bread was a luxury, for some families a Christmas treat only. An observer in nineteenth-century Brittany wrote that you could always tell a holiday feast from a regular meal because the bread was white, not black.

Whatever its color or composition, bread inspired reverence. The feeling came partly from frugality, almost a religion among the French peasantry, and partly from a desire to honor God's gift of sustenance. Then, too, bread was sacred, representing Christ's body in the Communion rite. The symbolism continued at the table. Saying grace meant thanking the Lord for bread. The man of the house cut a cross in each new loaf before either he or his wife sliced it, thinly, and served the family. After the meal, she gathered the crumbs. The tiniest fed the chickens, while the larger ones went into *panade*, bread soup.

If the word *meat* was traditionally synonymous with "food" in England, it was otherwise in France. For most French people, meat meant bits of salt pork that reached the table perhaps only once a week. Bread reigned, in fact and in spirit, as many proverbs attest. Children who wasted anything were told that they didn't "know how the bread comes." Another saying went that youth gave you teeth but no bread, while old age gave you bread but no teeth. And good teeth were vital, because peasant bread wasn't the moist delicacy that today's specialty bakeries offer proudly. The food that inspired so much adoration was dreadful, partly because the French peasant baked under severe constraints. Many houses lacked ovens, which meant using communal ones. That, and the scarcity of fuel and labor, made baking a rare event. In good times, it happened every few weeks; in bad, once or twice a year.

Under such conditions, any baking would have been difficult. With the sheer volume of dough, weak or impure leavening agents, and bad flour, turning out decent bread was a miracle. It was more likely to resemble the Solognat barley and buckwheat bread that "holds the knife as it does the throat." In 1845, a man from Franche-Comté recalled the oat bread he had grown up with, which hardened in the oven "like tile." But even the best bread turned rock-hard when it had hung around too long. It couldn't be eaten by itself; hence the phrase *tremper la soupe* (literally, "dip in soup," but implying "to pour soup over bread"). The phrase had another, important context: To let someone *trempe la soupe* meant to feed him. Proverbs attest to soup's importance in everday life, as with "Soup makes the man, woman makes the soup." However, before pouring the soup, someone had to cut the bread, which, as the man from Franche-Comté said, "neither tooth nor knife" could do. Rather, the job required an ax. In some regions, a boy couldn't call himself a man until he could cut bread.

By the early nineteenth century, a well-off farmer in Alsace, for example, might spend about one-fourth of his budget on bread, or twice as much as he paid for meat. This farmer was fortunate, because he had his own grain, his own oven, and the wood to fire it. Rural laborers without these resources bought either the grain or the flour on credit. That was a painful bargain, even when the miller was honest, and folklore, if not experience, taught people to be cynical. Laborers thus might spend 50 percent or 60 percent of their budget on bread.

In such a fragile household economy, the potato's advantages seem obvious, a way of saving flour, bread, and money. Compared with bread, it was also much easier to prepare, to eat, and probably to digest. The French peasant appears stubborn indeed to have rejected the potato while preferring such a dreadful, expensive, and meager diet. Perhaps so, but bread wasn't the potato's only competitor.

Bouillie held a special place too. In the sixteenth century it even attained vogue at court, the nobility deigning to rediscover baby food. During the eighteenth century the middle and upper classes continued to eat it. When Tobias Smollett saw the bourgeoisie and petty nobility of Boulogne lunching on soup and *bouillie* and ascribed it to penury or stinginess, he was showing a foreigner's ignorance. In 1760s England, porridge was a sign of poverty or excessive thrift, but not in France. Ten years later, an Englishman who had read Smollett and pardoned his prejudices saw moderation, not avarice, in a lunch of *bouillie* and soup. Significantly, he also thought the French enjoyed life much more than the English and ate more healthily.

However, these two visitors only met people who ate *bouillie* by choice, perhaps once a day. Peasants ate it more often. Each region had its preferred kind, depending on which grain was cheapest or best liked. Buckwheat, corn, oats, and sometimes even wheat flour or rice might become *bouillie*. For instance, the Bretons said that buckwheat weighed on the stomach, staving off hunger for a few hours. During the later stages of cooking, it got so thick the Breton housewife couldn't stir it unaided. Before serving, she scooped a hollow in the *bouillie*, simmering in an enormous pot, and dropped in two pounds of butter. Each diner spooned *bouillie* into a bowl of milk, then put butter atop the porridge. It was thought gauche to let milk from one's bowl get into the butter remaining in the pot.

The Bretons' Norman neighbors also made *bouillie* from milk and buckwheat, but they felt differently about it. The Normans thought it couldn't keep away hunger long, not without other food beside it, which may say something about the austerity for which the Bretons were famous. However, nowhere in France did daily peasant fare approach the sumptuous feasts that gourmets now enjoy. For example, the Mâconnais, in southern Burgundy, stands out today for its "country" cooking. But until the nineteenth century ended, rural folk there typically ate soup and *bouillie*. The only difference was that corn was the usual grain, with buckwheat reserved for tough times. *Bouillie* served many purposes in the Mâconnais. It was supper, children's fare, food for heavy work days, or when the family needed a quick, satisfying meal. If the Mâconnais had a gourmet treat hidden amid all that utility, it was *bouillie* of white wheat flour. That delicacy was typically given to children, the sick, and women in childbirth.

Accordingly, the tuber had to assume the niche that *bouillie* occupied, or join it, as happened in the Mâconnais. The process took time, and by the mid–eighteenth century, it had occurred in few places. Two regions where it did were the Pyrenees and the Dauphiné. Both are mountainous, probably no coincidence, because the climate favored the potato. In the Pyrenees particularly, cool weather and mild sunshine provided a sound habitat where, for more than a century, the crop rarely failed. As for the Dauphiné (which today includes three departments and the city of Grenoble), it wasn't only the mountains that counted, but where they were. In the seventeenth century, the tuber reached the Dauphiné by crossing the Alps from Switzerland.

However, the potato's singular record in the Pyrenees and the Dauphiné couldn't have rested on geography and climate alone. If it had, other mountainous areas would have profited much sooner than they did. For instance, the Savoie, whose two departments today adjoin Italy and Switzerland, was well situated to receive the potato. As an Italian state (France first annexed it in 1792), the Savoie had seen potatoes near its borders before most of Europe. Yet it didn't embrace the tuber until the 1770s. Therefore, something else must explain what made the Pyreneans and Dauphinois among France's earliest committed potato eaters. Two related conditions increased the potato's influence there: fuel scarcity and less reliance on bread.

In the Dauphiné, the fuel shortage had become dire by the eighteenth century. The province had lost so much forest that some people had to travel two days to fetch firewood, a labor they couldn't always spare time for and one that depended on good weather. Sometimes they even abandoned their homes for want of fuel. In the Oisans area, people reserved wood for baking bread, and they fired their ovens only twice a year. The ovens were communal, because only in provinces where wood was plentiful could households maintain their own. For want of wood, brush and cow dung became everyday fuels. The scarcity profoundly affected daily life. The *veillée*, a custom in which neighbors gathered nightly to do light work while listening to stories, had a particular twist in the Dauphiné. There, the *veillée* met in the barn, where the animals' body heat made it the only place warm enough.

The Dauphiné was a hardscrabble province. It contained remote villages where, well into the nineteenth century, people produced almost everything they used. They wore wooden shoes and clothes woven of the hemp they grew. They ate buckwheat and rye bread, cooked soup of beans and cabbage, raised pigs, collected chestnuts, and made their own cheese, oil, and vinegar. With bread hard to bake and harder to eat, the potato suited their diet and their need to save fuel. It also fit the Dauphiné villagers' isolated, self-sufficient economy. To this day, French cuisine recognizes the tuber's traditional importance in the Dauphiné by calling baked scalloped potatoes *gratin dauphinois*.

Perhaps what also allowed the potato to make a strong showing in the Dauphiné was not only the difficulty of making bread, but that the bread wasn't wheaten. In some regions, the potato might replace buckwheat or eclipse it, but wheat was another matter. Superstition hurt the potato here. Like the English, some French peasants believed that if they planted potatoes in a fallow field, the wheat they sowed there the following year wouldn't grow. This was because, they said, the potatoes sapped the soil's vitality. But such beliefs aside, wheat was supreme because of its social position. It was the aristocrat of grains, almost literally, because the best bread was wheaten, and only the "best people" ate it. If wheat evoked nobility, virile beauty, or masculine power, the potato, as one author has pointed out, evoked women, and not the sexy ones. Common recipe names even imply this, as with *bonne femme, menagère, grand-mère* (old woman, housewife, grandmother).

What's striking about the Dauphiné is that, at least during the century before the potato's arrival, the province produced second-rate wheat. Buyers scorned Dauphinois wheat because it was brown and mixed with rye grass. They avoided feeding it to their chickens. Moreover, eggs that came from hens that fed on such wheat brought lower prices than those raised on other grain. Of course, provinces like Brittany, where buckwheat reigned, were slow to adopt the potato, so wheat's absence or poor quality was not necessarily the deciding factor. Nevertheless, where wheat held court, the potato was less likely to find ready favor.

The Pyrenean peasant had always eaten grains other than wheat—corn and buckwheat—and prepared *bouillie* from them. The first mention of the tuber, called the *patano*, dates from 1744, but it may have arrived earlier. By

1780 it had become the Pyrenean highlands' chief food. People ate it boiled, mixed with a cabbage soup, or mashed with milk, a dish known as *machado*. The valley populations quickly adopted potatoes as well, so that by the early nineteenth century, the area was exporting them. In 1812, a government official wrote that even in good years, the peasants sold their grain, keeping the tuber. And 1812 was a terrible year, bringing one of the cruelest famines in memory. For anyone who cared to see, the Pyrenees provided a lesson, because the potato spared the region from the worst.

Outside the Pyrenean cities, bread ruled in only one place, near an iron mine. In that district, the blacksmiths ate butcher's meat and white bread and drank Roussillon wine. The bread was called "blacksmith's bread," and only they ate it, a fitting privilege, perhaps, for those who practiced that most virile profession. The miners ate bread too, but just on feast days, and it was black, the wheat flour having been mixed with rye, corn, or millet. Buckwheat *bouillie* was their usual fare.

The Pyreneans favored starches other than bread probably because, like the Dauphinois, they had nothing with which to bake it. The cutting down of forests, especially to stoke the iron forges, caused serious fuel shortages. As in the Dauphiné, the distance people traveled to gather wood cost them dearly, as did their lack of convenient transport. Those living near forested estates defied the law to cut wood there, and an illicit trade in charcoal grew up. Those who had no access to that under-the-table resource, however, had to solve the scarcity in other ways. For example, in 1745, the townspeople of Foix heated their homes with roots. Most peasants used brush. An English visitor to Perpignan in 1775 remarked on how expensive and scarce wood was in that town. "I frequently saw," he wrote, "mules and asses loaded with rosemary and lavender bushes, to sell for firing."

What kept the potato down, then—or, in some areas, raised it—was the point at which practicality met tradition. Not every area that lacked fuel grew potatoes, and not every area that grew potatoes lacked fuel. But the mechanism of the tuber's advance is only part of the story. The other part is why the mechanism clanked along so slowly. The tuber ran smack into centuries-old customs that decided two of the most basic questions of peasant life, what to put in the soil and on the plate. Existence was fragile enough without letting in what was new and uncertain, even though what was new might help. The fear of change ran so deep that people were ready to die rather than alter their ways.

Not just the French, either. When a famine struck Naples in 1770, people refused to touch a boatload of potatoes sent as a gift. In Switzerland, the physician Daniel Langhaus wrote *The Art of Self-Healing*, in which he proposed that bad food and lack of exercise caused scrofulous diseases. He pointed out that such maladies rarely appeared in the potato's absence. Similar beliefs existed in Prussia, where peasants feared that the tuber would bring scrofula, rickets, and tuberculosis. They felt so strongly that when Frederick the Great ordered them to grow it as a safeguard against famine, they argued. In 1774 the town of Kolberg sent him this message: "The things have neither smell nor taste, not even the dogs will eat them, so what use are they to us?" The king insisted and his subjects gave way. But seven years later near the Elbe, self-respecting servants still preferred to change masters rather than accept potatoes as part of their board.

In Russia, Catherine the Great decided that potatoes would be a good thing, overruling Orthodox fundamentalists who objected to growing a plant not mentioned in the Bible. Some regions responded to imperial prompting, but peasants in central Russia were convinced beyond her persuasion that the tuber caused cholera. Russia didn't truly become potato territory until 1850, when Nicholas I forced it on those who were still unwilling.

France didn't have a Frederick or a Catherine, but it did have Parmentier. A singular figure in history, Parmentier once wrote that his "perpetual object" was improving "the principal food of the people"; he came to that goal from firsthand experience. As an army pharmacist during the Seven Years' War (1756–63), he was taken prisoner by the Prussians and lived on nothing but potatoes, or so the story goes. (To stay healthy, he would have needed milk too, but legend says his captors gave him gin.) Whatever the literal truth was, Parmentier's miraculous survival convinced him of the tuber's value, and when the war ended, he returned to France, where he studied chemistry and applied its analytic principles to his favorite vegetable.

Disaster gave him an opportunity to spread the word. During the famine of 1770, he won an essay contest by arguing (wrongly) that potato starch was nutritious and made good bread. Louis XV noticed the onetime pharmacist's apprentice and gave him a sinecure that let him write and research. Parmentier used the king's favor as a passport to court, where he pressed his case. Parmentier saw the potato as his country's salvation, and for forty years he never missed a chance to say so, whether to king, landowner, councillor, or peasant. No matter how much resistance he saw, he never gave up, a campaign that seems to have sprung from a passion that was personal as well as intellectual.

The potato wasn't his only project—the fifteen thousand pages he penned included discussions of sugar beets, bran, and chestnuts—but perhaps it seemed that way. One wonders whether courtiers who didn't share M. Parmentier's obsession found someplace else to go when they saw him coming. Yet what little commentary survives about him suggests he was an engaging, lively man. Arthur Young, for one, thought him charming and wished more Frenchmen had his "fire and vivacity." Perhaps those qualities were what had led Parmentier to invite Young and other guests to a dinner in which all twenty dishes consisted of potatoes.

Parmentier's finest hour as a royal servant came under Louis XVI, whom he induced to wear a potato flower in his buttonhole. Marie-Antoinette thought the purple blossoms looked well on her too, and suddenly the court had a new fad. Parmentier exploited his opening, persuading Louis to endorse a public experiment. Because people had been saying that the potato ruined the soil, Parmentier wanted to prove that it would grow in the worst land available. That turned out to be fifty acres at Sablons, a sandy waste on Paris's outskirts. In 1786 he had potatoes planted there and made the field conspicuous by posting a guard, but only during the day. As he hoped, peasants visited at night to steal the tubers, a ruse Parmentier was proud of and used often.

These triumphs earned him a medal from Louis and praise from other scientists. But as Young remarked, when it came to agriculture, the French spent too much time on theory and not enough on practice. And as sure as the Lord made frost in springtime, French grain failed in 1788, and famine struck once more. By then, it was too late for the ancien régime, but the Republic listened. In late 1793, the Commission on Subsistence and Provisions, which oversaw the food supply, gratefully accepted Citizen Parmentier's counsel and printed ten thousand copies of a pamphlet he wrote advising on potato cultivation. These went to administrators in every commune, ordering them to publicize the contents and to foster the raising of that most useful vegetable, "too long ignored and even scorned." With rhetorical flourish, the commission appealed to Republican patriotism. Growing the tuber on lands once kept fallow to amuse the nobility—heaths, parks, rabbit warrens, and the like—would promote agriculture and help erase the legacy of wasteful idleness. This was a curious twist: casting as an instrument of vigor a vegetable elsewhere thought to inspire laziness.

The portrayal underlined what the new antiaristocratic philosophy said about land and its functions. Food production was politically vital. Counterrevolutionaries, unnamed but presumably France's foreign enemies and their sympathizers at home, hoped that famine would bring down the Republic. The potato would help plunge "the dagger of despair" into their hearts. Accordingly, if the peasantry still hesitated to plant the tuber, good Republicans must explain not only how useful the plant was, but that it would preserve the farmers' newfound political freedom against those who would take it away. *Vive la pomme de terre.*

Rehabilitating the potato didn't please everyone, though. When Parmentier's name arose for nomination to a municipal post, one elector objected, "He'll make us eat potatoes, he's the one who invented them." Parmentier lost the election, but he may have been lucky to be considered, let alone keep his head. The medal Louis XVI gave him, says one historian, caused him trouble among revolutionaries who suspected he had too close a tie to the late king. Nevertheless, Parmentier outlived the First Republic, just as he had outlived the two Louis. And he was vindicated when potatoes became politically correct. Within a year after the food commission distributed his pamphlet, a cookbook appeared with the charming title of *La cuisinière républicaine* (*The Republican Cook*). It offered twenty potato recipes and invited the public to submit more. Alas, the responses have been lost.

When Napoleon took power, he, too, noticed Parmentier. For military reasons, the emperor wanted France to become as self-sufficient as possible. This need assumed greater urgency after his ill-advised Berlin Decree of 1806, which declared an economic embargo on Britain. The policy not only failed, it provoked a counterblockade that worked all too well. Whether from hardship or common sense, the Napoleonic era saw potato production rise sharply, possibly as much as fifteenfold. Further, the emperor financed several of Parmentier's projects, including a factory to process sugar from beets. He also awarded him the Legion of Honor and named him to direct the health service. But these laurels came late, and Parmentier was failing. He died in 1813 at age seventy-six, while a terrible famine was proving, again, the wisdom he had preached. Today, his name survives chiefly through potato recipes, as in crêpes Parmentier. He couldn't have hoped for a more fitting epitaph.

How tempting to wonder what might have happened had France listened sooner, if the Bourbon monarchy had pursued a coherent, consistent policy to increase the food supply. Parmentier's sermons would have become official gospel, and potatoes the first food of the land. Marie-Antoinette would be famous for saying, "Let them eat *pommes de terre*," the French people would have enjoyed fuller bellies, and the Bastille would still be standing.

Not quite. Louis XVI's reign was known neither for coherence nor sure-handed governance. Even had it cared to address the problem Parmentier's way, any official effort would have run into the same obstacles the erstwhile pharmacist faced in his one-man campaign. Besides, as the English were realizing around that time, food habits cannot be legislated or changed at will. For most French peasants, life without bread would have lacked substance, in many senses. Had the government lobbied for the potato, especially to replace grain, people might well have thought they were being cheated. Finally, to suppose that more food would have prevented the Revolution is to reduce that complex event to a single cause, a debatable notion at best.

But if Parmentier's vision couldn't have saved the monarchy, it could have saved lives. Too bad more people didn't share it sooner.

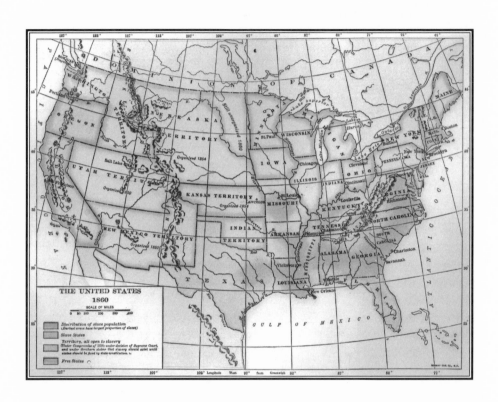

THE UNITED STATES
1860

SCALE OF MILES
0   50 100   200   300   400

Distribution of slave population
(Darkest areas have largest proportion of slaves)

Slave States

Territory, all open to slavery
(Under Compromise of 1850, under decision of Supreme Court,
and under Southern claims that slavery should exist until
states should be fixed by state constitution.)

Free States

5 The Democratic Table

I sometimes eat it [meat] two or three times a day . . .
it is the fashion always to have meat on the table.
OHIO TRAVELER

IN SEPTEMBER 1774 John Adams portrayed the struggle for American independence in clear, passionate words. Writing to his wife, Abigail, he said he would prefer the deepest poverty to obedience to Britain. "Let us eat potatoes and drink water," he said, "let us wear canvas, and undressed sheepskins, rather than submit to the unrighteous and ignominious domination that is prepared for us."

As far as this historian knows, from the late seventeenth century to the First World War, Adams's outburst was the only time an American ever attacked the potato in print—and he did it in private. Why English-born colonists forgot their potato prejudice once they crossed the Atlantic is hard to explain, yet they must have done so. Infant America, especially New England and the Middle Atlantic colonies, loved the tuber. Given the silence on its reputed defects, people probably never even stopped to consider whether it might be harmful or lower class.

Adams came close to that. But if the future second president was a potato-hater, a poll of other chief-executives-to-be reveals a different opinion. George Washington had the tuber planted on his estate in 1767;

Thomas Jefferson ate potatoes as early as 1772 and listed them in his farm journal for 1794. Contrast these actions with the likelihood that King George III's household never substituted potatoes for bread during the crisis of 1795, and a tiny corner of a large picture begins to emerge.

The potato is said to have reached colonial North America as early as 1613, in Bermuda, then gone to the mainland in 1621. If so, however, the destination was probably Canada, because the first hard evidence of American colonial potato growing dates from 1685. William Penn, describing Pennsylvania for those who might wish to emigrate, mentioned "Irish Potatos" in a long list of familiar grains and vegetables that throve in his colony. Further, a colleague of Penn's wrote that he hoped "to have a brave increase [of potatoes] to Transplant next Year," suggesting that they were or would soon be a field crop. The name *Irish potato* distinguished it from several other roots that were called potatoes though they were different plants. (Among them was the sweet potato, popular in the South, which accounts for the persistent use of *Irish potato* there over the next two centuries.)

Penn's letter may have gladdened his brethren in England, but its existence must dismay the archivists of Londonderry, New Hampshire. Londonderry has long claimed to be the first place to grow American potatoes, courtesy of Scots-Irish immigrants who brought them there in 1719. The town reportedly erected a plaque, whereas Philadelphia, where the first potatoes actually grew, seems neither to know nor care. One historian has tried to let Londonderry down easily, saying it probably had the first permanent crop, but the record suggests that Pennsylvania wins there too. In 1705, a twenty-year-old Philadelphian wrote his brother in Ireland, telling him that crossing the Atlantic was unbearable without potatoes; he had dreamed of them every night. If the brother should emigrate, the Philadelphian advised him, stock up for the voyage. What he didn't say was to bring some to Philadelphia, presumably because they still grew there.

Moreover, the potato spread so rapidly through the northern colonies that an introduction before 1719 makes more sense. Chester Township,

Pennsylvania, was growing it no later than 1725. Within ten years or so, the tuber had reached places as far apart as coastal Maine; Poughkeepsie, New York; and Salem, Massachusetts. A Narragansett, Rhode Island, clergyman began keeping an account book in 1743, in which he frequently mentioned potato harvests. By around midcentury, potatoes were "quite common" in the New Sweden settlement along the Delaware River. In 1751 fishermen and sailors in Kittery, Maine, counted themselves poor because they could only afford enough land around their houses to grow a bushel of potatoes and a hundred head of cabbage. Three years later and some forty-five miles up the coast in Portland, insects ate the potato harvest. By then, the crop was important enough so that the loss was a calamity worth noting.

If what one contemporary agricultural writer said was true, the potato's rising popularity was especially remarkable, given the nasty flavor. Samuel Deane, whose *New-England Farmer* first appeared in 1790, recalled that until 1740 there was only one kind, "of so rank a taste it was scarcely eatable." Concerning later decades, Deane also separated "table potatoes," meant for humans, from the "hog potato," fit only for fodder. Confusingly, the latter was also called the "Spanish potato," what the English called a sweet potato. So when Samuel Lane of Stratham, New Hampshire, told his diary in 1763 that the neighborhood had an "Abundance of Spanish Petatoes," he wasn't really saying the climate was warm enough to raise the sweet treat.

Midcentury travelers said that potatoes grew all over America, but that was a slight exaggeration. Virginia, like its southern sisters, imported potatoes from northern climes, a situation that changed only in the late 1760s. "Irish tators" eventually crossed the Shenandoah Valley into wild Kentucky, where a delighted traveler found some in 1775. (The word *tater*, by the way, was relatively new, having come, perhaps, from Wales.) By then, if not before, the tuber had won wide acclaim as a delicacy or a nutritious food. Dartmouth College students ate it, and the *Boston Gazette* advertised "choice English White Potatoes," just in from Maine. When the Continental armed forces went to war with Britain, the tuber went too. Soldiers often drew it in their rations; the Rhode Island General Assembly even set land aside for potatoes to feed its troops. As for the navy, in November 1775 the Continental Congress specified that sailors would eat turnips or potatoes three days a week, as part of the "daily proportion of provisions."

That the tuber went from newcomer to standby in less than a century would be astonishing by itself, but it's even more amazing when compared with what was happening in England. Where the English hesitated to raise it in quantity, colonials had no such qualms. Samuel Deane and Jared Eliot, two of eighteenth-century America's leading farm experts, said that the tuber enriched the land. Further, while Arthur Young railed against English farmers for not making money off the potato, colonial farmers needed no prodding to sell or barter it.

Amelia Simmons may have unwittingly drawn the sharpest contrast between the two nations' attitudes. In 1796 she published *American Cookery*, believed to be the first cookbook of American authorship written for an American audience. Only a year after Britain's Board of Agriculture passed around its "Hints," Simmons gave the potato first place among American vegetables, "for universal use, profit and easy acquirement." Even more significant, unlike the Englishwoman Hannah Glasse, whose *Art of Cooking Made Plain and Easy* appeared the same year, Simmons made no attempt to dress the potato up or hide what it was. Where half of Mrs. Glasse's recipes treated it as a dessert or as a side dish that might be sweetened, Simmons saw it primarily as a garnish for meat or fowl or an unsugared side dish. She, too, gave several potato dessert recipes—her dessert section is quite long—but she appreciated what the potato did best. Her cookbook may have been the first written in English to do so.

In trying to figure out why people of predominantly English heritage did something so un-English as to like potatoes, it's easier to discard theories than prove them. Some of the discards sound like common sense, but the facts don't fit. The following statements aren't true but seem as if they should be:

The Irish made the potato an American institution. This is partly correct, in that the Irish helped the potato take root in American soil. Irish Quakers numbered among Pennsylvania's early settlers, and Scots-Irish immigrants, such as those at Londonderry, planted the tuber in their new homes. But the Irish presence in eighteenth-century America, though substantial, was only a fraction of the total population. By 1790 almost 450,000 people of Irish stock had settled in the United States, but according to that year's census, such a figure counted for 11 percent of the white population. Most Irish immigrants who arrived before the Civil War came between 1815 and 1851.

Immigrants from another country must have done it. The only likely candidate here is Scotland. In their own land, the Scots were slow to accept the potato, supposedly because it wasn't mentioned in the Bible. Once they did, however, it spread rapidly and became a staple. But that didn't happen until the 1740s and 1750s, too late to have created a colonial trend regardless of the number of immigrants. Similarly, significant immigration from other potato-loving regions, such as Scandinavia or the German-speaking countries, didn't occur until the nineteenth century.

Frontier life was such that people either quickly abandoned their former food prejudices or learned the hard way. No doubt this was true in general, but specifics are in order. Despite a greater array of vegetables—and to some extent, fruits—than the English typically enjoyed, American colonials followed custom and revered meat. Some outdid the English and served meat at every meal. A traveler in the Ohio Valley in 1790 wondered whether he really needed to eat it for breakfast, let alone two or three times a day. Yet eating meat was "the fashion," he said, and if meat was set before him, he took it. In 1794 the Martinique-born French traveler Moreau de Saint-Méry counted fifty-two kinds of game and meat at a New York market.

The difference was that when Americans ate meat, they often had a lot else besides, including vegetables. Among well-to-do Philadelphians in 1798,

Saint-Méry noted ham or salt fish at breakfast, with coffee or tea and bread or toast. Lunch was broth, an English-style roast with potatoes, and fish, salad, pastries, cheese, and fruit. Supper, luckily, was light; tea and its accompaniments. A few years later, a tourist at Niagara Falls marveled at a breakfast of mutton chops, waffles, berry pie, bread, preserves, onion salad, coffee, tea, and sugar. It wasn't the meal's size that impressed him but its delicacies and variety, "hardly to be expected in such a depth of wilderness."

One prejudice the settlers did abandon was that against corn, a crop that ruled human and animal diets and governed prosperity if not survival. This devotion, too, is surprising. Corn didn't grow in the British Isles, and one leading agricultural authority wondered how digestible it was. Mixed with wheat, he said, it made good bread, but otherwise was most useful during shortages. That American colonists ignored this probably had something to do with how hard it was to raise wheat. Starting in the 1660s, Massachusetts settlers noticed how wheat caught "the blast," a smut that spoiled harvests and made the milled grain coarse and black. Corn, though requiring intensive labor, was less risky. It was also more versatile in the kitchen. It furnished the mush—"hasty pudding" in English (and New England) parlance, *bouillie* in French—and the hominy, johnnycakes, or biscuits that appeared at every meal. Late in the eighteenth century, the use of potassium carbonate as leavening expanded corn's culinary possibilities, as with quick breads.

Therefore, the colonists built a cuisine around food that, where they had come from, was little known and disdained. Further, though corn was king, it didn't crowd the potato off the table the way grain did in France or England. It also wasn't a question of replacing corn with potatoes in bad times, because American settlers ate spuds with corn mush and cornbread. In the South, corn's chief supporting starch was the sweet potato, whose cultivation and storage qualities may have fit the climate better, and whose sweetness perhaps suited the cuisine more closely. Still, that preference didn't exclude the Irish potato—witness its importation by colonies that didn't grow it.

Well, then, if American colonists made an exception for corn, they made another for the potato. It's that simple. Unfortunately, it isn't, because they didn't put the potato in the same class. Odd though it sounds, Americans didn't mind eating the same food their animals did and seem to have resisted doing anything else, even during corn shortages when they might have used potatoes as fodder. Samuel Lane's New Hampshire diary says that 1737 was a dreadful year for corn. People begged to buy it, "Not Sticking at Any price," and since there wasn't enough, they fattened their pigs on beech nuts. Twelve years later, a spring drought caused another dearth of corn, and Lane said farmers drove their cattle forty, fifty, even sixty miles to browse in meadows in the woods. True, Lane failed to mention potatoes by that date, 1749, which leaves open the possibility that there weren't any in the neighborhood. But that's very unlikely, given how early southern New Hampshire had the potato and how far the farmers went to graze their cattle.

Seven years later, an English agricultural expert wrote the oft-quoted opinion that potatoes were good for none but swine, and even then not worth much. No doubt he would have been curious that the Stratham farmers had met him halfway. They were willing to eat potatoes but not feed them to their livestock. Whether this was from prejudice or because the potatoes were too valuable to use as fodder is unclear. But the American tradition of putting corn in the trough and potatoes on the table persisted for the longest time. Diaries and journals reveal that well into the nineteenth century, farmers grew both crops but let their animals eat only one.

Why, then, did acceptance come so easily? No doubt isolation played a part. The United States in 1800 counted, on average, only 6.1 people per square mile, compared with 148 in England and Wales. Where Europeans desired self-sufficiency, Americans had no choice. If they couldn't grow what they needed or harvest it from Nature, they went without. Merchants were few and scattered, and cash to pay them rare. Cultivating as many crops as possible made sense, in case one failed, and for sale or barter. Then, too, lack of population density wasn't all bad. It meant that land, scarce and expensive in Europe, was much more plentiful. Given enough labor, and the potato took little, American farmers could choose more varied crop rotations, worrying less about having wasted arable on a perhaps dubious plant. The European habit of putting potatoes in the worst ground need not have been a concern.

In addition, abundant, varied food was the American style, even then. The bountiful America that has impressed visitors during the twentieth century also did so during the eighteenth and early nineteenth. Then as now, not every American benefited, something that observers have been known to overlook. Salt pork and corn meal were many Americans' daily lot, a routine neither nutritious nor interesting. Still, America past offered people who weren't rich a diverse diet that, in England, France, or Ireland, would have appeared only in wealthier homes. This was remarked on early, as when William Penn wrote how prolific the land was. Forty years later, the settlers who planted potatoes in Chester Township were similarly amazed at the bounty. "Scarce an house but has an Apple, Peach & cherry orchard," says their journal, "[and] as for chestnuts, Wallnuts, & hasel nuts, Strawberrys, Billberrys & Mulberrys they grow wild in the woods & fields in Vast Quantities." When James Birket visited Portsmouth, New Hampshire (population: four thousand), in 1750, he was impressed at the abundant meat, fish, and vegetables. English townspeople then, except the wealthy, had no access to such variety, which included asparagus. Amelia Simmons's 1796 cookbook discussed eleven vegetables besides nine kinds of beans and six of peas. The edition of Hannah Glasse's cookbook published the same year mentioned almost as many vegetables but provided no commentary and offered recipes for them primarily as Lenten fare or for people who lived too far from a meat market. Mrs. Glasse meant her cookbook to "instruct the lower sort," but she was reflecting English taste while failing to grasp the constraints under which the poor lived. Meanwhile, Simmons surely came closer to writing for cooks from "all Grades of Life."

Around the time her book appeared, foreign visitors commented on the varied American table and how little it cost. English travelers noted how cheap food was in Philadelphia and New York. William Cobbett, a political writer who spent ten years in the United States, believed that any American could have all he wanted to eat "if he will be *sober* and *industrious*." He further remarked that American food was better and cheaper, including luxuries like chocolate, which even poor people ate. Félix de Beaujour, who published his account of the United States in 1814, echoed Cobbett, writing that even day laborers ate what would have been luxuries in France. He was thinking of city people, but an upstate New York farmer expressed much the same idea, if with a different perspective. He recalled his early life, just before 1800, as "plain, coarse and primitive," until his family got tea and coffee. Neither he nor de Beaujour could have known that another eighty to one hundred years would pass before coffee became common in rural France.

If poor Americans could stock their larders with many foods, dietary distinctions were likely fewer than in Europe, or at least less important. It's hard to imagine that if laborers could afford chocolate, they would face disdain for eating potatoes too. Further, when so much was fit for the table—berries, fish, game, a cornucopia of vegetables—a loathing for any one thing would have been harder to justify. Not that all Americans ate everything, or that frontier democracy forbade food prejudices (or notions of class). However, Americans overlooked defects that would have stopped a European cold. For example, an English visitor to Philadelphia in 1791 complained that milk and meat tasted of "an ugly weed": garlic. It may have been a common problem, because in upper New York state, cows ate wild leeks, giving the milk and butter a particular taste. The best way not to notice it, said one resident, was to eat leeks before drinking the milk.

Taste aside, the potato brought advantages that were hard to ignore. Stored in the cellar when the house had one, otherwise beneath the floorboards or in a pit, the potato, if dry, kept through the rude American winter. That quality alone may have made it a cash crop and barter medium in, say, New Hampshire. Since refrigeration didn't exist, most foods wouldn't last the lean months without drying or salting (and salt was precious). Further, the potato lent greater ease to cooking where equipment lacked. The young Philadelphian who advised his brother about emigrating urged him to bring two large pots, one for each of them. The upstate New Yorker whose cows ate leeks said there was a single pot in the entire settlement. That was probably not unusual. Under conditions where the simpler the meal the better, the potato was a self-contained package that cooked whole in hot coals or cut up in the only pot.

Similarly, the dearth of utensils made the potato useful. A French traveler noted in 1805 that Americans used forks only while carving and ate with knives that had rounded ends. That would have made it hard to eat Pennsylvania Dutch "tossed" potatoes—fried in butter, thickened with flour and cream—a late eighteenth-century dish. But people who lacked forks, which perhaps included most lower-class Americans, or who had no heavy skillet in which to toss their potatoes, might enjoy them roasted or boiled instead. After all, what today's restaurateurs call finger foods are a time-honored American habit.

Which may put the potato in a long list of things that eighteenth- and nineteenth-century Americans weren't fussy about, having very different notions of class and manners from their English cousins. English visitors to the United States repeatedly remarked how crude and coarse Americans were, especially at the dinner table. A celebrated critic was Frances Trollope, the novelist's mother, whose book *Domestic Manners of the Americans* was published in 1832 and created quite a stir. Mrs. Trollope called attention to "the voracious rapidity with which . . . viands were seized and devoured" and "the frightful manner of feeding with . . . knives," which she saw on a New Orleans riverboat. No doubt she was telling the truth, but the tone of her book supported the popular British idea that Americans were boors and ruffians. Similarly, it told the Americans what they already knew, that the English were stuffy and put on airs.

It was the stuffy society that rejected the potato, while the crude one accepted it. This isn't to say that had American colonials been more genteel the way English people defined it, the potato would have traveled a harder road to popularity. No one can predict what would have been shunned or accepted in that improbable situation. Rather, the English seemed more conscious of the niceties connected with what one ate and how one ate it. And it was that kind of outlook that had, in previous times, so often worked against the potato.

As it was, like many foods in eighteenth-century America, the potato was neither primary staple nor outcast. It was simply there. Americans never charged the nightshade root with evil or occult powers, despite old-time herbalists' lore. Amelia Simmons could write, in 1796, that garlic made better medicine than it did food. How extraordinary, then, that in the "uncivilized wilderness" where terrors abounded, the fear of potatoes never evoked a tremor. Moreover, of the potato's sins—"insipidity," coarseness, baseness, filth, and so forth—not one ever aroused feeling in the United States. On these shores, the potato's only fault was "its overworked condition," how one late nineteenth-century writer described its too-frequent appearance at mealtime. By then, it had been feeding Americans for two centuries.

6   He Would Rather Be Hanged

. . . the only time I have Been in Prison was . . .
for getting a Poor Old widow woman a Bundle of Sticks . . .
JAMES HAWKER

"**I**T IS THE FASHION," wrote William Cobbett scornfully in 1818, "to extol potatoes, and to eat potatoes. Every one joins in extolling potatoes, and all the world like potatoes, or pretend to like them, which is the same thing in effect."

That any English commentator could report such a dramatic turnabout, and so soon after the agonies of 1795 and 1800, is astonishing. What isn't astonishing is that England's most influential radical thinker did the reporting, from which he concluded that the country was going to hell. Little escaped Cobbett's gimlet eye, and even less escaped his censure. A brilliant polemicist who began his career in 1800 writing under the name Peter Porcupine, Cobbett had one love, the welfare of England's small farmer and farm laborer, and a thousand hatreds, including cities, Quakers, Parliament, taxes, tea drinking, class-biased election laws, Shakespeare's plays, and Jews.

As for the potato, Cobbett was its deadliest enemy in human form. He called it the root of "slovenliness, filth, misery, and slavery" whose rise had naturally attended the "increase of the paupers." The potato was social and spiritual death, and its proponents must be either blind or wicked. For having allegedly brought the potato to England, Raleigh "was one of the greatest villains upon earth," but, fittingly, "He was hanged at last!" From there, Cobbett found it only logical to declare that he would rather see English laborers hanged too, "and be hanged along with them," than see them live on the "lazy root."

Today, this sounds absurd. But Cobbett was a passionate reformer whose views on government and society cost him one prison term and the subsequent threat of a second, leading to temporary exile in the United States. Several ideas he championed, such as revamping the electoral system, were national concerns that later shaped the Reform Bill of 1832—after which, incidentally, Cobbett ran for Parliament and was elected. Consequently, his tirades against the potato are more than amusing oddities. Not only was he a prophet warning of the tuber's growing power, he assumed that the change represented a larger pattern in which England was, in fact, going to hell.

To many people that was an accurate way to describe the upheavals that accompanied the industrial and agricultural revolutions. The population was swelling rapidly, land tenure was casting off old, comfortable rules, cities and manufactures were booming, traditional social bonds were breaking, and people were having to earn their sustenance in new ways. Poverty and dispossession seemed on the rise, especially in rural England. It was suspicious that the potato's success coincided with these happenings, doubly so that, as always, the privileged classes lived above the fray. Cobbett was furious that anyone would take the injustice lying down. "I despise the man that is *poor* and *contented*," he wrote, adding that such a disposition was "the enemy of all industry, all exertion, all love of independence."

With this statement, however, he unwittingly explained why England (and other Western societies) were embracing the tuber, and why that affected far more than the dinner table. Contrary to what Cobbett thought, the potato was a tool that allowed a degree of independence (which is why some landowners tried to check its use). Moreover, independence was no longer defined by what a family produced for itself. Time and space were shrinking as the nation grew and modernized, while the workload was as large or larger than before. Life would move faster no matter what Parliament enacted or rejected; people needed a way to cope with everyday problems, and the potato provided one. It stretched the household budget, the food supply, and that most precious commodity, time, thereby permitting more exertion, not less. Accordingly, had the potato not existed, nineteenth-century England would have been hungrier and harder pressed.

In rural England the changes that eased the potato's way had been happening since the eighteenth century, so the tuber's rise to prominence was somewhat less dramatic than it appeared. The most important change was enclosure, the process by which landowners reorganized small, fragmented farms into larger, more compact units, and thereby remapped living and working space. The arrangement that enclosure replaced, open fields, resembled Irish rundale (though open fields divided the land less and imposed fewer communal or familial restraints). Widespread, systematic enclosures began around 1750, with the bulk falling between 1793 and 1815. From 1750 to 1850, six million acres were enclosed, perhaps one-fourth of all English farmland.

Enclosure was a useful advance in many ways. With open fields, going incessantly from plot to plot cost the farmer time, rigid crop rotations wasted fallow land, and balks separating fields had to go untilled. Tenants had little or no incentive to maintain the soil or improve livestock, kept in a unified herd. Yet if one animal caught a disease, there was no safeguarding the others. Small wonder, then, that the Board of Agriculture reports for 1794 generally recommended enclosure.

However, it wasn't enclosure's agronomic beauties that enticed landowners. Between 1760 and 1810 food prices were rising steadily, encouraging tenant farmers to produce more and to rent more arable land, especially for wheat. Efficient, larger fields became desirable, and landlords who had enclosed their holdings could charge higher rents for them. Such were rural economics that, by 1815, rents were often twice their prewar levels. To cash in on this bonanza, however, a landowner had to take some trouble. Enclosing an estate usually required a private act of Parliament, an expensive and time-consuming procedure. Nevertheless, many landowners thought the effort was worth it, because some two thousand such acts were passed from 1793 to 1815 alone, when food prices were their highest.

Lost in these numbers is how enclosure affected people on the land. Landowners and large farmers gained, and small farmers sometimes did too. Parliamentary enclosure compensated anyone who owned land or dwellings or who had legal, as opposed to customary, right to graze animals or cut firewood. Such people could, for a modest investment, acquire a compact holding in the consolidated estate. That holding promised to be more profitable, less hampered by wasteful rules, and, under law, possibly free of church tithes. Also, where enclosure went, better roads and improved drainage followed. To those who could participate, enclosure offered clear advantages. But the key notion was prior ownership, because the law didn't protect former tenant farmers or those whose rights had derived from unwritten tradition. These people might still get farmland where enclosure functioned humanely, but that was pure chance. Often, they lost their tenancies. In that case, if they were lucky, they became wage laborers on the land they had once leased or got factory jobs in a nearby city. The less fortunate went on parish relief.

For obvious reasons, enclosure was controversial, pitting progress against the needs of those left behind. Historians remain divided over what enclosure did, and for whom. It's widely accepted that rural poverty and underemployment increased during the first half of the nineteenth century, especially in the east and south. Whether enclosure caused that is another question. The midcentury agriculturalist Sir James Caird, for one, blamed population growth and the land's inability to absorb it. He pointed out that relief rates were highest not where enclosure had occurred but where industrial jobs lacked, as in the heavily agricultural south.

What enclosure undeniably changed was the ways in which many people fed themselves and kept their homes. Where they once might have raised their own food, they now bought it out of wages. How high those wages were, how much their money bought, and whether laborers had extra sources of food or income helped decide how well they lived. Those circumstances, in turn, partly resulted from how the land was divided. With enclosure came the custom of leasing garden allotments to those who had lost various rights. Whether the landholder granted allotments, how large the parcels were, how fertile the soil was, and how much rent was charged depended on whim. When, in 1795, the Board of Agriculture suggested leaving "such angles and corners as might otherwise be neglected" for potato allotments, it did so because the practice was still unusual. The year before, for instance, the board's inspectors had noted that in Norfolk, Bedford, and Rutland, allotments were either very rare or somewhat so.

The nineteenth century saw allotments become more customary, but practices varied. North usually fared better than south, perhaps, as Caird suggested, because northern factories offered laborers an alternative. Yorkshire allotments, for instance, were sometimes even three acres, allowing cottagers to keep a cow, while in Northumberland, cottage and garden were sometimes rent-free. A survey in 1863 revealed that an allotment might include quantities of wheat, straw, cider or milk—or none of these. In some counties, laborers couldn't keep pigs, "lest they should steal from their employers" whatever the animals ate, but that restriction was rare. Geography wasn't the only variable, though. At midcentury laborers in Dorsetshire, a poor southern county, had allotments and free firewood, whereas their more northern cousins in Oxfordshire were renting allotments for twice what the surrounding land went for. Even at that, the farmers worried that their employees might spend too much time and energy on their half-acre plots and either exhaust themselves or otherwise neglect the work for which they were paid wages. Too much independence was a bad thing, despite how much the reigning philosophy stressed the value of unfettered individual exertion.

Complicating everything was the huge appetite for bread, a food the laborer might not produce. The author of the 1863 farm survey, Dr. Edward Smith, a pioneer in nutritional public health, found that bread provided 40 percent of caloric intake in laborers' families. Each adult ate, on average, more than twelve pounds a week, and the family consumed almost fifty-six pounds, or fourteen loaves. Smith recognized that averages can deceive, but he had shown how bread dominated the laborer's table.

That dominance echoed in political life. In 1815, when food prices had fallen and farmers were overextended, Parliament revised the Corn Laws ("corn" meaning grain). The revision acted to prevent imports, in theory keeping the home supply low and protecting the price. Whether they achieved anything like that is unclear, because foreign grain was probably unavailable, at least at a competitive price. But the revised Corn Laws' true effects were a moot point. The poor believed the new laws enriched the farmers at their expense, and they demanded to know how Parliament could show such cruel indifference when so many people were struggling to buy bread. Accordingly, the laws caused political agitation and strengthened the push for widening the franchise and reforming Parliament. By the time the revision was repealed in 1846, thanks largely to opposition from industry, it had inspired much unrest, including violence bordering on rebellion.

Therefore, how (or whether) the laborer obtained grain was a highly charged issue, in practical and symbolic terms. Before the 1790s, laborers in grain-producing areas bought grain or flour from their employers, and, if they were lucky, for a compassionate price. But during the peak enclosure years, when grain sold so profitably, farmers were inclined to send every sack to market. A half-century or more later, Smith did find farmers who gave grain as part of wages or sold it below market value. But he emphasized that the amounts were limited, not enough to feed a family. The di-

minishing availability of grain affected the cottager in two related ways: It
helped kill home baking and made shops that much more vital. One historian has estimated that in 1800, 65 percent to 70 percent of the country,
rural and urban, bought food in shops or markets. Cobbett condemned
this state of affairs. Relying on a shop for daily supplies was "perfectly tormenting," because it represented the death of independence.

He meant that philosophically, but the torment had a mean, practical
edge. Smith calculated that rents averaged 1s. 6d to 2s a week, which meant
that laborers earning eight or ten shillings were hard put to buy fourteen
loaves of bread and might have to get by on less. Between the Napoleonic
Wars and Smith's survey, a loaf's average cost was almost always higher
than tenpence (a shilling was twelve pence). That underlined how hard it
could be to support a family on a single wage, let alone afford bacon, tea, or
cheese. Adding such "luxuries"—always in small, uneconomical quantities,
maybe at steep prices, maybe at short weight if the grocer was dishonest—
could easily force a family into debt. Spending their incomes a week ahead
of earning them, a plight called "one week under another," such unfortunates found themselves virtually enslaved to the shopkeeper. The slavery
could be complete if, as sometimes happened, an employer owned the shop
and gave regular work only to those who spent the most money there. Even
worse, laborers were often paid every two weeks or once a month, a custom
that Smith wanted to see ended.

With bread absorbing so much earning power, whatever else the family
ate had to come cheaply. This explains why the allotment was crucial to survival and why the potato was crucial to the allotment. Even a quarter-acre
plot could yield a winter's supply of food and, just as important, loosen the
storekeeper's grip on the family budget. Joseph Arch, a farm workers' union
organizer, recalled that during his Warwickshire boyhood in the 1820s and
1830s, his family and neighbors "had no hope" of allotments, and most had
no gardens. People stole turnips and potatoes, and "every other man you
met was a poacher." From these facts of life, young Arch learned hard

lessons about political independence, especially when local employers blackballed his father for refusing to sign a petition supporting the Corn Laws. Significantly, when Arch wrote his memoirs in 1898, after his election to Parliament, he hailed the abundance of potatoes as one reason the farm laborer's lot had improved.

Late nineteenth-century Oxfordshire as Flora Thompson described it in her engaging book, *Lark Rise*, showed just what the potato and the allotment meant to farm laborers. Even at that late date, they still earned ten shillings, paid a shilling or more rent, and got by on what they grew. They sowed half their allotments in potatoes, the rest in barley or wheat to feed their pigs, and bought their bread. Potatoes always appeared at supper, the day's only hot meal, joining garden vegetables, a fruit pastry called a roly-poly, and a small chunk of bacon, all cooked in separate compartments of a three-legged pot.

Allotments went far toward keeping people off relief—another aspect of independence—but that wasn't entirely the potato's doing. Having enough land for a cow was a big advantage, because milk and butter yielded protein and vitamins, and whatever the family didn't eat, it could sell. Laborers who had pasture land, as in some northern counties, probably enjoyed the healthiest diets in England. However, life turned on more than the presence or absence of the allotment. The laborer's skill and character played a role, as did the size and age of his family, whether his wife and children could also earn money, what the shops were like, and whether free or cheap fuel was available.

Still, the dietary roster is so short that it's hard to imagine what would have taken the potato's place had it not been there. For example, a report in 1843 said Wiltshire laborers ate mostly wheaten bread, potatoes, and tea, with beer and butter as luxuries. Sometimes cheese, bacon, and pig entrails reached the table, but these were less common. Such a diet meant true poverty, and Wiltshire ranked among England's poorest counties, but even more comfortable laboring families relied heavily on cereals and potatoes. The difference was that they had butter, cheese, bacon, and tea in larger amounts or more often. The potato's presence was merely a matter of degree.

Edward Smith's 1863 survey of 370 families put its influence in raw numbers. He found that potatoes were the second leading food after bread, appearing in almost nine of ten households. Depending on the season and whether an allotment rented cheaply, a family consumed fifty-six pounds or more a week. Smith recognized that the potato stretched income and the bread supply, and permitted pig raising. Further, he cited its nutritional value as contemporary medicine understood it, and noted how, by contrast, green vegetables were a once-a-week treat except during spring or summer. The potato, he said, also allowed a hot, inviting meal when the alternative might be less appetizing and saved the housewife from struggling with the onerous chore of cooking.

Smith's remark about pigs opens a window onto nineteenth-century English rural life. Meat was a luxury, weekly consumption averaging sixteen ounces per adult (though conditions varied and Smith's survey didn't account for irregular food or income, such as rabbits the laborer poached). Even so, 30 percent of the families said they never had butcher's meat, which meant they ate only bacon; nearly half the families had both. If, as sometimes happened, the bulk of it was saved for Sunday, leftovers usually went to the laborer, lasting as many days as thrift or quantity permitted. As a result, he might have meat daily, however small a morsel. This wasn't a rich diet, by any means, but the laborer himself didn't do as badly as the overall description suggests.

Bacon was vital, not only for eating but for flavoring a cuisine based on vegetables and cereals. In Thompson's village those who couldn't afford pig feed bought it from the baker or miller by promising them portions of the meat. Half the animal might be mortgaged this way. Thompson wrote that she heard people say, " 'Us be going to kill half a pig, please God, come Friday,' " an idea an outsider would have thought very strange. But the practice wasn't strange at all, having gone on in many places since the century began. What made it feasible, given the cost of grain, was the potato patch. Laborers were still wary of feeding pigs on potatoes alone, but their allotments had taught some measure of trust. This economics lesson was long overdue.

Yet much as the potato protected the laborer's diet, its rise *was* connected to the decline of bread's sacred, unique place. The potato triumphed partly because home baking died, and what killed it were the lack of fuel and an oven. Where home baking lasted longest was, again, northern counties like Northumberland, where coal was cheaper and wages higher. But laborers who could get coal didn't always bake bread, and coal's presence didn't always solve their fuel problems. Thompson's Oxfordshire village was no doubt much more prosperous in the 1880s and 1890s than when the century was younger. However, even then, she said that food and shelter weren't the dragons that gobbled the household budget. Coal, kerosene, and clothes were. For southern laborers during the first half of the century, the fuel equation was starkly simple. When coal was either too expensive or scarce, they were less likely than their northern neighbors to have warm houses or hot meals. Joseph Arch recalled that in the 1830s the village rectory gave the poor—those of whom the rector's wife approved, anyway—coals along with soup. Twenty years later, laborers at Salisbury (Wiltshire) were earning six or seven shillings, paying one shilling rent, and reportedly eating bread and water for supper. Some farmers let them have allotments and gather wood, "a very expensive article in a labourer's family."

Not everyone was so permissive. The Game Code forbade anyone to harvest or kill anything wild without the landowner's consent, and the war between poachers and gamekeepers was legendary. Critics wondered how Parliament could let rabbits and birds eat grain, and foxes steal chickens, while making anyone who harmed the pests an outlaw. Though the code acted primarily to keep milord's hunting sufficiently diverting, it also protected his woodlands. In 1847 one writer recalled that in 1800 rangers in Sherwood Forest hadn't been able to keep people from gathering wood or letting their pigs feed. Now, foragers were pursued, arrested, and fined. This comment carried tacit irony, because centuries before, Robin Hood had roamed Sherwood Forest, helping himself to the king's deer and fooling the lawmen, all to general mirth. Now, in the 1800s, such bandits did not go unpunished. Some years, two-thirds of all criminal convictions fell under the game laws. Most of the illegal activity took place in the south.

This isn't to say that every laborer faced the law on one side and cold food—or no food—on the other. However, England's respect for property had consequences for people trying to cook a hot meal or stay warm. Traveling in the 1820s, Cobbett once saw, to his horror, girls gathering wheat and bean stubble because they had no wood. "And yet foragers will be hanged," he remarked. In 1842 the Chadwick report, which surveyed living conditions for the Poor Law Commission, mentioned a Reading landlord who had given his tenants bundles of wood so that they would leave his hedges and trees alone. This self-interested generosity paid dividends, not the least of which was the tenants' gratitude. However, such landlords were rare. Arch wrote that time was, when a laborer was hired to cut timber, he could take home a basket of wood chips or dead branches. That perquisite died, he said, with the Poaching Prevention Act of 1862. This law allowed a policeman to search anyone on the road if it seemed that the suspect had just trespassed on private property. A man Arch knew was arrested for picking up two sticks forty yards from his own house. The village retained a lawyer and got the man acquitted, but Arch said this case wasn't the only one of its kind he knew firsthand. James Hawker, an avowed poacher who had many scrapes with the law, said the only time he went to jail was "for getting a Poor Old widow woman a Bundle of Sticks as she had no coal."

Even with enough fuel, baking bread was a chore, and not every homemaker knew how. Both Cobbett and Smith chided such women—Cobbett said they were "unworthy of trust and confidence . . . a mere burden upon the community"—but this judgment was grossly unfair. A laborer worked twelve or more hours a day. If his wages didn't cover the bills, his wife had to earn income, though perhaps working fewer hours than he. Given time pressure and the immense bread consumption, it's hard to see how she could have kept up. Perhaps in the past, tenant farmers less dependent on wages found home baking cheap and manageable. But now, life was simply moving too fast to permit it. Buying bread was the answer, and if laborers had to buy less of it, boiling or roasting potatoes was a convenient, fuel-efficient supplement.

Then, too, English rural kitchens were awful places to work. After visiting England in 1784, nineteen-year-old François de la Rochefoucauld wrote that "the worst thing that could befall you would be to go into the kitchen before dinner." The filth, he said, was "indescribable," turning the cooks "black as coal." Naturally, the young duke was referring to noblemen's kitchens, because he associated with people of wealth and social position. Laborers' kitchens were surely worse, even a half-century or more later. The Chadwick report harped on how lower-class houses were poorly ventilated, and the effect on daily living. "Damp, low, cold, smoky, and comfortless" went one description. Windows were often built not to open, which meant the door offered the only air. But when people had little fuel, "the door must be kept shut to maintain warmth," so the house filled with smoke because, as in Ireland, the chimneys drew badly. The report noted that, where cottagers had casement windows that opened and fuel receptacles, they lived better, regardless of their poverty.

As for baking bread, that would assume the cottager had an oven, a much sought-after item. Significantly, the Chadwick report described model cottages built in duplexes sharing an oven. It wasn't attached to the cottages but in a tile-roofed wooden outbuilding, suggesting that the designer understood how unpleasant it was to stoke a fire. The outbuilding also had a spacious fuel bin, an amenity that would seem obvious but, unfortunately, wasn't. Fifty years later, Flora Thompson's villagers had a similar arrangement, with the ovens built into the washhouse. It should be stressed that Thompson's villagers didn't live in the "garnished hovels" Arch had seen so often—ivy and climbing roses outside, near cesspools inside. Rather, Thompson's houses were made of stone or brick with slate roofs, and the windows opened. Yet despite this modernity, not everyone had an oven. Those who didn't borrowed a neighbor's. Fuel was too scarce to waste, so they baked many dishes at once—joints of meat, desserts, pork pies, cakes, potatoes—but not bread.

Where the death of home baking affected the bread supply, the demise of another custom, boarding in, reduced the amount of meat. Boarding in was the arrangement by which farmers fed their hired hands and sometimes housed them, paying them less in wages. The system began waning before 1750, though in 1863, Smith saw farms where it still operated. Its advantages to the laborer were many. Not only did it fill his household's presumably hungriest mouth, morsels might find their way home. Laborers depended on it as an adjunct to wages, especially during haying and harvest. The practice was part of the bond linking farmer to laborer; one couldn't succeed without the other's cooperation. Or so argued Edmund Burke, he who trusted the workings of private enterprise over anything else. In 1795 he wrote that the thriving farmer supplied "abundant nutriment, and cloathing, and lodging, proper for the protection of the instruments he employs."

When the Napoleonic Wars drove up food prices, more of Burke's "abundant nutriment" went to market, and less to the instruments employed to raise it. Except where industry provided competition, the laborer had no bargaining power, because enclosure and population growth swelled the labor pool, and farmers could dictate their terms. Some abused this power, occasionally to their cost. A Board of Agriculture inspector in Norfolk in 1794 criticized a farmer who was reportedly reluctant to pay board or more wages than he had to and delayed hiring enough laborers for the harvest.

Then, when he finally got them, he rushed the work and lost 10 percent of his crop.

A list of what boarding-in laborers typically ate suggests just how big a hole its absence created. To cite only one example from Smith's report, he found a Devon farmhouse serving up breakfast and supper of bread and milk (or clotted cream), fried potatoes, and pudding, or bread, cheese, cider, and cold meat. Lunch was mutton, pork, or bacon, with vegetables, bread, milk, and pudding. Such a spread was expensive, and farmers became reluctant to share it with hired hands, who might have large appetites and rude manners. Moreover, as farmers got wealthier, social pretensions demanded drawing rooms and dining rooms that excluded the help and where wives and daughters might associate with refined visitors. Therefore, boarding in endured mostly in pastoral areas, where livestock required constant, on-site attention, or where towns drained the labor supply. In 1851, boarded-in Darbyshire laborers could demand and get porridge, bread, cheese, meat, and small beer. In 1861, industrial Lancashire was still boarding in a sixth of its farm labor. Boarding in also survived in Scotland, where custom strongly supported it. The Scots diet, however, was cheaper (and probably healthier) than the English, its mainstays being oatmeal porridge and milk.

Without boarding in, the English laborer had to find another way to eat his fill. The potato, as a bulky starch, offered the best means available. In quantity, it also supplied necessary vitamins and minerals, not that anyone knew, and, if that ever-vital commodity, milk, were on hand, kept body and soul together. Moreover, the potato fulfilled an essential task within the family. In many homes, especially the poorest ones, it kept the laborer's wife and children alive. The family, who hadn't boarded in, had always depended more than the laborer on what the land produced, if they rented any, or on what his wages (and theirs) could buy. When boarding in ended, the laborer was now eating at home, and that often meant he got the choicest bits, particularly of extras like meat and cheese. As Smith observed, the laborer might have those daily, while his family got them once a week, at most. Accordingly, they ate more potatoes.

When one reads that the laborer ate the best food in the house, questions rush up from the historical depths. Was the practice new, or was it traditional, and no one had thought to ask? Did people accept or fight it, and what did that mean for family life? Smith, astonished by the custom, believed it was "not only acquiesced in by the wife, but felt by her to be right, and even necessary for the maintenance of the family." Whether that was wise or just, a different scenario emerged a quarter-century later. The novelist George Gissing, in *The Nether World*, envisioned a working-class London home where the children want the meat and cheese reserved for the men, not the bread and the "villainously cooked" potatoes à l'anglaise. Whether Smith or Gissing had perceived the larger truth—or whether the truth had changed—would make a revealing piece of history.

There was one truth that hadn't changed. Despite the potato's great strides in the century's first three decades, not everyone was a willing convert, or even a convert at all. In 1836 a farming journal reported that some southern laborers viewed the tuber "with considerable scorn" and demanded their traditional bacon, beer, and white bread. Cobbett, who had died the year before, would have approved. Richard Cobden, the famed Parliamentarian and a leading opponent of the Corn Laws, warned the House of Commons in 1842 that "a potato-fed race" would never "lead the way in arts, arms or commerce." Eight years later, Sir James Caird visited parts of Buckinghamshire where leases still forbade potatoes, and where no one who thought himself "a *good* farmer" grew them (or any other vegetable) for sale.

This traditional social code was reflected in England's finest kitchens. Charles Elmé Francatelli, Queen Victoria's onetime chef, had strict ideas about what potatoes were good for. In *The Modern Cook* (1846), his recipes called for sculpting the humble spud to resemble pears or olives—more elegant, expensive foods—or disguising it altogether, as in purées, for soup or ornamental borders. A few other vegetables suffered comparable tortures at Francatelli's hands, but from time to time, they also appeared in their own clothes. The potato did not. It was if one should never look down at one's plate and see such a sight—a startling throwback to the late seventeenth century, when potatoes, if served at all, never appeared au naturel.

Nevertheless, well before Francatelli's cookbook, the tuber had gone from pariah to "invaluable root." It was now a "most wholesome and nutritive food" that "prudent families" adopted to replace wheaten bread during shortages. By 1836 it was said that "two million persons who used to subsist on wheat flour" were now living chiefly on potatoes. The estimate was unofficial, yet there was no reason to doubt it. Consequently, about one-seventh of the nation now owed their lives to the tuber.

London alone, one midcentury observer believed, consumed perhaps three thousand tons per week, a remarkable total, particularly because railroads had yet to link distant farm counties with the metropolis. Wagons brought most shipments, though nearly half came by water. Whole warehouses held nothing but spuds. By 1850 the potato ruled London vegetable markets in tonnage sold, though figures purporting to say by how much were untrustworthy.

The potato's London triumph underlined a curious fact. Early nineteenth-century England was the world's foremost industrial nation and, even by 1800, more urban than any save Belgium and Holland, yet the country was predominantly rural, both in fact and in mind. Romantic notions glorified the English countryside, and some were rooted in truth. Victorian social statisticians believed the farm was healthier than the city, which mortality rates suggest was no fantasy. However, long before 1838, when nationwide mortality was first recorded with any accuracy, observers assumed the farm was morally healthier too (and further assumed that morality and disease went together). Rural folk were cautioned that they faced perdition if they left the farm to seek factory wages. Such wages might be double what the farmer paid, but, said the warning, all that glittered wasn't gold.

Factories, which placed men and boys alongside women and young girls for long hours in small spaces, had a bad reputation, with some cause. However, an agricultural expert surely exaggerated when he wrote, in 1796, that factory workers were "the dissolute of every age and sex, drawn together from all quarters, as if for the purpose of promoting dissoluteness, debility, and wretchedness." Cottage manufactures, he believed, were "highly beneficial," partly because they allowed people to do farmwork in addition, but factories were "one of the greatest evils any country can be afflicted with." In 1795 another writer, having studied Manchester, said that farms provided "neatness, cleanliness, and comfort," while factories offered "filth, rags, and poverty." He was specifically criticizing child factory labor, but the underlying message was clear. Just as soot from urban smokestacks tainted the snow and irritated the lungs, the city menaced the nation's pastoral beauty and choked its innocence.

This was where Cobbett came in. Rural innocence, embodied in self-sufficiency and a slower, simpler life, was what Cobbett fought to preserve. Once, he met a Wiltshire woman who didn't know the road to the next town, four miles away. He defended her, saying it was "a great error to suppose that people are rendered stupid by remaining always in the same place." Transportation was a "curse" that ruined people's diligence, morals, and happiness. Such a contrarian, extreme argument was typical of Cobbett, but, taken whole, his philosophy sounds more coherent. Moving from place to place, like buying food in shops or eating potatoes, corrupted the social order. No wonder that cities, where people depended on others for daily needs, where much labor occurred indoors and produced no food, and where populations crowded in suffocating masses, were sinkholes of immorality.

Where that put the potato, morally speaking, wasn't hard to figure, because urban dwellers depended heavily on it. One might guess that rural people needed the tuber more because their shops were less likely to carry a wide choice of foods, and because they had less money to buy them. But two circumstances argue the opposite. First, the population grew and shifted. Between 1801 and 1851, a mere fifty years, the population of England and Wales doubled, to number almost 18 million. Simultaneously, the proportion living in towns of twenty thousand or more also rose sharply. The figure was 17 percent in 1801, reached 25 percent in 1831, and hit a staggering 35 percent in 1851. Compared with France, by this yardstick only 10 percent urban in 1851, England and Wales formed one giant metropolis. Second, as English and Welsh workers clustered in cities, farming accounted for fewer jobs. At midcentury, barely more than a quarter of all working males were earning their livings from agriculture. Cobbett would have spat vitriol.

This suggests that even if a farm family relied more on the potato than its urban counterpart did, city dwellers and others who typically didn't grow their own food ate the greater quantity. To understand why that should have happened requires a look at how English city dwellers lived. Housing and labor conditions dictated a less varied diet than the workers' earning power might imply. Moreover, had a better-stocked larder been within their reach, like as not, they lacked the skill or resources to take advantage of it.

Reading about workers' tenements sends a Dickensian chill up the spine. The sensation was familiar even then, as portrayals of a single city, Manchester, illustrate. A doctor who saw its tenements in 1832 described "an air of discomfort if not of squalid and loathsome wretchedness" about them. The houses were "often dilapidated, badly drained, damp." Eight years later, another reformer saw only "the meanest comforts of life" there. He found no "decent furniture," only bricks, logs, and other makeshift devices, with a bag of wood shavings or pile of straw for a bed. Such wretchedness, he said, was neither temporary nor unusual. In 1844 Friedrich Engels visited Manchester and wrote a classic description of urban Victorian England. He reported seeing rows of houses "in bad order, never repaired, filthy, with damp, unclean cellar dwellings" and little or no ventilation besides chimneys. Many Irish immigrants lived in one infamous neighborhood, "behind broken windows, mended with oilskin, sprung doors, and rotten doorposts, or in dark, wet cellars, in measureless filth and stench." Engels concluded that working-class Manchester offered "no cleanliness, no convenience, and consequently no comfortable family life."

Skilled laborers commanded much higher wages than the people these observers were describing and often had the opportunity to live better. Nevertheless, had the horrific scenes existed only in isolated cases, England would have paid no attention. The reform movement in which Edwin Chadwick, who wrote the Chadwick report, played a part believed that poor housing and sanitation fostered typhus, tuberculosis, and other endemic plagues. He would never have had reason to think so, let alone convinced anyone else of it, had the conditions been rare or hard to credit. However, despite his efforts and those of journalists and novelists to portray the horrors of lower-class housing, change moved slowly. Some historians have said that this was because evangelical progressives who crusaded against slavery or for factory reform, high-minded causes, couldn't bring themselves to talk about garbage or crowded tenements. In any case, neither law nor custom favored lower-class housing. Industry was more profitable than residential real estate, and so the cheap production of pipes, woodwork, or brick remained uncommon until the 1840s. Until 1835 many British manufacturing towns had no strong municipal government to enforce a health code, and no city approved such a code until Liverpool did it in 1846. As for the nation, Parliament ignored Chadwick's findings six years before passing the Public Health Act of 1848, a law that fell far short of his recommendations.

Since few who had the means were willing to improve housing, it follows that kitchens remained dreadful for decades. The doctor who surveyed Manchester in 1832 found, in homes of the poor Irish, the "most scanty culinary apparatus," a chair or two, and a "mean table." A political activist who visited London's infamous Spitalfields district in 1831 entered many houses where "a saucepan or cup or two" were the sole cooking utensils. The journalist Henry Mayhew, who surveyed Spitalfields almost two decades later, noted that "cupboards and closets are nearly altogether unknown." No coal bins existed, and fireplaces, Mayhew said, were built without any concept of "convenience or comfort" for people who had to use them. A boarding-house kitchen contained so much smoke that light entering the window looked as if it were cutting through fog. A "respectable butcher" in London's Whitechapel district told a Chadwick investigator that lower-class houses were so crudely ventilated, meat his customers bought Saturday night sometimes spoiled before they could cook it Sunday. Of course, it might have been spoiled already; Manchester butchers were said to offer their poorer clientele diseased or "half-decayed" meat. But the respectable Whitechapel fellow added that butter kept in poorer homes quickly became rancid, and bread "dry and disagreeable," all because of poor ventilation.

Early nineteenth-century upper-class kitchens were no bargain either, and not as good as they would have been if upper-class people had sweated in them. In 1841, when Alexis Soyer became head chef at the Reform Club, London's best-known gathering place for liberal-thinking gentlemen, his first act was to rip apart the kitchens. Among his ideas was to install ventilators, something no kitchen architect had ever done for fear the food would get cold. So revolutionary was Soyer's design that it was published, and hundreds of people came to tour the club's marvelous kitchens. One writer expressed amazement at the "chemical laboratory" Soyer had created.

Most nineteenth-century urban dwellers, of course, had nothing close to a laboratory, even those whose income and living standard put them a rung or two above the unfortunates the reformers described. Forty years after Soyer's coup, when times were better for the working classes, a small oven cost thirty shillings, and a simple set of cooking utensils fetched five pounds. Such prices meant a heavy, if not unreachable, investment for workers earning less than a pound a week. For the most part, kitchen equipment remained a stiff expense despite the increase in real wages, which rose 60 percent between 1860 and 1900. In 1914, Maud Pember Reeves surveyed the London district of Lambeth, where wages averaged twenty-two shillings, an amount thought normal. She found that "one kettle, one frying-pan, and two saucepans, both burnt" often made up a kitchen's equipment.

Even if equipment had been cheaper, fuel was an ongoing problem. The urban poor, though much closer to the coal than their country cousins, couldn't always benefit. In part this was because cramped tenements lacked facilities for receiving and storing coal, which meant the poor spent proportionally more for it and used less. The absence of coal bins that Mayhew noticed wasn't peculiar either to London or to midcentury. The activist George Jacob Holyoake recalled from his Birmingham boyhood in the 1820s and 1830s that no houses he knew got coal delivered, only the baker and the tavern. On Saturday nights, he went to the coalyard, waiting to buy a barrowful—sixpence if filled level, ninepence if heaped—for the Sunday fire. Similarly, a York coal dealer remarked that during the winter of 1899, the poor paid 25 percent more for fuel because they bought it in bags, not by the ton. They also used a less efficient grade because it was cheaper, a habit that might have cost them more in the long run. Reeves's study of Lambeth noted how the rich spent less for coal because they had a cellar large enough to store it in bulk. To put that in perspective, around 1900, many Londoners had no space for themselves, let alone for coal. Just less than a half-million of them, almost one-eighth of the population, lived three to a room. Nearly one-third of the city inhabited conditions that, if more spacious, were nevertheless called "overcrowded."

Equipment and fuel weren't the only culinary necessities lacking. Many lower-class women didn't know how to cook because they had had little or no chance to learn. Their mothers, like them, had most likely worked in factory or domestic manufactures, leaving little time to impart whatever they knew, assuming that was more than the rudiments. Reformers were forever saying that such ignorance held the poor back. One, speaking of Manchester, stressed the physical and moral degradation inherent in consuming "coarse food," specifically potatoes. A group of Birmingham physicians whom Chadwick quoted said that the poor's "depraved domestic habits" included buying expensive, quickly prepared cuts of meat when they could afford them. Chadwick remarked that reports frequently mentioned how the "ignorance of domestic economy leads to ill health, by the purchase of unsuitable and, at the same time, expensive food." Many asked that the poor be given "instructions in frugal cookery."

The cookbook authors obliged. Esther Copley, whose *Cottage Cookery* was published in 1848, believed that many families were miserable "more from want of discretion in managing their resources than from the real scantiness of their income." To assist them, she offered such recipes as tea made from rue and strawberry leaves, bread of maize, barley, and rye, and mutton chitterlings. Soyer, whose *Charitable Cookery* appeared around then, offered sounder, less condescending advice. He counseled using vegetable peels to their best advantage and saving odds and ends for stews. Yet even Soyer missed the point. In his best-selling *Gastronomic Regenerator* (1846), he suggested that the stockpots, turbot kettles, braising pans, and so forth from well-to-do homes would be out of place in humble kitchens. He advised using "six black saucepans" instead.

Upper-class women might not know how to poach a turbot either, but they could hire someone who did or whom other servants would train. In 1851 in England and Wales, an estimated forty-four thousand cooks were employed, and the number more than doubled over the next twenty years. One might suppose, then, that an army of working-class women learned skills they later used in their own kitchens. Sadly, that wasn't the case. The food that servants prepared for their masters involved more expensive ingredients and paraphernalia than they themselves could afford. This fact was unwittingly underlined in 1884, when Sir Henry Thompson suggested in *Food and Feeding* that working-class cuisine might well include such dishes as bouillabaisse and pot-au-feu. Moreover, a wealthy Victorian household employed maids, butlers, governesses, and housekeepers, among others, who divided the labor. A lower-class housewife had to fulfill all these functions herself. Though her home was smaller and, in some ways, less complicated to run, she couldn't give the care to a single task that a servant could. For working-class women, then, the best cooking was usually the simplest and fastest.

The industrial world was moving faster in general, and the laborer had to move with it. The poacher James Hawker remembered that in 1842, when he was six years old, his father, a tailor, worked until ten o'clock at night. A pottery worker recalled of the same era that as a young child he labored fourteen or fifteen hours a day and then stumbled home, trying not to fall asleep on the road. His shop observed Saint Monday, but that was rare and becoming more so. In theory, home craftsmanship allowed some freedom from the rapid pace, but such businesses were losing ground to factories. Holyoake wrote that 1820s and 1830s Birmingham had many home manu-factories, his mother's buttonworks among them, but they died out. He mentioned this as a curiosity, which, when his memoir was published in 1909, it was. Consequently, as the century progressed, the nation's factories employed a growing percentage of workers—for example, power weavers outnumbered hand-loom weavers probably by the early 1840s. For the work-ers, that meant that as many hours as the machinery turned, they had to be there to run it. A survey in 1816 revealed that cotton mills hummed four-teen, sixteen, or even eighteen hours a day. One mill owner, considered a hu-mane employer, expected his apprentices to work thirteen hours, starting at six in the morning.

The Ten Hours Act of 1847 changed matters somewhat, setting the maxi-mum workday for thirteen- to eighteen-year-olds, and for women of any age. Further, because many machines required both child and adult opera-tors, by extension the act limited the adult male workday. Even so, the day remained long and grueling, particularly for women, also expected to cook at home. Since how well a family ate might depend on how many wage-earners it had, women frequently worked in factories or at domestic trades.

In 1835 half of all cotton factory workers were women and girls. The 1851 census, the first to count occupations in detail, stated that females provided more than 30 percent of the labor force. How accurate this census was is open to question, but if anything, the true figure was higher, possibly because women were reluctant to tell census takers what their outside incomes were.

Consequently, the hard-pressed working-class cook most often chose food requiring little or no preparation. Bread remained the favorite, claiming a third of the midcentury household food budget. The lopsided expense derived partly from volume, partly from quality. Londoners, for example, continued to insist on the best wheaten. "An artisan demands it as well as a peer," wrote one expert on London's food habits in 1856. Eating anything else was thought "derogatory to his position." The best wheaten meant the whitest flour, expensive because it required laborious milling. When the rolling mill appeared in 1872, the process moved faster, lowering the price. White wheaten bread lost its cachet, at least among the upper classes. But the taste for bread was still strong. In the 1880s Britain's per capita consumption—regardless of age or class—was 270 pounds a year, or five pounds a week. No doubt an adult worker ate much more.

Before midcentury, the second most important staple was potatoes, boiled or roasted. Manchester workers, wrote the doctor who studied that city in 1832, lunched on a "mess of potatoes" on which butter and lard were poured. Sometimes "a few pieces of fried fat bacon" flavored them, "but seldom a little meat." The food was put in one large dish, and everyone attacked it with spoons, devouring it quickly. Supper was tea, bread, and possibly potatoes or oatmeal. Twelve years later, Engels noted much the same diet and thought the proportion of bread and potatoes rose when a family earned less. The best-off families, he said, might have meat daily and bacon and cheese for supper. Both observers agreed, though, that meat generally played a small role.

Meat most often meant bacon, the third most important urban staple. Mayhew's midcentury Londoners craved butcher's meat, though they settled for bacon. A weaver's family he interviewed had "animal food" maybe once a week but no more, and never as a roasted joint, the Sunday tradition. An umbrella maker's family did somewhat better. Among six people they divided seven pounds of meat weekly, but of an inferior cut. The man of the house longed for good roast beef "with potatoes done under it," but said, "I shall never taste that again." For many Londoners, that gloomy forecast held much truth. Fifty years later, the poorest in the metropolis were still living mostly on bread and potatoes. To that they added "a little bacon or some fried fish"—the latter probably from a fish-and-chips shop—and "the cheap parts of beef and mutton when the money in hand goes far enough." The chief beverage was weak tea.

Cheese, butter, and tea appeared less often and in varying quantities, depending on how well the family was doing. Of all items in the urban diet, it should be noted that only potatoes, bacon, and tea needed a cooking fire, and not a lengthy one. A kettle or frying pan sufficed for preparing any of them. In their simplest state, the solid foods could be consumed without silverware, and tea in a cup. All could be purchased in small quantities, which was, as with coal, both helpful and damaging. The poor could spend less at any one time, comforting when they were buying on credit, but the habit cost them disproportionately more. This was "thoughtless extravagance," said the Birmingham physicians who contributed to Chadwick's report.

Sunday was the day the working poor could stop to breathe. Not coincidentally, that was when they had the time to prepare the only soup or roast likely to grace their tables. But Saturday shopping for that most important meal was a rushed job because many, if not most, employers waited until the last possible moment to pay their workers. Before midcentury, at least, that meant "nine, ten, and often eleven o'clock" at night, leaving just a few hours before the stores closed for the weekend. Holyoake complained,

"There seemed no end to this, and no way out of it." It was more than a nuisance because by late Saturday night shop shelves might be nearly empty, and what was left, though selling at bargain prices, was poor quality. Why employers inflicted the delay isn't entirely clear. Some may have acted out of sadistic whim; others wished to curb their workers' drinking. The theory went that laborers paid on Friday would imbibe that night and either miss Saturday's labors or perform them sloppily. More enlightened employers realized that the Saturday workday was restraint enough, and that paying earlier would actually funnel more money to the food market and less to the pub. But the practice didn't become general until laws imposed the Saturday "half-holiday," and workplaces closed in the afternoon.

It isn't fair to generalize from a single instance, but anecdotes do provide arresting insights. A Leeds manufacturer whom Chadwick thought enough of to quote related why he paid his workers early. He wanted to save them trouble and to keep them from drinking, but he had another compelling reason. If they bought from street vendors instead of shops, they would spend more and get less, but, more important, they might be tempted to buy on Sunday, when vendors were selling and shops weren't. Sunday was, of course, when all moral people were in church, and no Victorian needed to be told that denying people religious instruction was a great wrong. A truly benevolent employer, then, would pay his workers early. Whether the manufacturer—or Chadwick—knew they would get farther arguing for religion rather than for kindness and consideration is impossible to guess. But the belief that the educated, monied classes must set a moral example pervaded many theaters of life, not least the workplace.

Naturally, this paternal attitude had many problems, among them a mixed message. The Leeds manufacturer reported that in his city, employers commonly paid their workers in groups. Rather than give each one exact change, several were handed a banknote and left to sort matters out. This led, the manufacturer said, "to the public-house," where the publican made change. The manufacturer estimated that 10 percent of the workers' wives and children had to chase down their breadwinner there, or they would have never seen any money. A midcentury pottery worker confirmed that story from the other side. He recalled that the publican, in return for making change, pressed everyone to buy drinks and a hot roll and cheese. "Those rolls and cheese were devoured with rare gusto," the potter said, but the change only appeared when the publican saw enough workers settled down for a night's drinking. Moralists would have found much in that scene to decry—drinking, juvenile laborers in a pub, the publican exacting ransom. It would be interesting to know how much blame went to the workers for surrendering to temptation and how much, if any, to their employers for putting it in their way.

Another detail sticks out about that scene. The potter remembered that the children eating rolls competed to see who could make them last the longest. That glimpse of working-class life says much about how fast food served that growing industrial society and others since. Leaving the week's labors with pockets jingling meant being able to assuage hunger with food hot off a cart or shop stove. No doubt the late hour and the week's grind made cooking or waiting for a meal seem pointless. The street vendors whom the Leeds manufacturer (and others) warned about understood this quite well, for they thronged working-class neighborhoods when the Saturday night shift got off. Competing with the shops, the traders hawked market produce bought earlier that day and "little savoury knick-knacks that may serve for a supper, or for a penny treat." In London, these offerings included hot pies, chestnuts, bottles of ginger beer, stewed eels, buns, pastries, and baked potatoes.

The "baked 'tato man," with his "brightly polished, hot and steaming" equipment, "redolent of large potatoes and strong butter," occupied the London scene for eighty years, starting around 1820. According to the journalist Henry Mayhew, potatoes were a specialty item like roasted chestnuts until about 1835, when the trade boomed. In 1851, three hundred vendors were plying London's thoroughfares and outdoor markets from mid-August to early April, selling ten tons of baked potatoes daily. Many were tradesmen or laborers who couldn't find regular winter work. The job required standing outside on cold nights, entrepreneurial hustle, and a few pounds up front, but weekly profits averaged thirty shillings, sometimes more, an excellent wage for the time.

Given the lack of fuel and kitchen equipment, a vendor had to be daring and a bit ingenious. Renting an oven on occasion was an established urban custom—Holyoake's family had pies baked that way—but to succeed, the potato vendor had to see beyond the small-quantities-are-best horizon. Buying potatoes by the hundredweight, the vendor paid a baker to bake them in large tins. Having had the potatoes baked, the vendor then put them in a tall can built for the purpose. It had a firepot and boiler inside, a pipe to let the steam escape, a small compartment for butter and salt, and another for fresh charcoal. Some cans, Mayhew said, were fancy pieces of craftsmanship. The most handsome one, he thought, was made of brass mounted with German silver and decorated with three colored-glass lamps.

The baked potato played a special role in London working-class life. An "eminent divine," Mayhew reported, praised them publicly as "among the best of modern improvements," a cheap luxury for the cold wayfarer. A newspaper seller whom Mayhew knew probably spoke for many when he said the potato vendor's cry always gladdened him, because the hot spud would turn what would have been just a snack into dinner. That hot spud, Mayhew said, had another use, too, as a handwarmer. So it did for many years. The botanist and potato historian R. N. Salaman remembered that until just before the First World War, barrows "with great brown and crusted tubers impaled like heads of traitors on [their] triangular spikes" frequented London's most crowded districts. If a man and a woman were together, Salaman said, and the weather cold, the hawker would recommend the man buy her a baked potato. This advice was often taken, and the potato placed inside her muff.

Certainly, this was a novel use for a vegetable, and that it conjures up images of the hot coals or bricks that served as bedwarmers says something. Forever practical, the stolid, lumpy potato resolved life's mundane problems, but it wasn't attractive or interesting. It had no gentility, no style, which held it back until its liberating advantages became too compelling to ignore. However, though probably no one realized it, the gleaming baked-potato cans marked the last stages of a long, roundabout journey in which the tuber had crossed many barriers of class and manners to find its true English home. From garden crop and occult nightshade, the potato had become a plant for neglected corners, then a meager substitute for bread, a low-class interloper with no proper place, even among the lower classes.

The city gave the potato wider scope. The population explosion, life's quickening pace, the faults of lower-class housing, the lack of fuel, the want of cooking skill, the potato's cheapness and bulk—these made the tuber an urban blessing. However, these are also practical considerations, and the baked potato had a social impact beyond utility. Like the hot rolls or eel pies, the steaming baked potato doused with butter and salt was a delicacy. That many cooks or kitchens couldn't produce them was probably only part of the attraction. There is something gratifying about fast food, especially if it fills the stomach and adds color to a festive occasion, such as celebrating the weekend. For the upper classes, such gustatorial pleasures probably confirmed how improvidently their inferiors sated their brutish appetites. Certainly, much of the food had dubious origins and offered little or no nutrition. But the very idea of eating food in the street was enough to arouse snobbery, a view that lasted long after the pushcarts had become shops.

Consequently, the baked potato's London triumph displayed the tuber as a lower-class item, but the lower class no longer minded. The potato was now good food, not as good as bread, but worthy, and no longer debasing those who ate it. It could be eaten publicly, even with the hands. This was significant, because eating with the hands was a habit for which English observers criticized the Irish, yet baked potatoes seemed to arouse no fear of comparison. What's also odd is that the trade never reached Ireland—at least not according to any sources this historian has seen—where it wouldn't have raised any eyebrows.

Nevertheless, despite the potato's new acceptance, how the vendors plied their wares suggests reverse class-consciousness. Mayhew noticed that they typically gave their businesses gaudy names, often with blue-blood associations. Such legends as "Royal George" or "Prince of Wales" decorated the sellers' cans on suitably engraved brass plates, a genteel touch like the colored lights and silver fittings that caught Mayhew's eye. Or the name might be "Original Baked Potatoes" or "Old Original Baked Potatoes," pretense of a solid, long-standing tradition that had never existed. Businesses often publicize themselves this way, but usually the humbler, hustling ones. For the potato vendors, this behavior might have been a glaze for street peddling, commonly thought disreputable. Or perhaps it reflected the product they sold, just lately rescued from social exile.

Either way, street food would never be the same, nor would the English worker's diet. And perhaps this was the baked-potato trade's greatest contribution, showing that the tuber could have a career in the street and anticipating the french fry, what would one day be the world's most popular fast food. Some forty years after the brass cans with the florid names emblazoned on them appeared, the french fry joined another street food. Together, they formed a great working-class institution, without which British life would be much poorer: fish and chips.

7   A Fortress Besieged

*We always have our praties hard, they stick to our ribs,
and we can fast longer that way.*

IRISH PEASANT

From the countless books, pamphlets, and government reports published about Ireland during the eighteenth and nineteenth centuries, among the millions of words and tons of printed paper, perhaps the most concise summary came from the English traveler Philip Luckombe. In 1780 he wrote that "landlords first get all that is made of the land, and the tenants, for their labor, get poverty and potatoes."

Like all one-sentence profiles, Luckombe's was glib. Nevertheless, he had outlined an all-important truth that would apply even more strictly as the country headed toward 1845 and the Great Famine. Land, poverty, and potatoes were variables in an excruciating social arithmetic problem. No two people agreed on which variable mattered most, but one thing was sure. If any single variable were to change, the others would have to follow; yet that was impossible. If the potato had to give way before poverty diminished, some other food would have to replace it. But peasant land tenure wouldn't function without a crop that produced so much on so little land, especially when an expanding population shrank the amount of land available. As for land tenure changing to accommodate the poor, that was infeasible too.

However bizarre Irish land laws and practices were, seemingly designed to hamstring both tenant and landlord, sorting them out would have meant land reform. And since landowning was the crux of the social order, Parliament would have none of that.

Consequently, the social arithmetic problem was insoluble. Ireland was left to go where it would, while, for much of the population, only the potato kept them this side of disaster. They could have done worse, because the potato was more reliable and nutritious than its critics said. Still, as long as the tuber was the staple (or the only) food and also the peasant's only asset, too much was riding on it. When the harvest sufficed, the Irish didn't starve—extraordinary, considering how many millions of people the potato fed. But it alone could never provide more than that barest insurance. Real progress was out of the question.

Much of the difficulty rested on one crippling fact. Where the nineteenth-century Irish peasant saw land as the means to subsist, the landowner saw it as the path to wealth. To say so is to state the obvious, because Ireland was agricultural and European aristocracies were founded on landholding. In England, though wealth and power increasingly came from other sources, landed interests held sway. The phrase *gentleman of property* denoted more than money. It conveyed influence, lineage, and social position to which the wealthiest merchant or manufacturer had no claim. Humbler, poorer folk lived worlds below. As the fiction of Austen, Dickens, and other writers attests, such attitudes were instinctive and defined the world. In 1852 the English economist Nassau William Senior began a book about Ireland with this: "The great object and the great difficulty in government is the preservation of individual property." Senior meant all property, but land was primary. Whoever owned it deserved favor and represented the nation's interests.

Given Ireland's historical reputation, it's not surprising that the favored hands were few. What is surprising is just how few they were, and how many lives and fortunes depended on them in a very small space. The 1841 census counted almost 8.2 million people, in an area roughly the size of Maine. However, 8.2 million is seven times the state's 1992 population, so to re-create Ireland's population density, everyone in New Hampshire and Massachusetts would have to move to Maine. Then, all the land worth having would have to be divided among eight thousand landlords. Since that number would equal 0.1 percent of the population, it's easy to see why Ireland possessed a vast, crowded, many-tiered tenantry whose standard of living was often tenuous.

Class privilege naturally followed similar lines, but the divisions went even deeper than in England. When Arthur Young wrote that a landlord in 1770s Ireland could not invent an order that a laborer or cottager would dare refuse to carry out, he meant it as a contrast. The lowest English peasant had his dignity and basic rights, or so it was said. An infamous, much-quoted anecdote reported by Edward Wakefield in 1809 showed where the Irish peasant stood. At Carlow, Wakefield saw a gentleman strike a man with a whip, "with less ceremony than an English country squire would a dog," rather than ask him to move aside. The blow laid the victim's cheek open, yet bystanders didn't so much as murmur. As one historian has aptly noted, in Ireland the "poor were below the law and the propertied above it."

With land ownership went a distinctive lifestyle. The idle, spendthrift landed gentleman was a recognizable type. Types are caricatures, but nevertheless, profligacy drove many Irish estates into bankruptcy or crippling debt. Young condemned the landowners' extravagance, especially that of the petty gentry. He called them the "pest of society" and said their routine was to "hunt in the day, get drunk in the evening, and fight the next morning." Most historians think he exaggerated, but his central point merits attention. Many landed proprietors, not only the Irish, associated landholding with leisure. The object was to possess land for the wealth and privilege it conferred, not to make the soil productive. To such proprietors, farming or managing land was business and beneath a gentleman's notice. The people who actually worked it lived in another universe.

Some observers said this emphasis marked the landscape. "The Irish gentry have been spoiled by indulgence," wrote a visitor to Munster in 1830. He found mansions run down or deserted, lands abused, tenants angry or vindictive, and estates in litigation. A few years later, another commentator was glad to see lavish hospitality on the decline, because he thought it had led to prodigality. However, that prodigality had already done its work. By 1844 more than 1,300 Irish properties, with a combined annual rental of nearly a million pounds, were under court receivership.

Two landowners, both English-born, set down their thoughts about this. In 1842 Elizabeth Smith, a county Wicklow proprietor's wife, told her diary that agriculture needed "intellect, knowledge, and capital," and that "*gentlemen* must turn to the profession of farming now that Law and War are out of favour with the times." This new kind of gentleman farmer would employ "the thews and sinews of those used to labour" and pay them well. Moreover, with that change, she hoped "ostentation will by and by give way before good sense." To her mind, her husband ran their estate along these sober principles. However, even as she was urging everyone to do likewise, she was tacitly honoring a social barrier that prevented it. To speak of "those used to labour" as distinct from members of her own class was precisely the problem.

Another critical voice belonged to William Bence Jones, a county Cork landholder who published a memoir in 1880. Its title was significant: *The Life's Work in Ireland of a Landlord Who Tried to Do His Duty*. Part of that, as he saw it, was to improve his property and manage it. This was hardly fashionable during the 1840s, the period he was recalling, but it wasn't just fashion that led other landowners to laugh. Desirable as improvements were, they were impossible, and any landlord foolish enough to implement them himself would soon give up. Jones thought he had the last laugh, which entitled him to criticize. In particular, he condemned his fellow landowners' neglect and unfair manner of dealing, and he called those who couldn't live within their means "showy paupers."

Some landlords did treat their property more seriously, either managing their holdings themselves or hiring a competent agent. The Devon Commission, a British government panel that surveyed Irish land tenure in 1844, noted "the increasing interest which many landlords, particularly some amongst the largest proprietors, take in their estates." Nevertheless, the statement implied a recent, welcome change. And in case anyone thought all was rosy, the report stressed that "there is much that requires alteration and amendment."

The upper-class attitude filtered downward. The observer who favored the decline of hospitality noted how merchants loved country houses. "With few exceptions," he remarked, "a Dublin tradesman who has realized £10,000 or perhaps a greatly less sum, is above his business, gets up his jaunting-car, becomes the possessor of a villa, and entertains company." The poorer classes couldn't dream of such things, but they evinced their own social compulsion about land. Describing land tenure in 1848, one writer noted that a small farmer struggling to subsist on a few acres would do anything to avoid becoming a wage laborer, a great comedown. This was true despite what numerous Devon Commission witnesses said, that a laborer with steady employment was better off than a small farmer. One witness, a landlord, said that the small tenant "has such a horror of becoming a labourer, that he would rather do anything than fall into that class."

Of course, bitter experience had also taught the need for a secure food supply, particularly when regular, wage-paying employment was rare or nonexistent. But that practical lesson doesn't explain why the laboring poor apparently borrowed upper-class values. Jones thought tenants saw a farm as a sort of inheritance, not a business. He was a hard-nosed landlord, and he may have known little outside his corner of county Cork. Still, other eyes saw what his did. An economist wrote that neither tenant nor landlord in Ireland acted as if they had a "permanent interest in the soil." Smith waxed indignant because the "lowest ranks" admired how their betters behaved and imitated them to whatever extent their means allowed. She added that "they had not the slightest idea" they were being neglected or oppressed—a remarkably naive comment, to put it kindly.

If the poor did imitate the rich, it was understandable. The rich offered the most visible signs of success. In certain rural districts, especially where farms were small, few people belonged to the middle class except for middlemen, who could be harder and greedier than the landlords. Such behavior did not, of course, encourage lower-class aspirations. To contemporary observers, therefore, the Irish countryside revealed society in clear-cut terms. The French visitor Gustave de Beaumont, who saw the country in the late 1830s, wrote, "The traveller in Ireland meets only magnificent castles or miserable hovels . . . there are only the rich and the poor." Like many descriptions of midnineteenth-century Irish poverty, this one overstates the case, but the gulf between haves and have-nots was impossible to miss.

What was also obvious was that, longings or pretentions aside, land functioned differently for the lower classes. Without land, there was no food or place to live. As de Beaumont remarked, this time with no exaggeration, without land the peasant could only starve, beg, or steal. One dispossessed tenant told the Poor Inquiry in 1836 that "the poor would rather lose their lives" than "quietly submit" to losing their land. With no other means of living, they "would be starving wanderers through the world, as even their relations and former friends would turn their backs upon them, considering them an encumbrance." Nine years later, a landlord told the Devon Commission that in his district, the story went that evicted tenants had "died of a broken heart." His version differed slightly. He knew what really happened because "they died in my neighbourhood, being obliged to leave their warm cabins, and build houses on the road side."

Such makeshift roadside houses had an infamous reputation. Young had called the dwellings "hovel[s] much worse than an English pigstie," and said their denizens "support themselves how they can, by work, begging and stealing." If they were lucky, they found work or the neighborhood ignored them, in which case, Young said, "the hovel grows into a cabbin." A half-century later, a naval doctor visiting county Tyrone saw hovels built into a heathy embankment and thatched in heath for camouflage. Doors were two perpendicular sticks with five crosspieces, resembling a gate, with straw ropes covering the cracks.

The name given an unfortunate living in such a dwelling was *spalpeen*, a word that conveys disrespect for the landless. *Spalpeen* derives from *spal*, "scythe" or "sickle," and *spalp*, a man who wielded one. Initially, *spalp* was a term of honor, signifying an experienced worker. During harvest season, when extra, less practiced, and generally younger men joined the work crews, they were called *spalpeens* (-*een* is an Irish diminutive). Given their reputation and that they earned half of what established men did, the word came to describe migrants, generally from Connacht, who sought employment in England every year. That it also came to mean laborers who held no land and lacked a permanent, sanctioned home conforms to the way land operated as a social gauge. Fittingly, too, the *Oxford English Dictionary* says the word meant a "low or mean fellow; a scamp, a rascal."

Of course, no one would willingly become a spalpeen. Dearth of paid work made the threat real, even when eviction wasn't an issue. As someone said of Connacht in 1825, "No bribe will tempt the poor man to leave his own ridge to plant for another." And, she said, he was right, because whoever offered work couldn't promise it year-round. It was thought better to have one's own potato supply than to live from hand to mouth. It was better, too, to be from somewhere, even the worst acre on a mismanaged estate, than to live like a rat in a roadside lean-to.

Land was also a social asset, without which grown children had trouble finding suitable marriage partners. Not that lack of land prevented marriage or removed any chance of a dowry. As a county Galway man told the Poor Inquiry in 1836, "There are few men so poor . . . but that when their daughter comes to be married they can manage to give her a few pounds as a fortune." Nevertheless, a few pounds were easily spent, and livestock, which often changed hands in marriage settlements, were perishable. An-

other Poor Inquiry witness said girls in his county Waterford district wouldn't marry boys without potato land, because they would starve during the summer, when potatoes were hard to get. Small farmers were similarly choosy, though they had bigger prizes in mind. The Devon Commission was told that young men in county Sligo couldn't get permission to marry without showing their prospective fathers-in-law leases for their land and receipts proving they made a good living from it.

No wonder, then, that when a landholder put a parcel up for rent, swarms of would-be tenants applied. "If I now let it be known that I had a farm of five acres to let," one county Galway landholder told the Poor Inquiry, "I should have fifty bidders in four-and-twenty hours, and all of them would be ready to promise any rent that might be asked." A county Leitrim man remarked that peasants who lived by subsistence had a hard life, but that of "the peasantry who stand every day in the streets of towns, looking for employment is far more wretched; they are oftener disappointed than engaged. I don't know really how they exist." In describing these alternatives, de Beaumont said that Irish land resembled a fortress, always under siege.

Sharpening the problem was population growth. Despite efforts to reclaim mountain or bog land, the amount of arable increased little, so the supply shrank as more people tried to live on it. Dividing and redividing a holding was partly responsible. As one county Leitrim witness told the Devon Commission, "If a man thinks he is near death, and he has six acres, and three sons, he will give them two acres a piece, and they will do the same; so that the holding is dwindled away to a cabbage garden." As a result, he said, neither tenants nor landlord could prosper. A tithe commissioner testifying before the Poor Inquiry thought subdivision was the single most important drag on agriculture. As an example, he said that in 1822 he had visited a thriving area that comfortably supported twenty families. Revisiting the place thirteen years later, just before giving his evidence, he saw seventy families living in misery.

Subdivision was hard to stop, sometimes impossible, and occasionally risky, as when the dispossessed tenants resorted to violence. Other landholders either didn't mind subdivision or encouraged it. Certain middlemen allowed it shamelessly, charging the new tenants more per acre than they themselves paid the landlord. By the 1840s such practices were rare, but the damage had already been done. The 1841 census revealed that Ireland averaged 217 people per square mile of arable. Among Ireland's crueler ironies was that in Connacht, where the soil was least fertile, the square-mile average was 386. Sixty-four percent of all Connacht holdings larger than one acre were smaller than five. Connacht was a hardship case, but even in more fertile Leinster, returns from four counties showed that more than 25 percent of all landholders held less than one acre. By a broader comparative measure, for every hundred hectares, Ireland averaged a hundred people. In France, the figure was sixty.

Subdivision gave the landless a chance to maintain themselves, but it also squeezed them. Prospective tenants knew that if they balked at paying a high rent, someone else would get the property, so they promised more money than they could reasonably pay. As a result, remarked a county Kerry land agent and surveyor named John Wiggins, the land went backward. The tenant struggled to get by and exhausted "the capabilities of the land, and the landlord's patience, about the same time." Wiggins proposed a remedy, explaining that English proprietors viewed excessively high rent bids with "alarm and suspicion." To prove it, he cited instances in which the more capable applicant got the tenancy despite bidding less. Irish landowners would profit by doing the same, he said. But that was an enlightened opinion.

Landlords or agents who tried to stop subdivision or reverse it through evictions had to proceed cautiously. Groups like the Whiteboys, becoming more concerned with land tenure, responded violently to evictions or consolidations, against tenants who profited from them, and agents believed to have abused their authority. Often, the Whiteboys got their way, and the evictions or consolidations stopped. Witnesses to the crimes—beatings, arson, and murder, sometimes committed in broad daylight—seldom testified, either from sympathy or fear of reprisal. As a result, the Whiteboys remained a potent force until midcentury, when improved law enforcement, active disapproval from priests and the middle class, and the Great Famine destroyed their power.

The Whiteboys' methods and even their existence marked the battle lines between lower-class tenant and landlord as sharply as anything did. In a country where land meant wealth and power to one and bare subsistence to the other, the two sides were deadly antagonists. Moreover, the Whiteboys were fighting for the potato as a way of life, whereas the landlords wanted to replace it with something they thought more acceptable. Britain had a huge appetite for Irish cattle and grain, but the tuber was neither an export commodity nor a cash crop. Also, unlike grazing or grain tillage, potato cultivation wasn't gentlemanly farming. Landlords tolerated it to guarantee their rents, but the tenantry relied on it to satisfy their two hungers, for land and for food. With the stakes so high, there was bound to be war.

Where the potato accommodated land hunger is obvious. Since even a tiny farm could support a family, holding that land accorded not only the self-sufficiency that comes with a ready food supply, but the ability to grow it expending little effort. Many people concluded from this that the Irish peasant was lazy, but in fact the low-maintenance potato freed the laborer to accept part-time day wages if he could find them. Many couldn't, and no doubt some preferred not to. Still, the potato's influence wasn't as easily defined as its critics thought.

Then, too, often the cottier had to work off the rent, a system open to abuses that helped lock the peasant into poverty. Trying to climb out of constant debt, known as "working for a dead horse," was a common strain in Irish peasant life, much as it was in England. The potato was what let the laborer squeeze by, in normal times, at least, because it left room for raising cash crops or animals. The saying went that the pig paid the rent; but the potato fed the pig and its owners.

Moreover, it did so reliably until 1845. Admittedly, that is a controversial statement, because local crop failures occurred every several years, on average, and general famine struck too, most cruelly in 1800–1801, 1817, and 1822. During the famines of 1817 and 1822, people resorted to eating nettles, wild mustard, and other weeds, or drawing blood from cattle and mixing it with oatmeal. Sometimes, in desperation they dug up their seed potatoes, though that ended any chance of having food the next season. In the summer of 1822, hunger was so bad and work so scarce—even men willing to work for food alone might not find any—that people pawned their clothes. "Heaven only knows what will become of them in the winter!" exclaimed one witness. On the coasts, people were eating seaweed. The death tolls during 1800–1801 and 1817 were each between forty thousand and sixty thousand, mostly from typhus. The famine of 1822 killed far fewer.

Despite the deaths, these famines were less severe than those of the eighteenth century. That in no way diminishes the misery involved, but the comparison matters. Once the tuber had taken universal hold in Ireland, it sustained the nation somewhat better than other crops without it had done beforehand. It wasn't that there were no serious famines between 1740–41 and 1845, as some have said, but that the outbreaks caused fewer deaths. Further, as with Ireland's worst eighteenth-century famines, the troubles of 1817 and 1822 resulted not from potato failure alone but from other harvest losses too. An observer in Connacht noted how wheat and oats had done poorly in 1817, and that oats fetched an "enormous price." Similarly, heavy autumn rains in 1821 ruined hay supplies, which made it harder to keep livestock.

To be sure, many contemporaries, including agricultural experts, thought the tuber was prone to fail. They spoke of the potato's tendency to "degenerate" or otherwise turn traitor. "Degeneration" was another name for curl, but the term implied a flawed background. Whenever the tuber was the subject of economic, political, or scientific inquiry, talk of heredity wasn't far behind, a striking comment in an age conscious of bloodlines. From the 1770s, when curl began ravaging Europe, the notion of degenerate stock had gained adherents even among the potato's champions. Parmentier, for one, remarked on degeneration and urged using seed balls to prevent it, the right move for the wrong reason. Degeneration was an especially popular theory during the Great Famine, as when a public-health advocate blamed the tuber for its "hereditary fault," a tendency to succumb to a "latent germ of disease." This pernicious idea had serious consequences, not the least being a belief—much like a wish, in some quarters—that the potato would fail for good.

The tuber's critics couldn't have realized what that would mean, nor did they understand what a remarkable job the potato had done. All crops fail. England's string of bad harvests during the Napoleonic Wars proved that, sometimes with results very much like famine. Supporting a poor population the size of Ireland's was no mean feat, though of course some called that the problem. However, much as they might will the poor not to exist or curse the lazy root they lived on, that root was all that lay between survival and catastrophe. By 1845 Ireland contained an estimated 65,000 farms of no more than one acre, on which the spade was the only tool and potatoes the only crop. The historian Austin Bourke calculated that 3.3 million people, or almost 40 percent of the population, were living solely on potatoes. In farm communities, each person consumed more than a ton a year, on average. No wonder a proverb said, "Potatoes in the morning, potatoes at noon, and if I got up at midnight, it would still be potatoes."

Nevertheless, citing the potato's remarkable staying power and high yields isn't to deny Ireland's danger. Rather, it's to counter the popular impression that a disaster the magnitude of the Great Famine was really just a larger version of what had already been happening. To repeat, nineteenth-century Ireland wasn't perpetually starving. Depending on a single crop was more than risky, but high rents and the dearth of wage income had made the potato the only choice. Grain wasn't an option because, like pork, it cost too much to eat; peasants who farmed enough land to grow it often had to sell it to pay the rent.

Where the potato came up wanting was that it went bad faster than grain and was harder to ship. The Poor Inquiry noted that while an acre of potatoes yielded more food than one of grain, weight for weight, grain lasted a family longer and was much less bulky. As a result, want and plenty sometimes existed side-by-side for lack of freight. "It frequently happens," said a witness from county Sligo, "that the peasantry in one district are in a state of starvation, while potatoes are in abundance in the neighboring district." Others reported the same or similar conditions; in one case, the two contrasting districts were only eleven miles apart.

Even more serious was the spoilage problem. In theory, cultivars like the Irish Apple solved that, but reality was more disappointing. The Apple kept one year, hardly ideal but granting some protection. However, as land became scarcer, so did the Apple. The so-called lumper received far wider use, especially among the poor. It came from Scotland in 1808, where it had been strictly animal fodder. The Irish grew the lumper as human food, mostly because it was prolific. Several witnesses told the Poor Inquiry that land producing fifty or sixty large barrels of Apples per acre could yield seventy or eighty of lumpers. The lumper would also grow in poor soils and was reliable. A decade before the famine, it outperformed one hundred other cultivars in tests. Further, it needed less manure than other potatoes.

Despite all that, the lumper was much maligned. Outsiders especially could not get over its former status as animal food. Charles Trevelyan mentioned that "coarsest and most prolific" potato in the same breath as the lazy bed, leaving no doubt what he thought of Irish agriculture. Even in Ireland, it was said that pigs would sniff among the potatoes put before them, rejecting the lumpers until last. Laborers given board were allowed to dig only lumpers for their meals. A ditty about bankrupt Napoleonic War profiteers went like this: "Our gentry who fed upon turtle and wine / Must now on wet lumpers and salt herring dine." Lumpers and salt herring were a common diet in Connacht. A Galway man told the Poor Inquiry, "Never believe them that would want to make you think that we'd eat *wet lumpers* if we could get good bread." Rarely was such treason spoken against the national vegetable, at least to official ears. But a man from county Sligo did say that having Apples would make the pure potato diet less monotonous.

Perhaps the lumper would have been forgiven its sins had it kept from one harvest to the next. Instead, it went bad usually around June or July, though some people said that could occur in May or even April. From then until the new crop came in, August or September, starvation threatened those who had no other food. Had earlier-maturing cultivars existed, this threat would have lessened considerably, but it was Ireland's luck that the modern, early-maturing tuber wasn't bred until after the Great Famine. As it was, the county Kilkenny diarist Humphrey O'Sullivan wrote that with good reason, July in Irish meant "yellow month." The fields were yellow, as were "the faces of the paupers" from sickness. A Poor Inquiry witness ascribed the skin color to eating wild mustard. The year before, 1834, in county Wicklow, charitable citizens had anticipated a bad summer and collected a relief fund. When they distributed food, they found families who hadn't eaten for forty-eight hours and who would have starved otherwise. Hundreds would have perished "of absolute famine," one witness told the Poor Inquiry. He added that the same want had arisen twice before within the past seven years. Much other testimony referred to privations during the "meal months."

The time of shortage had that name because, if potatoes were unavailable or too expensive, people had to buy other food, generally oats. Since they had no cash, that brought on the so-called gombeen men. They were merchants who sold food on credit—typically oats but potatoes too if they were available. As collateral, they accepted the forthcoming crop, which they had the right to seize and sell for nonpayment. They could also demand, before granting a promissory note, that someone such as the parish priest stand as guarantor.

For this privilege, the gombeen merchants charged usurious prices. The Poor Inquiry cited an instance in county Kilkenny of gombeen potatoes costing 10s 6d per barrel when the open market asked 4s 6d. That was only the most drastic example. In county Wicklow, the gombeen agent might insist on the highest market price of the season and then manipulate that price upward. Elsewhere, the markup might be a straight 30 percent or 50 percent. Much has been said about English Protestant landlords, often absentees, who abused their Catholic tenantry. Gombeen agents were usually Irish Catholic and, unfortunately, ever-present. When summer came and the potato displayed its greatest weakness, misery and the gombeen agent were bosom partners.

The meal months showed how relying on one crop stressed the Irish peasant to the limit and often beyond. These sufferings also underlined how the diet had eroded until the potato was, for many people, the only food. It hadn't replaced meat, as some critics assumed, but greater or lesser quantities of oats, beans, barley, herring, or even bread, which had once joined milk and dairy products on the table. Traditionally, the strict potato-and-milk diet, with the milk often buttermilk, was an object of ridicule. A poem from the 1770s belittled it, as did a proverb saying the poor person's food was "small scabby potatoes, and milk having its brains beat out with a stick."

As the Napoleonic Wars ended, the lower-class diet shifted. Oats and beans receded in importance, and potatoes assumed a greater load. O'Sullivan remembered when, before 1800, every "able-bodied farmer" sowed peas and beans; by 1830, few outside the gentry did. Wakefield wrote that throughout Connacht, people were wretched because oatmeal was a luxury. That was Connacht, but even in more prosperous county Wexford, where beans were raised, he remarked that a potato crop failure would be as disastrous as a bad rice harvest in India. He did see bread in several southern counties, a recent addition, but that wasn't typical. As for herring, that was likely to be salted, because, Wakefield said, people thought it went farther.

For the same reason, he also noticed how some laborers' families cooked their potatoes only partway. They called this "leaving the bone" in, a wistful image for people who ate little or no meat.

Far more ominous, however, was the gradual disappearance of milk, obvious even to a casual observer. A woman who summered in Ireland during 1814 and 1815 not only said that oatmeal was a delicacy, and "much more prevalent" in the north than south, but that having buttermilk with it was a great treat. Seven years later, a doctor traveling in Leinster saw, not real milk, but something called "bull's milk"—again an ironic name. Bull's milk was unsifted oats left to ferment in water. When the water was poured off, what was left tasted like weak vinegar. Perhaps its purpose was to make half-cooked spuds more palatable, because that's how people ate them. "We always have our praties hard," they said, "they stick to our ribs, and we can fast longer that way."

The following decades showed that milk and what came from it marked a social gradation. A visitor to Munster remarked on the butter trade, which accounted for so much road traffic. "The sour milk," he reported, "is consumed at home, or, if a town be in the neighbourhood, taken there to sell." As for cheese, only the rich ate it, as a luxury. That was in 1830. For the small producer, the pressure to sell more dairy foods and keep fewer rose along with rents. For the consumer, the expense sometimes priced milk and butter off the table. To one observer in 1834, if small farmers in Leinster were better off than laborers, that was chiefly because the farmers had a little buttermilk to go with their potatoes. The same thing separated laborers who found regular employment from those who didn't. In county Wexford he saw farmers holding forty or fifty acres, the sort who might have eaten meat in Young's time. Now, though they were well off, high rents kept them from "rolling in plenty." Still, they lived in cottages or farmhouses, not cabins, and had buttermilk, sweet milk, butter, and barley bread with their potatoes.

Government surveys heard a lot about the laborer's diet. The Poor Inquiry recorded daily potato consumption figures higher than Wakefield's

5.5 pounds, pointing, perhaps, to the tuber's widening role. Meat and eggs were a rare indulgence, even for those who raised chickens. Small farmers did little better; eggs appeared more often, and a lucky few occasionally had their own bacon. As for milk, county Galway laborers thought buttermilk "a treat," and even farmers who kept two cows couldn't afford to eat their butter. County Limerick laborers had milk sometimes but more often not. Of Ireland, the Devon Commission concluded that "in many districts their [cottiers' and laborers'] only food is the potato, their only beverage water . . . and that nearly in all, their pig and manure heap constitute their only property." The most eloquent testimony came from county Donegal: "Those who have buttermilk are considered independent." Most ate potatoes and salt fish. For much of Ireland, jokes about the potato-and-milk diet were no longer funny.

The hunger for milk was closely connected to the hunger for land. Milk was an expensive purchase, so for the working poor, producing it was the only way to get it. Young had noted, with approval, how the county Donegal peasantry kept cows. With time, land division made that beast a luxury. Many laborers and cottiers held less than the three acres necessary to keep one, or lacked the money to buy and maintain it. This may account for the frequency with which it reportedly figured in dowries. For those who couldn't keep a cow, a pig—or if there was already one pig, a second pig—took its place. The pig required less space, no pasture, yielded manure, and ate what the family threw away.

It was also profitable. The lack of a cow was a nutritional hazard but not necessarily an economic one. Ireland's pork trade boomed, especially with England, and as one observer noted in 1830, the steamboat shipped live pigs across the Irish Sea. Production of pigs and potatoes became interlocked, so that when potatoes were cheap, pork prices fell, which discouraged pig farming. One agricultural historian has estimated that, by 1845, a third of Ireland's potatoes fed pigs. Moreover, cottiers and laborers raised many of those animals, because a third came from farms of an acre or smaller. So it was that contemporaries measured prosperity by the pig's presence in the cabin. It was respected enough that no record exists of the Whiteboys killing any, though they destroyed every other kind of livestock.

Undeniably, however, milk would have made mealtime more pleasant. It would also have supplied vitamin A in the absence of eggs, butter, or meat. Fish would have done instead, but many of the poorest had their potatoes with no accompaniment except salt. Three times a day if they were lucky, twice if not, the drained, cooled potatoes were dumped on the table, if there was one, and peeled. Then the diners dipped the potatoes into the salt, kept in a saucer on a nearby stool. They called this "dab at the stool" or "dip at the stool." Or, sometimes, "blind herring" or "herring up the road," because they pretended there was fish to eat. An American visitor in 1844, watching children avidly dip their potatoes in salt, embarrassed herself by blurting out, "I am happy, my lads, to see you so pleasantly employed."

Naturally, the better off didn't "dab at the stool." Among large farmers, having meat less than three times a week was a sign of poverty. Middling farmers counted their blessings by having more bread and fewer potatoes. The diary of O'Sullivan, a modestly successful businessman, gives a glimpse of how the middle class lived in the 1830s. The O'Sullivans had oatmeal porridge with milk in the morning, wheaten bread with milk at lunch, and dined on potatoes and meat or butter. The potatoes were probably their own. Even people who weren't farmers held land and used it, and even the well-to-do liked the tuber. They laughed at the poor who ate nothing else, but O'Sullivan didn't. He remarked that whereas his family had chicken and ham for Easter, when the poor bought meat for Christmas, they had to be content with "pig's heads, soggy beef, joints of old cows' loins, and small bits of old ram."

Consequently, the laborer and cottier occupied a fragile position. Not only was their potato the chief or only food, it assumed functions it was never meant for. As one commentator wrote during the Great Famine, it substituted for investment capital or money in places where neither existed.

This statement implied that in much of a mid-nineteenth-century Western European nation, united to the world's leading industrial power, a barter economy existed, and with feudal overtones to boot. There's no doubt he was right: The rural Irish economy operated largely without cash changing hands. As Jones said of his county Cork district, "a complete truck system prevailed." The small farmer, Jones said, gave his laborer subtenant a cabin, unmanured potato land, grass for sheep, a small patch of flax, and the right to gather turf. The laborer repaid him through labor, receiving potatoes to eat during the workday. That way, the farmer got his fields prepared and tended, the laborer got what he needed to live, and neither touched a red penny. This version of events sounds almost impossibly idyllic. The laborer received a dwelling, land for animals, the wool they yielded, and the fiber with which to weave linen—all this, for only his labor.

Other observers and the government commissions cited more straitened circumstances. Laborers commonly had to work off their rent one to three days a week, often at sixpence a day, a low wage even for Ireland—and if the employer supplied "diet," wages were a penny or two less. Nevertheless, they couldn't go so low that no one would want them. In 1830 a Parliamentary committee estimated that between 20 percent and 25 percent of the population was unemployed. Many anecdotes relate how huge crowds answered calls for labor, suggesting that most would have been happy to find regular, year-round employment paying sixpence. In 1842 Thackeray heard of a county Kildare farmer known as a philanthropist because he paid women and children eightpence and sixpence year round. He may have deserved the reputation, too, because he also housed them for free.

Whether Jones's description or the commission's was more accurate, the laborer had little or no cash, and without wages, no chance of getting any. Therefore, his only capital was the labor that nobody wanted and his potatoes, likely his sole tangible good. Moreover, as with all farm commodities, value fluctuated with the market and wasn't realized until harvest. Accordingly, the laborer wagered all on the crop, which, besides its other functions, was his collateral if food ran out. As a relief committee report remarked a few years after the Great Famine, "The labourer thus became a commercial speculator in potatoes." Unlike most speculations, however, this one was for stakes much larger than those found on a common balance sheet. The blight would prove that.

With such limitations, it was perhaps only natural that a system like conacre should arise. The name, probably a corruption of *corn acre* ("corn" meaning grain), applied to an arrangement by which a person hired land for the right to raise and harvest a single crop, generally potatoes. The plot was small, frequently a rood (quarter acre) or less. Circumstances varied, but usually the landholder renting out the conacre, most often a small farmer or middleman, prepared and manured the land. The renter, often but not always a laborer, had only to sow, weed, till, and harvest, and need not pay rent until after the crop was in. For these advantages, the renter paid dearly. Rents of £6, £8, or even £10 or more per acre were common, double what the small farmer paid for land of similar quality. The cost was lower for unprepared conacre or if the tenant paid cash up front, an unusual case. Rents were exorbitant, especially considering wage rates, yet available land didn't go begging. A county Cavan landholder told the Poor Inquiry that when he rented out thirty acres of conacre, there was competition for every half rood of it.

The system was ripe for abuse. It allowed small farmers to act like the rack-renting kind of middleman. They didn't even have to set the price. Since holding conacre was "often a question of life and death," farmers knew that someone would be glad to offer a fat rent. If the farmers leased out enough conacre, their tenants would wind up shouldering most or all of the rent burden. In addition, farmers who could have leased multiple-acre holdings sometimes thought conacre a sharper deal. The Devon Commission heard about a county Meath district where farmers were said to like "a man worse off in his circumstances, because they are able to get a greater hold of him." They rented out conacre, whose tenants they hired as laborers.

Conacre had many critics, not least for allowing penniless people to marry. A Galway man told the Poor Inquiry that conacre was an "unmitigated evil," yet couldn't be ended because so many people depended on it. Evil or not, however, conacre was ingenious. For the tenant, it was "a species of savings bank." Though the rent was likely to equal what buying all the potatoes would have cost, the laborer still gained. Conacre freed him from having to acquire potatoes during the winter, when the market was high, higher yet if there was a shortage. The market might also be far from home, requiring transport.

Further, by cultivating his own crop, he earned the security he craved, psychological as much as economic. A half-rood plot was small (in statute measure, equivalent to seventy-five feet square), absorbing relatively little labor and allowing him to work for wages. Yet it was enough land to raise a pig, whose sale could pay the rent. Moreover, since the rent didn't fall due until six weeks after the harvest, more time than he would have had had he bought potatoes on credit, conacre acted like a short-term interest-free loan. If the crop didn't fail and the pig's sale fetched enough money, the laborer had squeezed through another year. Without a pig, the equation was harder to satisfy, because the crop had to cover the rent. If it didn't, the tenant starved or "took the country," meaning to go begging.

For the farmer who needed labor but couldn't pay cash, conacre offered a solution. Such farmers might provide manure and lower the rent, presumably choosing tenants for their skill and energy, not whoever promised the most money. In general, farmers profited from conacre, but so did young single men working as their servants. They often received conacre as part of wages, and since they also got board, they could sell their crop, waiting until the market was highest. Even town merchants took conacre, no doubt for similar reasons. However, anecdotes about the few who profited underline what happened to the great majority who didn't. Conacre couldn't provide a good living. The holdings were too small, and the system made sense only when potatoes were expensive, because otherwise the high rents were unjustified. Therefore, conacre was a safety net that gave subsistence to people who wouldn't have had it any other way. It couldn't encourage better agriculture, and it certainly couldn't stimulate a stagnant rural economy.

The Poor Inquiry, looking for something to furnish that stimulation, asked what it would take for grain to supplant the tuber or at least become its partner. The surveyors, it seems, believed that grain was a more reliable crop that, at a stroke, would supply better food, make subdivision infeasible, slow down population growth, and introduce prosperity. But if this was the dream, the testimony dashed it. Witnesses said that grain could never become a lower-class staple while holdings were small and employment scarce. As one put it, "A rood of potatoes pays as well as an acre of oats, and a man cannot eat the meal and pay his rent at the same time." Another remarked that storing meal within a cabin required a cupboard, which people didn't have. They also lacked the kiln to dry the grain, the rickstand to safeguard it from pests, granaries to store it, and the oven with which to bake bread. Then, too, without potatoes, keeping pigs would cease to be economical. To accommodate grain, the peasant's whole world would have had to change.

More enlightened critics approached the problem based on how that world was put together. As one argued, dependence on the potato was the result of poverty, not its cause. The Irish lived on the tuber because it was the cheapest food available, and they couldn't afford anything else because they couldn't find regular wages. Since land laws and practices caused the lack of employment, reworking land tenure was the solution. However, Queen Victoria's charge to the Devon Commission suggested how tricky that would be. The commission's purpose, she said, was to study land tenure and taxes to see whether laws might be passed to improve agriculture and tenant-landlord relations. Such laws, however, must show "due regard to the just rights of Property."

Since Irish land tenure imposed utter confusion and inefficiency, Her Majesty was asking a great deal. Tenants, especially the small holders, fought an uphill battle to survive. Their biggest grievance was insecurity, meaning of the land and any investment in it. By 1845, though most land was under lease, most tenants held it "at will," with no written guarantee. If the landlord decided to switch from tillage to grazing and wished to convert the tenant's land to pasture, down went the cabin. Wiser landlords offered compensation in that case, but most counties didn't require it. Similarly, if a tenant improved his farm or dwelling, the landlord could raise the rent, but when the tenant left the holding, his expenses could go unreimbursed. Expert opinion divided over whether such practices inhibited improvement, or whether tenants used them as excuses not to bother. The Devon Commission, true to its charge, urged Parliament to provide a remedy, noting that bills for that purpose had failed as recently as 1843 and also in 1835 and 1836. In any case, tenants either wouldn't or couldn't improve, and landlords generally didn't pay. This custom reportedly differed from that of England.

Other practices that hindered the tenant abused either the letter of the law or common decency. Since a tenant's goods could be seized for nonpayment of rent, unscrupulous agents or bailiffs misused that power, though without the landlord's knowledge, it was said. A magistrate told the Poor Inquiry about an estate steward who withheld wages from seventeen laborers to put them in debt. To keep them there, he levied fines "upon the slightest pretence," which he deducted from wages. Then he sold the men food at gombeen prices. As a result, the labor cost the steward about half its real value, and he pocketed the difference. The magistrate said such practices were common in his district.

Landlords who needed money often preferred to rack the tenants than improve the estate, assuming they knew how. A county Sligo landowner told the Poor Inquiry that most landlords would squeeze the tenantry to pay their own debts. Other landlords confirmed this. Middlemen might behave the same way, though legend has colored how much this practice actually went on. In fact, middlemen sometimes did what a conscientious landlord would have done and which too many landlords didn't do. A county Cork land agent told the Devon Commission he knew middlemen who encouraged the tenants with advice and even loaned money for improvements.

As with middlemen, legend has accused absentee landlords of myriad evils, only some of which were real. If no authority was resident, bad tenants were as likely to be favored as good ones, creating turmoil and, perhaps, corruption. Possibly, too, as some critics then and now have claimed, absentees spending their money in Dublin or London instead of on their lands hurt the economy. However, certain absentees' estates were better managed than residents' because a good agent was on site. Absenteeism was highest where the land was least fertile and the chances for productivity lowest—poor Connacht!—but where the soil offered promise, more landlords resided. This disproves the myth that all landlords would have rather lived abroad or in Dublin. However, to the cottier or laborer, where the landlord lived probably made little difference. The tenant might even see the absence of authority as a blessing, because it meant less interference.

And interference aptly describes how law and custom often viewed an improving landlord's efforts. It was easy to ruin or neglect an estate, as the heirs to it often found, but fixing it was much harder. An Ulster nobleman spent one-fourth of his gross rental income servicing his predecessor's debts. A county Roscommon lord mortgaged much of his property before he was finally declared insane in 1835. These are only two examples of infamous profligacy, self-inflicted wounds that weren't allowed to heal, sometimes because the law prevented it. An estate in arrears was nearly impossible to buy, sell, or modify, which meant the land lay ailing while the lawyers fought over it.

Jones inherited a county Cork estate his grandfather had never visited and his father had seen just once during his whole life for a half-hour. Making changes in such a place, Jones wrote, was a daunting job. Not only were neighboring landowners waiting, if not hoping, to see him fail, the task was huge. There were no roads, rents hadn't been collected properly in years, and farm equipment was sorely lacking. A friend who took over an eleven-thousand-acre estate in 1822 told him that a wheeled vehicle had never entered it. Once, when the friend got lost while bird hunting, the peasants had to send two miles for someone who could direct him home in English, a measure of the cultural barrier between the classes.

Because that barrier existed, it's often hard to decide whether landlords' complaints about their tenantry speak more of blind prejudice or what they truthfully perceived. The agent John Wiggins said that when he first went to county Kerry in 1807, "The people were certainly as wild as the country they inhabited: quarrelsome, violent, and litigious; great lawyers—yet though fond of law, not very ready to obey the laws; little accustomed to labour." That he was quick to add how he admired the people and enlisted their help to revive a dying estate suggests he was not merely reciting his prejudices. More suspect, perhaps, are comments from Lord Monteagle, who said that "the Irish tenant is not to be trusted with a lease. His instinct is while he is alive to sublet the land, in order to have an income without trouble, and on his death to divide it among his children."

Nevertheless, if Lord Monteagle unjustly ascribed motives to people he didn't understand, the actions he was talking about did take place. Subletting and subdivision were common. Whatever social benefits they conferred, they reduced farms to where potato subsistence was the only prospect, and sometimes put even that tenuous future in jeopardy. They also tangled landholding relationships so badly that tenants were constantly suing one another. And despite all that, landlords and agents had no end of trouble keeping the land undivided. Some lost their lives trying, though the animosity that could lead to that depended on personalities, perceived intentions, and diplomatic skill. Still, even those landlords who had their tenants' trust spoke about how hard it was, if not impossible.

No one likes a landlord except another landlord, but sympathy for Ireland's oppressed tenants shouldn't obscure their shortcomings. Ireland's failings in agriculture may not have been of their making, but they bear a small responsibility in holding back progress. Some changes the Irish balked at were anything but newfangled. When Elizabeth Smith's husband asked his overseer—Irish-born, though many landlords preferred foreigners—to plant turnips and to use seed drills for potatoes instead of a spade, the man threw a fit. Similarly, the Devon Commission heard again and again that green crops, meaning turnips and clovers, had only appeared recently. The landlords couldn't be the only ones to blame. It was also not their fault that paring and burning continued despite the law and common sense, especially among tenants whose tenancies were almost up and who didn't care whether they exhausted the soil. Then, of course, there were the inevitable wrangles over rent. Both Smith and Jones said that tenants would offer any excuse for nonpayment, even if they had the money.

But Whiteboy activity was the most significant, obvious landlord complaint. How much the Whiteboys hindered general progress, or even whether they did, has never been proven, because tales of ruffians roaming the countryside by night or murdering by day were sensational. It's striking, however, that the classic Whiteboy victim among landlords and agents was the improving kind. The big question is whether the Whiteboys scared off badly needed capital, presumably from England. The Poor Inquiry thought so, though not every witness agreed. The Devon Commission heard similar ideas and condemned the violence, but without explicitly blaming it for discouraging investment.

However, as one historian has argued, manufacturers didn't need to build factories in Ireland when Irish immigrants flooded Liverpool and Manchester and were willing to work for low wages. The Liverpool Sanitary Act of 1846, the model for Britain's national public-health legislation, was enacted largely because of Irish immigrant population pressure, which worsened already miserable living conditions. Secondly, as another writer has shown, a reputable property insurer charged no higher premiums for Ireland than for England, despite the rates' sensitivity to arson or vandalism. As far as this company was concerned, doing business in Ireland wasn't a bad risk at all.

Still, perceptions matter, especially concerning a flighty creature like investment climate. Imagine what a capitalist looking for venture opportunities would have made of outbursts like this one, from the respected economist J. R. McCulloch:

> A landlord who should attempt to introduce an improved system on his estate, would run a very great risk of being shot; and it is really astonishing that any individuals able to live elsewhere, should continue to reside in such a country. It is wholly unfit for any save a military government....

The language was particular, but the thought behind it widely held. Senior, the influential economist who believed that government's chief object was to protect property, reproved Ireland for failing to do so. Neither he nor McCulloch knew the country well, even for outsiders, but their readers probably knew it less. The opinions that these two and other noted critics expressed fit what observers had been saying for centuries: that the Irish were violent, fractious, unruly people. Since capital is conservative, the logic of the time, or perhaps any time, dictated that the smart money should go elsewhere.

Which was the final blow to hopes of redeeming Ireland's lower classes from poverty. If neither tenant nor landlord improved the land, farming would never rise above the subsistence level. The standard of living would drop as the population grew, land hunger sharpened, and more people were thrown on tiny, unproductive farms or, worse, conacre. The landlord-tenant relationship would become even more antagonistic, as a relatively small but growing group of improvers reorganized their estates and evicted tenants for whom they were unwilling or unable to find room. Those evicted had few choices: emigrate, beg, starve, fight back. None of those hard choices fixed anything.

Such troubles were no secret. When the Devon Commission heard evidence in 1844, it was the thirteenth Parliamentary survey of Ireland in twenty-five years, not including three censuses. Many private pens had described Ireland's miseries in heart-rending detail. But all the information in the world couldn't change one simple fact: No one knew what to do. In every direction stood an impenetrable wall—the potato as staple, unworkable land tenure, wretchedness that seemed beyond help. Besides, imposing an answer was unthinkable. The reigning ethic stressed self-reliance, respect for property, and belief in an unintrusive government, principles still familiar today. Add the unshakable conviction that the social classes differed and didn't wish to be treated alike, let alone deserve it. What solution could possibly balance that morality against Ireland's seemingly irrevocable suffering? This question, too, is familiar.

Not that solutions weren't offered; many were. The Devon Commission heard a particularly daring plan from John Wiggins (which he also set out in a book). Wiggins's scheme required no acts of Parliament, no government intrusion, no disrespect for property, and nothing to hamper the poor person's initiative. On the contrary: His agenda encouraged the Victorian virtues and made money. Perhaps most remarkable, it unshackled the peasant from the potato, making the tuber part of agriculture but not the whole. In other words, Wiggins tackled Ireland's social arithmetic by altering each variable a little, but none too radically.

By his own account, Wiggins had succeeded handsomely in county Kerry, turning a cursed tract into something as close to rural utopia as Ireland could have. Hard-working tenant farmers lived in proper houses, not cabins, attended music and reading societies, and even owned horses. Meanwhile, the landlord earned a good profit. All Ireland could do likewise,

Wiggins boasted, though his system would fare "as well in Russia or in the Indies."

His ideas rested on three key principles. First, he thought that if tenants wished to improve and if the landlord agreed, the landlord should pay some of the expense. Were the tenants better off, Wiggins said, that wouldn't be necessary, but Ireland's landlords had no choice. If they didn't, their properties would remain ill used or neglected, the occupiers would become apathetic if they weren't already, and the country would go backward if it moved at all. Second, Wiggins said any landlord who charged more than a moderate rent was injuring himself, his tenants, and his property. Tenant and landlord were "of one and the same family," meaning the landlord had to aid his tenant because their interests coincided. Third, Wiggins believed in involving the tenants in decisions that concerned them, though without, of course, yielding control. Rather, giving them a voice was how he guided them where he wanted them to go. They did their own work, but he earned their goodwill and compliance. "A very essential portion of my system," he said, "is to make the tenants the executive. I would not build a wall for them on any account."

For example, when he reapportioned fifteen thousand acres' worth of subdivided, scattered holdings, he didn't redraw the map himself. To reassign the land, he called together the several hundred resident families, who appointed a committee he then consulted. Kinship and friendship shaped the decisions, as did convenience, soil quality, and the tenants' perceived ability to make it pay. The committee voted on the changes, with individual members withdrawing whenever they had a conflict of interest. As a result, Wiggins persuaded several hundred families to consolidate their farms without resorting to wholesale evictions. At his request, they did expel fifteen or twenty "bad characters," mostly sheep stealers whom nobody mourned, he said. After the consolidation, he oversaw improvements that sound much like those of English enclosure. Roads and outbuildings were built, and a supply of lime assured. Oats joined potatoes in organized crop rotations, returning to the more balanced agricultural economy that had probably existed in the late eighteenth century. The estate revived and the tenants prospered.

The commissioners listening to this astonishing tale cross-examined him carefully, with more apparent zeal than usual, perhaps because he seemed so cocksure. Most witnesses were politely diffident when expressing their views, but this man acted the prophet iconoclast. They pressed him to say why his system wasn't universal if it worked so well. And why didn't everyone invest for the long term if, as he said, the benefits were self-evident and the alternative disastrous?

Wiggins needed little prompting. He condemned "the selfishness, and short-sightedness of men, who usually look for immediate benefits, rather than remote ones." Landlords refused to see that asking lower rents would repay them in the long run, and that spending on improvements wasn't a waste but a wise investment. He understood such things because he was "a man of business," but they weren't. "The clergyman tells us of our future interests," he said, "but we do not pay so much attention to him as those interests require, and so it is in a great measure with landlords and their lands." Moreover, he noted, land agents were unlikely to play clergyman. It was much easier not to persuade the landlord to do what he didn't wish to do and risk being blamed if anything went wrong.

He might have added that there were social barriers at least as formidable as the economic ones. Wiggins's system required active, shoulder-to-shoulder dealing with tenants, asking their opinions and listening to the answers. (It must be said, however, that Wiggins wasn't resident, so how much on-site knowledge he had is open to question.) In any case, only a confident agent could deal that way, one who was comfortable with his social standing and knew that contact with laborers and cottiers wasn't a threat. Further, it meant observing the tenants closely and seeing them as people, which many of Wiggins's class or the class he served found difficult. Also, if land agents lacked experience at these tasks, social prejudice wasn't solely to blame. Estate management in Ireland had only recently emerged from the time when agents—the honest ones, anyway—did little but collect rents. What Wiggins was suggesting demanded not just agricultural expertise but diplomatic gifts. Much depended on the individual people involved, who apparently had to be extraordinary.

Most important, he was proposing this as a man of business, and so he was doomed to fail. Gentlemen of property did not wish to involve themselves in business matters. That was why they were gentlemen. Wiggins knew that, of course, and he was speaking as one who would spare them from dirtying their hands. Nevertheless, he was pleading for business sense from a class that had rarely displayed any and found the very idea demeaning. And when he said that gentlemen belonged to the same family as their ragged, barefoot peasantry—well, that was radical, preposterous nonsense, even in the purely metaphorical sense in which he meant it.

About a year after John Wiggins testified, the blight came.

8 A Passion for Thrift

Morsel swallowed has no more taste.
FRENCH PROVERB

WHEN THE FRENCH NOVELIST Pierre Gascar recalled his youth in
rural Périgord, he said he felt as if he had grown up during the Middle
Ages. The family wore wooden shoes and spoke a dialect that dated from
the thirteenth century. They lived in a common room blackened by smoke
and lit by kerosene lamps. The house was cold because only the hearth provided heat, and then only if you stood close by it. Gascar's grandmother
probably never washed her head, and no one knew what a shower was. They
ate bread baked once every two weeks, the center of which crumbled from
improper leavening, while the surface was hard enough to break a tooth.
The sole physical comfort recognizable to an outsider had to do with the
beds, whose mattresses contained down as well as corn stalks. Gascar's family didn't buy the down, of course, but plucked it from the geese and ducks
they raised.

Those fowl also supplied the livers that went into pâtés. The farmers
never tasted them. Nor did they sample, except on the rarest occasions, the
truffles that added so much to the pâtés' mystique, flavor, and expense.
Such a commodity fetched ready money and was too precious to consume.
Truffles reached the table only in parlance: *Truffe*, the French word, meant

"potato" in the local patois. The substitution aptly described an existence in which one might speak of luxuries but not enjoy them. Appetite was an urge one controlled; indulging it caused extravagance, a sin. Gascar perceived this attitude in the way his grandmother treated the geese and ducks. Following time-honored practice, she force-fed the birds so that their livers would enlarge. Cruel as this was to the animals, it was also painful irony for herself, because she had performed the chore throughout a life during which she had seldom satisfied her own hunger. "It makes you pitiless," he wrote, "when you have to force-feed an animal: It is just, in your eyes, that satiety becomes a punishment."

Such was the ethic of a people who remembered and expected famine, who saw life as severe and unyielding, and who worshiped utility. How ancient these beliefs sound, and how fitting that they should emerge from smoke-blackened, single-room farmhouses. Gascar's invoking the Middle Ages seems perfectly natural. And yet it wasn't, because he moved to the Périgord in 1924, when he was eight years old. Within a few years, Lindbergh would fly the Atlantic, and Paris would toast Josephine Baker. What is most remarkable, however, isn't that time had stopped in the Périgord. Rather, it had dawdled a decade or so at most. Not only does Gascar's description tally with others of rural France between 1900 and the First World War, the essential details go back much farther. Except for objects such as kerosene lamps, his sketch would have rung true before 1850.

No one in 1920s France would have been startled to hear that traditional peasant life still existed. It was well known that France had remained largely agricultural up to the war. The 1906 census revealed that farms employed almost 44 percent of French workers, a proportion more than three times that of Britain. Moreover, it wasn't simply the number of people who tilled the land, but that they held such tiny pieces of it. France was famous as a nation of small farmers, many of whom owned their homes and perhaps five or ten hectares nearby. To some, the land-tenure mosaic assumed legendary stature, as when the geographer Paul Vidal de la Blache called it evi-

dence of a "solidity," an attachment to the soil that France's more industrial neighbors lacked. The year was 1911, and he was likely anticipating a
war against those neighbors, but nationalist fanfare couldn't drown out a
painful everyday truth. Generations of small proprietors had slaved away in
self-denial, chasing after self-sufficiency and freedom from a consumer
economy that might ruin them. As Gascar's recollection so vividly attests,
such a mindset even outlasted the conflict whose means and outcome depended far more on the industrially cast sword than the plowshare.

The peasant outlook says much about the tuber's curious career in
France. The conservatism that suspected anything new, especially anything
that meant risking land, labor, or the bread supply, had kept the potato
down in the eighteenth century. Ironically, conservatism raised it in the
nineteenth. Once it had proven itself a reliable standby that disturbed nothing, absorbed few resources, and so encouraged thrift, it had enemies no
longer. Of course, urban dwellers had different food habits, but these people were less numerous, and anyway, they had quickly appreciated the
potato's cheapness and culinary advantages. So rapidly and completely did
the tuber conquer France that by 1840, a visitor knowing nothing of the recent past would have sworn that the potato was as close to a saint as a vegetable could get.

The memory of famine, so vivid that decades of relative security couldn't
erase it, formed a large part of what inspired the peasantry to save and con-
serve. The threat of want settled under rural roofs like a despotic house-
guest whose orders must be followed despite inconvenience or suffering.
Even during the 1880s and 1890s, when French agriculture had arguably
reached its most prosperous point of the century, people were still recalling
disasters from the Restoration era. In Haute-Marne they talked about 1816,
when they had to eat barley bread made with beans, which rattled around
inside the loaves. A villager from the Gard said that everyone kept famine in
mind because you could easily count the houses where people ate well. Sto-

ries circulated in the Mâconnais about the hailstorm of 1817, which destroyed the grain and forced the most desperate to try to make bread out of ground-up walnut shells.

But it wasn't necessary to reflect on the past; the present could be terrifying. Like the English and Irish peasantries, the French constantly battled debt and a bare larder. Arthur Young was told in 1790 that sharecroppers in Berry "almost every year borrowed their bread of the landlord before the harvest came round." It was bad bread, too, he said. As for their Limousin counterparts, he heard that they did no better. Half of them were deep in debt to their landlords, who felt obliged to turn their tenants out and take a loss. Sharecropping covenants typically favored the landowner, but even without that disadvantage, the farmer's resources were easily stretched. Needing money, he might have to sell his grain right after the harvest, when the market was lowest, only to have to buy it back after the price had risen. Laborers who had little or no land were even worse off, because their wages didn't always cover their needs, as an 1848 inquiry discovered in the Nivernais. The economy did improve during the century's second half, but debt remained a danger. A woman who grew up in the Nord in the 1890s recalled that everyone in the family earned wages—they even worked on Christmas—yet they still lived all winter on credit. A man born near Chartres in 1897 remembered that his mother earned fifty centimes a day sewing, while land rented at twenty-five francs the hectare (a low figure, incidentally). To make ends meet, his parents "worked almost like serfs." Joseph Cressot, who grew up in late nineteenth-century Haute-Marne, remarked that the land let you live if you lived simply. For Cressot's family, who were poor but not hungry, simplicity sufficed. For the less lucky, it didn't.

As in other peasant economies, cash was scarce. Farm wages were low. Many laborers lived with their employers, who paid them in money and kind, and gave free board, lodging, and laundry. The arrangement sounds more generous than it was. In 1852 annual money wages averaged anywhere from less than 100 francs to slightly more than 200, depending on local custom. Ten years later, the national average approached 200 francs, a needed improvement. Nonresident workers in 1862 earned anywhere from 1.15 francs to 2.50 francs per day, but perhaps only half that if their employers also fed them. In the Deux-Sèvres commune of Mazières, which seems to have mirrored rural France in miniature, live-in farm servants earned 150 francs a year. For the same money, a farmer could buy a large barrow.

Thrift may have helped immediate survival, but in the long run, it also hurt. French agriculture was notorious for lacking investment. A forward-thinking observer in Mazières noted sadly in 1830 that most farmers raised too few animals and left too little land in pasture. That, he said, resulted in less dung and therefore a weaker grain yield. However, cattle fetched real money in Mazières—bulls cost 350 francs, and cows, 100—a huge expense for a small holder, conceivably forcing a choice between having the animal or hiring much-needed human labor. Besides, the emotional and economic pressures to grow food, especially grain, argued against conceding arable to pasture.

Such conservatism, which included the reluctance to buy equipment or better seed, was well known, but the peasants weren't the only ones to resist change. For centuries, leases had forbidden planting anything but grains. The potato was shunned because people still feared it would ruin the land for wheat. Moreover, leases were usually three, six, or nine years, hindering tenant and landlord from making permanent investments. Young was appalled at how little care or money French landlords, even members of agricultural societies, expended on their holdings. But labor was cheap, and the peasantry hungered for land. The conventional landlord had no incentive to pay for drainage or even the simplest tools, especially where farms were too small to allow an economy of scale. The sickle, for example, didn't fade from use until the late nineteenth century—and it yielded not to the mechanical harvester, but to the scythe.

As in England and Ireland, landowners' social pretensions encouraged a laissez-faire attitude toward the soil and contempt for the people who worked it. A trenchant description comes from *The Life of a Simple Man*, Emile Guillaumin's classic novel of the rural Bourbonnais, published in 1904. Guillaumin was a peasant, and he depicts the mid-nineteenth-century countryside with unusual realism. His farmers are stubborn, illiterate, hard-working cynics who struggle through life, asking no quarter and giving none. The landlords are bourgeois townfolk who delight in making the tenantry bow and scrape, and whose interest in the land goes no further than a steady income, earned without bother or expense. One such landowner warns Tiennon Bertin, the novel's sharecropper protagonist, not to ask for repairs: "It's a principle of mine not to do any." Much as Tiennon dislikes this—his roof is falling apart—he dislikes the "improvers" more. Some are dishonest, others spout half-baked plans that he must follow, and either way, he loses. However, he needs the land more than they need him, so he must endure their behavior in silence.

The peasant's solution was to become one's own master, which offered freedom from intrusive, possibly ignorant landlords, and financial security beyond the pittance of wages. Contrary to popular myth, before the Revolution peasant ownership was a cherished dream and a frequent reality. By 1789 perhaps a third of France's arable lay in peasant hands, though regionally the proportion varied from 22 to 75 percent. However, many holdings were so small, their proprietors had to hire themselves out as laborers. Therefore, the goal wasn't only ownership, but to buy enough land to be self-sufficient and to bequeath it. Under the ancien régime, this was difficult because feudal laws restricted commoners' rights of inheritance. The Revolution, though it delivered far less land reform than it promised, did sweep away those laws, and so assisted the impulse of legacy.

Consequently, the peasantry's thrift had a vital, tangible object: to buy land and pass it on. In that, the French differed from the English or Irish, who faced many social and economic barriers to owning land or who preferred to invest their savings elsewhere. Young said he was glad that the English lower classes didn't do as the French, caught in an intense competition for land that became ever more subdivided and less productive. He wished the French would use the land they had rather than covet the neighbor's parcel. The advice made sense, particularly because obtaining enough land to farm efficiently was unlikely. But such ideas couldn't satisfy people whose status had recently changed from subject to citizen. The Revolution may not have given them land, but it gave them their country. Bequeathing the soil therefore tapped into traditional desires. The word *héritage* ("inheritance"), wrote Vidal de la Blache, had infused French culture for centuries. Linking the ideas of land and identity, he said *héritage* literally materialized in the soil. During Joan of Arc's time, he added, the word had even meant the kingdom itself.

To share the *héritage*, her nineteenth-century successors went to agonizing lengths. If necessary, they defied their terror of strange places to migrate where wages looked more promising, spending weeks, months, or most of a year away. They stinted themselves to an appalling degree, of which no more graphic example could exist than one reported by the renowned historian Jules Michelet. "To have a few feet of vineyard," for a fee a Burgundian woman takes her own infant from her breast and nurses a stranger's instead. Her husband tells the child, "You will live or you will die, my son; but if you live, you will have land!" This ideal surely wasn't what Vidal de la Blache intended when he said that in agricultural France, the land remained the "nourishing mother of her children."

Statistics are less eloquent than Michelet, but they outline what land hunger looked like in panorama. In 1826 real estate accounted for two-thirds of all inheritances, while movable goods amounted to one-third. The figures balanced only in 1896, suggesting that throughout the century, most people habitually put their faith (and savings) into the most durable investment first, and then into other possessions. By then 69 percent of the peasantry owned their homes, twice the proportion found among city-dwellers. In places the figure reached 80 percent. Meanwhile, the peasantry was also buying arable, and partly as a result, the number of landless laborers fell, especially after 1860. Statistics before that time are unreliable, so tracking peasant ownership is tricky, but it was clearly increasing. The agricultural census for 1872 revealed that nearly half of the 18.5 million people active in farming lived on or cultivated land they owned, up from an estimated (though possibly inaccurate) 35 percent in 1851. But ownership didn't always bring the independence that was so prized. An unknown percentage of small proprietors traded their labor to those who held larger farms, in return for wages or the right to borrow equipment.

Moreover, though ownership spread, large tracts remained in few hands. In 1826 sixty thousand proprietors owned one-fourth of the land, much of it prime. Neither that concentration nor the overcrowding it caused among smaller holders approached the situation in Ireland, the country with which France was sometimes compared. Nevertheless, as landowning ranks increased, French farms became smaller, the middle-sized category often being the one to give way. By 1862 about 75 percent of holdings were ten hectares (twenty-five acres) or less. Farms of forty hectares or more would have seemed like plantations; they accounted for less than 5 percent of holdings. To put those numbers in perspective, half of England's farms were less than eight hectares, and more than one-fourth were between eight and forty.

Besides security and inheritances, land provided dowries. Saving for dowries was a chief reason for thrift, because marriage was a business transaction, not a romantic indulgence. When Tiennon wants to marry Victoire in *The Life of a Simple Man*, her parents oppose him at first because he has no land. Only when he agrees to match the cash portion of the dowry, three hundred francs, do they relent. No special passion binds the pair, but the bargain is well made. Thanks to his father-in-law's contacts, Tiennon gets a sharecropper's lease, which means he won't be a wage laborer all his life. To Victoire, he brings his hard-working, responsible nature, qualities lacking in the men her elder sisters married. That is his only collateral, but he thinks it made her parents willing to take a chance on him.

Marriage customs were rooted in practical concerns. In 1840s Limousin, wedding gifts were almost always edible. An inventory of Mâconnais marriage contracts reveals that the bride's family was expected to provide soup pots and caldrons. In Mazières the gifts were a bed, linen, and a chest. Such formalities persisted throughout the century. A man born in Puy-de-Dôme in 1888 remembered seeing his mother's notarized marriage contract. It specified a bed and an armoire—which, compared to a chest, was a sign of modernity. The memoirist from the Gard, recalling that period, said that dowries were vital, otherwise a young woman couldn't get married. What counted wasn't beauty, but whether she had property and was strong, courageous, capable, and honest.

The emphasis reflected her domestic responsibilities. Though many wives had a servant, and women seldom went to the fields except to deliver meals or lend a hand with haying or the harvest, they labored hard. In Guillaumin's novel, Victoire cooks, cleans, tends the children, and cares for the poultry and pigs. She sells milk in a nearby town, and, when the cows produce enough, churns the surplus into butter and makes cheese. When Tiennon has to take her sales rounds because she's seven months pregnant and can no longer manage the containers, he's laughed at for doing a woman's job. So large was the workload women bore that an observer in midcentury Brittany reported that they actually liked bread baking, an enormous chore, because it was communal and allowed them a few hours' conversation.

The home where the housewife did most of her work says much about what happened there. Peasant cottages were dark. They had no windows or perhaps only one or two, possibly no wider than several inches and difficult to open or shut. Breton homes, for instance, were somber even at high noon on a sunny day. And even if a house had more windows, the clasps were so poorly made that prevailing winds often prevented siting homes to take advantage of sunlight. Frequently, the doorway furnished the most reliable light and ventilation, including the exit for smoke. Between the darkness and fumes, seeing one's way could often be impossible.

For lighting, the housewife had tallow, made of animal grease, which smelled awful. Around 1840 wax candles came in, but they were expensive. Kerosene lamps appeared a decade later, but they were unsafe, especially under thatched roofs. By the 1870s and 1880s, lamps improved, but hemp oil was cheaper than kerosene, and the peasantry was slow to change over. The man from Puy-de-Dôme remembered a lamp fashioned from a hollowed-out potato. Walnut oil fueled it, and cotton strands from an old shirt provided the wick. Just before the First World War, a girl from the Vaucluse accompanied her father on a business trip to a town. It was there that she first saw electricity—at home, the family relied on a kerosene lamp and candles.

The darkness partly explains why French hearths sometimes covered an entire wall, and why they often supplied the only light or heat. In the north, they were where field hands stood to dry off, *veillées* took place, and grandpa put his armchair—the most luxurious seat in the house. The fuel might well be peat, wood, or, as the century progressed, coal dust mixed with marl. The woman who grew up in the Nord in the 1890s said the latter fuel emitted a smell that made her think of death. But whatever the fuel—coal, straw, wood, or brush—it was precious. A saying went in the Gard that wood fires heated a house so badly, even the lice wouldn't stay. Cold was such a problem that, with the notable exception of Flanders, farm animals frequently inhabited the house: The extra bodies added warmth. In certain areas of the Pyrenees, the practice lasted at least until 1893.

The fire, therefore, assumed immense importance. Lighting it was the woman's first task on waking, and protecting it her last before retiring. Damping it for the night needed a deft hand and the right cover, heavy enough to keep the fire from burning actively, but not too heavy to smother it. Come daybreak, if the coals had died and she couldn't revive them, she borrowed embers from a neighbor. Lighting a fire was also a tricky business. Puffing on it too much would make it smoke and burn out, but if left alone, it would die before reaching the main log. Like cutting bread, managing a fire was a mark of competence. Those who couldn't do it were good for nothing, not even to marry.

This meant the cook had exacting work to do in a room in which she could barely see and that might be cold and thick with smoke. It was also cramped. Most peasant houses had a single story, though in the north especially, they occasionally had an upper floor. Sometimes the main floor had two rooms, the larger one often called *la maison*. It held almost everything to sustain life: washwater jugs, a large table for eating, a bed, two chests, the fireplace, a tiny table for food preparation. There was no vertical space, either. Ceilings in the Sologne were so low that even a person of average height couldn't stand erect, while visitors to Breton homes were wise to duck on entering. The size of *la maison* varied, but to cite one example, the man born near Chartres in 1897 said it was four meters square. The second room, *la chambre*, was just large enough for a bed, which he shared with one sibling. He thought himself lucky that, unlike his friends, he came from a small family.

The issue of family size points out how the French peasant was perceived. Nineteenth-century France, despite its often alarmingly low birthrate, had its share of critics who blamed the peasantry for marrying on nothing and having children they couldn't feed. These critics included Young, of all people (though he was writing in 1790, when France was Europe's most populous country). However, he never went so far as to say that this habit derived from laziness or fecklessness. On the contrary: He remarked that "no commendation would be too great" for the "conspicuous" and "meritorious" work ethic the peasant displayed. Young was notably more sympathetic to humble farmers than many of his contemporaries, but this viewpoint stood. For the next century, the French peasant was called many things—ignorant, slow, superstitious, dirty, stubborn, cautious—but not lazy. And despite the attacks on improvident marriages, the peasantry's reputation remained that of wariness and thriftiness.

This differs from what observers said about the English and Irish poor, and about their staple food, the potato. Where those populations struggled under the moral censure that poverty hung around their necks, the French appear to have accepted their lot with far less shame. Being rich meant wearing solid shoes and eating one's fill. No one scorned a poor person who lived modestly; the sinner was someone who had squandered a fortune on enjoyments. This attitude had its drawbacks, but it did remove the stigma from what appeared on the dinner table. Where the English and Irish poor were thought to eat the potato because they couldn't afford anything else, the tuber kept its lower-class status. It substituted for real food, for wholesome food. No such distinction applied in nineteenth-century France. Once the potato was deemed fit to eat, it didn't matter who ate it. It couldn't be the lazy root, because no one in his right mind could call the peasant lazy. Nor could it substitute for real food; it never replaced bread, and to the poor, all food was respectable.

Which raises the question of why the French finally decided to respect the potato. Their way with vegetables was typically cautious, testing them in their gardens first. Peas and beans underwent their garden trials in the late eighteenth century, and other vegetables had their turn later—much later. Around 1900, farmers in Mazières tried out asparagus, artichokes, and radishes. In 1910, they experimented with tomatoes. But as a field crop, the potato had spread much earlier, much faster, suggesting that caution had nothing to do with it. A few historians have said the famine of 1812–13 persuaded the doubters, and in places such as the Morvan, it may have. Nationally, however, there's no reason this famine should have wrought overnight what sixteen others over the entire eighteenth century couldn't. Besides, it seems the potato took off in the 1790s, to judge from contemporary comments, including myriad requests for seed tubers received by the Commission on Subsistence and Provisions of 1793. Farm statistics support this timetable, particularly because production boomed right after the Napoleonic Wars, and it didn't come from thin air. Between 1815 and 1821, potato yield almost doubled, reaching 42.9 million hectoliters (about 124 million bushels), a total the United States wouldn't match for a half-century.

Consequently, Parmentier's pamphlet for the Commission on Subsistence and Provisions may have had important long-term effects. If so, the reason wasn't only the sizable printing, ten thousand copies, or that the Republic was more likely to demand an accounting from its local administrators than the monarchy had. Possibly the pamphlet found a more receptive audience because the Republic's military was draining farm manpower (and Napoleon would do worse). The potato, because it yielded heavily and absorbed little labor, was a remedy. Most important, the potato coincided with the Revolution's demand that land, especially wasteland, be set free for productive use. Consequently, when the commission linked the potato to the campaign to reclaim wasteland—after all, it would grow in any soil—this statement spoke to a subject near the peasant's heart. Waste was a sin, and the potato would help wipe it away.

The potato won friends because it fit a culture in which people stretched every resource, buying only what they couldn't make or raise. Most hard evidence for such self-sufficiency comes from the mid–nineteenth century or later, but that has to do with the widening focus of social commentary, not the sensibilities it was reporting. The peasants of 1789 were no richer than those of 1889, and surely both sensed the perils of assuaging appetite. "Rich cooking is poverty's neighbor," went one proverb; "Morsel swallowed has no more taste," warned another. A third said, "The fatter the kitchen, the thinner the last will." During the nineteenth century, the most obvious way to follow these maxims was not to go to the grocer. This meant that honey or jam sometimes replaced sugar. Vinegar came from discarded apple cider or, for those who could afford it, wine. The merchant provided salt and pepper but could sell oil only to those who harvested neither walnuts nor olives nor churned butter. Some people bought candles, but they left matches, which were taxed, on the store shelf. As the century lengthened, coffee—as chicory—made the shopping list, but those who drank it rationed its use.

The farmer fashioned his own tools, of wood. Clothes also came from the land, as wool, flax, canvas, or hemp. Colors were dark, fabrics rough. Joseph Cressot recalled that hempen sheets scraped the skin despite repeated washings, underwear was indescribable, and shirts billowed when you bent over. Like many rural youths, he got leather shoes only to celebrate his First Communion, wearing *sabots* up until then and again afterward. In many places, until the century waned, wedding clothes were the only ones a person bought, and they were expected to last. Martin Nadaud, a mason born in the Creuse in 1815, wrote that the only shawl his mother ever wore was a wedding present. Emile Guillaumin's Tiennon and his brothers attend different Masses on Sunday because there aren't enough good clothes to go around. Looking back from old age, Tiennon says that at one time, a man wore the same suit to his wedding and his funeral.

Without tongue in cheek, it may be said that the tuber entered French life through the *marmite*, the soup pot. Bread was the diet's spiritual center, but soup was what satisfied hunger, or was supposed to. Many homes weren't equipped to prepare much else, with kitchen equipment fitting into a small cupboard—a *marmite* or two, a frying pan, a spoon, a few crocks. Moreover, since cooking was one of many chores and probably unpleasant in the surroundings, simplicity was the goal. Putting a *marmite* on a slow fire saved fuel, time, energy, and care. Soup was a daily fact, as the shape of tables in late-nineteenth-century Gard suggests. Sometimes they had rounded depressions, removing the need for plates and any doubt about the menu. In some regions, dining from the communal *marmite* was the rule—dishes were scarce —and the only utensils were spoons and knives. Forks took the longest to become popular; in the Breton department of Finistère, they were rare until 1890.

Soup appeared two or three times a day. Even in 1960s Mâconnais, people ate it twice daily in winter, once in summer. In nineteenth-century Brittany, breakfast meant cabbage soup with milk and butter; hired hands brought their own spoons. Near Châteauroux (Berry) in 1823, William Cobbett's son, James, saw an innkeeper's family beginning the day with cabbage soup and red wine. Limousin peasants breakfasted on a vegetable soup flavored with bacon, while the Bourbonnais Tiennon started his day with onion soup. For the man from Puy-de-Dôme, it was leek and potato, seasoned with a bit of lard. The peasant's morning soup didn't give way to café au lait until the century was almost over.

Ingredients for soup varied by season, region, and which meal it was for. Almost everything went into the *marmite*: chestnuts, apple cider, beans, cabbage, leeks, bread, and milk were common constituents. In Franche-Comté if a person or thing was too hard to work with, the saying went that you couldn't make good soup out of him/it. But however varied the soup's chief ingredients, the base was almost always the same—water, bacon or other fat, and salt. Unknown were the rich stocks that today's cooks buy or prepare, thinking nothing of the expense. How well off the peasant household was decided the amount of fat, or even salt, available for flavoring. In poor homes the soup risked being thin stuff, especially when the housewife poured off the broth, serving it and the vegetables as separate courses.

Not only does the potato make excellent soup, it adds bulk and readily absorbs essences like bacon grease. Simple fare, but people treasured it, to judge by the rituals and childhood memories associated with it. In parts of Brittany one ate potatoes by crushing them against the side of the soup plate and spooning up the milky broth with each piece. In 1890s Gard a soup "that held the stomach" contained cabbages, leeks, potatoes, chestnuts, and milk. After the soup came the bacon that flavored it. For one family at least, that was dinner. A woman from turn-of-the-century Vaucluse fondly recalled the soups her mother made from salt pork, sausage, and potatoes—and her family had a more varied diet than many. From late-nineteenth-century Cévennes comes a recollection of a soup so marvelous, just smelling it on a cold day made one feel warmer. The secret was mashing the potatoes with a fork partway through the cooking, then adding a leek, a carrot, and a celery stalk and letting everything simmer. Probably for similar reasons, because the potatoes supplied bulk and thickened the broth, soups in the nineteenth-century Mâconnais traditionally contained potatoes. Only the other vegetables varied.

Bread appeared with the soup. Having to eat soup without bread was a scandal, and eating bread without soup was often physically impossible. Beyond that rule, however, what else the peasants ate depended on what the land yielded and how much they could afford—or allowed themselves—to consume. Modern-day cookbooks and restaurants give the impression that French cuisine would be incomplete without cheese, eggs, butter, and other dairy products. But people who didn't produce these items most likely couldn't buy them, and those who did produce them usually sold them, keeping back little or none. In midcentury Limousin an omelet was a delicacy; a cheese omelet was a luxury. Butter in certain Nivernais cantons cost twice as much as it did in others, and cheese sometimes came from other departments altogether. A family in a Nord mining village in 1891 gave the midwife who delivered their daughter a pick-me-up of an egg in coffee. Otherwise, eggs never appeared in the house, and the drink was chicory. When the baby girl stopped feeding at her mother's breast seven months later, that was the last time she tasted milk at home. However, memoirists from the Gard and the Vaucluse recalled that eggs appeared regularly in the diet. Other writers remembered homemade cheese that the family often ate. Then again, in the Mâconnais, farmers almost always sold their eggs, though they occasionally reserved some for quick meals.

Accordingly, the common thread in the French peasant diet wasn't the cuisine, but the attitudes toward it. These feelings emerged most strongly over the two costliest items, bread and meat, the potato's traditional enemies. However, though the hallowed pair helped define the diet in both France and England, the French view diverged strikingly from the English. And despite what certain contemporaries thought about meat's apparently lesser role, the difference had nothing to do with taste. The French worshiped bread, but they also loved meat, revering the pig in particular. Many peasant families slaughtered one for home use, a second animal if they were better off. The yearly pig-killing was the occasion for a feast. After that indulgence, however, sobriety set in; the leftovers had to flavor a year's worth of soup. Butcher's meat was a luxury. People craved it and ate it every chance they got. But they wouldn't mortgage themselves for it, nor did they think themselves disgraced for not having it.

In such areas as Normandy, butcher's meat had its place, but not in the usual sense. Twice a year, the Normans prepared beef fat and preserved it in crocks, saving it to flavor soup and to spread on bread when butter was lacking. The well-off sometimes had chicken on Sunday, but even they sent their plumpest fowls to market. An observer in Rouen remarked in 1863—when the rural standard of living had begun to rise—that even a "healthy laborer" could buy no more than half a kilogram (a pound) of meat weekly. Another Rouennais who observed daily life closely was Gustave Flaubert. *Madame Bovary* is about unslaked passions, and the author includes the yearning for meat among them. At Emma's wedding, a handful of guests who have consistently missed out on the choice portions take revenge by gathering at one table to whisper ill about their host.

Perhaps Guillaumin nodded toward *Madame Bovary* when he portrayed Tiennon and Victoire's wedding feast in *The Life of a Simple Man*. Unlike its Norman counterpart, this scene shows everyone getting plenty to eat. In fact, stews, roasts, fowl, brioches, and wine are such powerful temptations that the elderly guests remain at the table, gorging themselves, while the younger ones dance. It's hard to blame them. The normal diet is soup, bread, baked potatoes, beans, and dumplings, with a bit of bacon sometimes during the summer and on holidays. The only variety comes on baking days, when there are pies and *galettes*, a sort of pancake.

The passion for meat was such a part of life that those who didn't feel it stood out. When the mason Martin Nadaud and his father left the Creuse in 1830 to seek work in Paris, the fifteen-year-old Martin took up a bizarre habit. He exchanged whatever meat he was given for vegetables and cheese, saying he preferred them because his mother had always fed him soup, bread, buckwheat *galettes*, potatoes, and dairy products. Nadaud senior was annoyed, believing that his son's quirky tastes would leave him unfit for heavy labor. The argument had more to it than food prejudices or parent-child tensions, however. At that time, the Nadauds numbered among more than twenty thousand Creusois masons who migrated to large cities looking for high wages. Competition was fierce, and if the migrants didn't earn enough, their families back home would suffer. To the father, then, Martin's trading away a hard-won luxury might well have seemed an insult, especially since so much was riding on his ability to keep up with a physically demanding profession.

No doubt most people would have thought Martin Nadaud was crazy. Meat was only a Sunday treat in Franche-Comté; otherwise, food was potato *bouillie* and a few slices of cheese. In midcentury Sologne, the poorest workers' families added bits of salt pork to their vegetables only on Easter and New Year's. Matters didn't improve until 1900. Similarly, Mazières had no butcher until the mid-1880s. The Cévennes memoirist recalled that her family ate no butcher's meat, only their own bacon. They cut it in small dice and put it on bread, "with great respect," taking small bites to make it last longer. In Joseph Cressot's Haute-Marne, vineyard laborers had bacon four times a day, but butcher's meat was strictly for illnesses or celebrations. The butcher was an important person who made weekly deliveries to the curate and the gentry. Anyone else seen going over to his cart became a target for gossip.

Unlike meat, bread was essential, but eating it evoked similar feelings. French peasants hungered for good bread, or to eat as much as they wanted of it, but the prevailing custom was to avoid doing so. Even some people who could have afforded fine wheaten bread cut their flour with rye or barley. An observer in Brittany just before midcentury asked farmers why they ate barley bread when wheat was about the same price. They replied that they would enjoy eating it too much and so consume more than they should. An incident in *The Life of a Simple Man* suggests that this fear transcended regional borders. Tiennon, who says that "every pleasure must be paid for—often rather heavily," has nevertheless craved white wheaten bread ever since he was a boy. But Victoire refuses, saying they would get too fond of it. So he arranges privately with the miller to have the bran extracted and discarded—normally, the miller would have given it back—while pretending to Victoire that it's a mistake. As Tiennon has shrewdly foreseen, once his wife has tasted the finer loaf, she indeed becomes too fond of it to want anything else.

Cressot's mother baked ten eight-pound loaves at a time, and they didn't last a week. Which prompted his father to say of the children, "What devourers, better to kill them than to feed them!" But he did nothing to restrict their appetite, which made his household unusually liberal. It was reportedly the fashion in late-nineteenth-century Foix, a Pyrenean town, to lock the bread cupboard. That suspicious brand of tight-fistedness was probably rare, but rules governing bread consumption were common. The memoirist from the Gard wrote that in his father's home, each person might have four or five slices per meal, a generous ration, perhaps, but it was forbidden to dip into tomorrow's supply. When Pierre Gascar's grandmother brought him to visit his extended family, who lived even deeper in the Périgord, it happened that at every house, the baking cycle was in its final days. Since that cycle was three weeks long instead of two, the bread served young Pierre was even more durable than that at home. Naturally, his hosts didn't disrupt their calendar by moving up the baking day, nor would anyone have expected them to. But they did try to make up for it by offering the visitors a treat, *confit* of goose or duck.

In this world of thrift, simplicity, and self-denial, the potato offered potent advantages. Besides slipping neatly into a soup-based cuisine, it let people fill their bellies while stretching the bread supply. As Parmentier had predicted, the potato also fed the pig, with profound economic effects.

Where farmers had once bought acorns or beechmast or foraged their animals in the woods, sometimes incurring fees, the tuber made pig-raising a more independent enterprise. That put an extra layer between the peasant and the cash economy, but it also carried risks. Whenever grain failed, the farmers had to eat the potatoes they would have used as fodder, causing pig husbandry to decline. But the alternative, relying only on grain, was worse. Gambling on the potato at least saved labor and money, because it required no threshing, no curing, and no grinding. Harvesting was so easy a child could do it.

The French were neither the first Europeans to discover these advantages, nor the only ones to benefit. But French cooks went farther than anyone else to exploit the potato's culinary versatility. What made this particularly unusual was that the greatest experimenters weren't, at first, the chefs of haute or bourgeois cuisine. Ere Napoleon saw Elba, fine Parisian restaurants were serving potatoes as a garnish, but otherwise the tuber seems not to have captivated the beau monde. André Viard's *Le cuisinier impérial*, among the era's most enduring cookbooks, possibly because its title changed to reflect which government was in power, offered a modest sampling of potato recipes. The 1837 edition, the fifteenth, counted only nine, about half the number in the *La cuisinière républicaine* of 1794. Urbain Dubois and Emile Bernard's *La cuisine classique*, which appeared in 1856, hardly mentioned the potato in seven hundred pages.

By contrast, a random cross-section of lower-class cuisine shows that potatoes found their way into soups, salads, purées, *galettes*, stews (with or without other vegetables), omelets, and savory tarts with eggs. They were steamed, boiled, roasted on embers and then buttered, fried, and roasted with bacon and onions. This appears to distinguish the French from their English or Irish contemporaries. But that doesn't mean French peasant fare was always tasty or that, as with any nineteenth-century cuisine, it would please the palate today. The memoirist from the Gard said that the surest way to get something good for dinner was to invite a guest, a strategy that probably worked in many homes. Moreover, a custom like the Irish "dab at the stool" was known in France. In 1904, no less, an Ardèche innkeeper was seen feeding his family with a bucket of potatoes, which he emptied on the table and crushed with his fist, and salt, which he ground under a bottle. Still, the French had a reputation for culinary skill that touched all classes. Young thought they particularly outdid their English counterparts in presenting a diverse menu. It happened especially at wealthy tables, he said, but even those less well off managed to do it "by means of cookery only."

That last remark is important. With only a few exceptions, the potato recipes listed above called for everyday ingredients, and none demanded unusual equipment. The discovery that the potato could provide varied fare despite these restraints almost certainly contributed to its influence. This is because the food the tuber most easily displaced was *bouillie*— potatoes need less processing, they save grain, and porridge is always porridge, no matter what you do to it. However, to what extent the potato completely replaced *bouillie*, or even at all, is open to question. As the century progressed, acreage under potato cultivation increased, but so did that for grains—much more so, in fact. Further, when *bouillie* began leaving the diet, probably in the decades after midcentury, foods like macaroni, meat, and eggs were becoming more available. But there again, the choice pitted variety against tradition.

This is the portrait of a society where nothing changed fast but where people had to labor just to stay in step. Where life moved more rapidly, the pressures were perhaps even greater. Midcentury Lille textile workers, for example, lived in one-room dwellings four meters square and two meters high with a storeroom attached. They had no running water or private toilets. Communal pumps and toilets were the rule, the latter usually holes in the ground. Holes in the floor received used wash water. The roofs, lacking gutters, funneled rainwater inside through broken windows or leaky casements. Keeping these houses habitably warm was a struggle.

Lille had plenty of coal—its soot permeated the air and coated the leaves on trees—but it was expensive for the lower classes. Wages might be twelve francs a week, while a month's supply of coal cost nine, and renting the stove in which to burn it, two. When the household budget became too tight, people used footwarmers, whose smoke emitted dangerous gases and added to the dirt. The general filth attracted bugs, which people tried to kill by mixing black soap with pepper and applying it to the walls. In 1856 a public health inquiry reported, "The relative cleanliness of the inhabitants does not manage to make these human habitations as healthy as certain stables."

As for the urban working-class diet, it was hardly richer than the rural one. When Louis François Benoiston de Châteauneuf calculated Paris's food consumption in 1817, he offered grim tidings. He said that of Paris's seven hundred thousand souls, the people who most needed "restorative food," meaning meat, were workers who could least afford it. Meat appeared on their tables in small amounts of sausage, which, he pointed out, were relatively cheap and required no outlays for fuel or utensils. With the sausage, workers ate bread and vegetables, chiefly potatoes. Parisians also loved their coffee, but for the lower classes, that meant chicory. Coffee was vital too in Lille, where a popular song named it as a consolation for life's troubles, and where coffeepots were rarely seen in pawnshops. There, too, the drink was really chicory, perhaps with some coffee mixed, and bought at the pharmacy or grocer's, possibly dampened to make the customer pay more.

Lillois fare of the late 1830s probably hadn't changed for decades and wouldn't again for several more. Alongside bread came sausage, thin soups, potatoes and other vegetables, a little butter, cheese, or milk—but usually only one of these foods per meal. White bread was for holidays, and served like cake; daily bread was gray, made of inferior wheat, sometimes adulterated with copper sulfate. Eggs were too expensive, at fifty centimes the dozen (potatoes were five to fifteen centimes the kilo), and only better-off workers could afford the occasional beef stew. In 1855, an official report said, "Workers talk about food, not politics."

They were most likely talking about meat—good cuts of beef, priced within their means, not the second-rate stuff butchers fobbed off on the poor. In the Nord, even a kilo of diseased meat, whitewashed to hide the putrefaction, cost more than one franc, or half the daily wage. At least potatoes were honest. With them so cheap, workers organized banquets around them, and street vendors sold them boiled. In 1860 a family of six ate more than ten pounds of potatoes a day. The peels fed rabbits, which apartment dwellers raised in rooftop or basement hutches, and which furnished meat for special occasions. *Pommes frites*, what Americans call french fries, appeared on city streets in the Nord around 1870, and the oil that fried them usually came from horseflesh, meat the lower classes ate. The vendor had a stall, roofed to protect against the rain, and served his product in a paper horn, as the English fish-and-chips sellers were also doing then. The hot oil smell permeated the air and clothing, mingling with that of roasting chestnuts, another favored street food.

As in England, industrial life left its mark on the domestic scene, again partly because women participated in both: The 1851 census counted more female textile workers than male. Not all worked in urban settings or factories, though, because, again as in England, home and workshop manufactures developed before more centralized industry. Many workshops were located in the countryside, employing a workforce that was slack during the winter. For example, a young girl in the Nord left school after six years for a winter job weaving handkerchiefs in a basement. The hours were 4 A.M. to 10 P.M., with an hour and a half off for meals, for which she earned two francs a week. She was so little she had to wear wooden blocks on her feet so she could reach the pedals of her machine. That was around 1900, long after English factories had absorbed home manufactures. Her case wasn't unusual, either, because about that same year a girl in the Cévennes took a job on a spinning machine. Her workday was much shorter—8:30 to 6:00, with two hours off for meals—and she was fourteen, older. But in entering the workshop, she performed a valuable service: She replaced her mother, who could then return full time to her household chores.

The potato's reputation in nineteenth-century France illustrates a quirk of the human mind. Like its Irish counterpart, the French peasantry lived in miserable hovels, went barefoot much of the time, ate vegetables rather than meat, and was called stubborn and hard-headed. Both countries were heavily agricultural and predominantly Catholic. Large portions of both populations were illiterate, and many couldn't speak the official language (in 1863, almost one-fourth of France spoke no French, only regional tongues). Agriculture in both nations was deemed backward, partly because law and custom divided the land into minute pieces. To many who saw Ireland (and some who didn't), the potato was somehow mixed up in that country's ills, especially laziness, from which everything else sprang. Curiously, that charge was never leveled against France. In fact, James Cobbett decided that the French didn't eat many potatoes and was offended when the proprietess of an inn at Le Mans served him a bucketful.

What was easier to see in France was that the potato encouraged thrift. Much of Ireland's reputation had to do with political and ethnic prejudice, to be sure, but France's example shows how the potato was an economic weapon. The French peasantry suffered much, and perhaps they would have done better had they stinted themselves less, but the tuber provided another means to that choice, and so they embraced it. By 1817, said Benoiston de Châteauneuf, only five departments did not produce potatoes, and per capita production equaled more than 120 pounds a person. Yet in 1840, the tuber occupied only 3.6 percent of French arable. This tiny fraction was a far cry from Ireland's case, of course, but in 1843, France produced almost half a million bushels on it, the largest crop before the Franco-Prussian War. According to French sources, this figure most likely represented the largest yield on the Continent and possibly the largest in Europe. In about a half-century, France had gone from a nation that hated and mistrusted the tuber to a leading disciple of faith in it. Parmentier would have been proud.

Unfortunately, the two countries had one more thing in common. In 1845 a blight descended on potato fields throughout Europe. For the next five years, an economic crisis gripped France, punctuated by revolution in 1848 and the short-lived republic that followed. Unemployment increased, debts rose, and less currency circulated. Agriculture was particularly hard hit, as grain continued to fail. Rural violence broke out, as people seized harvests and forced sales of food. The potato blight recurred and caused severe losses, amounting to about a third the usual crop for 1845 and 1846, an eighth for 1847, a quarter for 1848, and three-quarters for 1849. As a result, people relied more on grain, which drove up the cost almost to the century's highest point. People suffered worst where they had depended most on wheat, rye, and potatoes, as in the Morvan. Where corn and buckwheat ruled, people fared better. Demographically, the crisis had perceptible effects. The marriage rate dropped, and so did the birthrate. Mortality rose, possibly because the weaker diet left people less resistant to disease. Never again would the French countryside show the dominance it once had.

This was nineteenth-century France's last full-scale famine. It had many immediate causes, of which the potato blight was only one. The damage was serious and memorable but not crippling. Ireland, as the world knows, underwent a much deeper tragedy.

9 The Lumpers They Were Black

. . . God help the people;
the roads are beset with tattered skeletons . . .
ELIZABETH SMITH

THE POTATO BLIGHT that invaded Europe in August 1845 was the most vicious, least predictable the world had ever seen. Diseases such as curl were commonplace, but this blight didn't behave like curl. It killed suddenly, without warning symptoms, and spread faster than cholera did among humans. No cultivar was safe, no matter how reliable or hardy. Even tubers in storage fell victim, removing an early harvest as a possible remedy. Crossing borders with frightening speed, within weeks the plague had reached England, Belgium, France, Germany, and Poland. Dr. John Lindley, a distinguished botanist and editor of Britain's leading horticultural journal, *The Gardeners' Chronicle and Horticultural Gazette*, admitted with alarm that science was helpless. "As to cure for this distemper there is none," he wrote in an editorial. "One of our correspondents is already angry with us for not telling the public how to stop it; but he ought to consider that Man has no power to arrest the dispensations of Providence. We are visited by a great calamity which we must bear."

As yet, Ireland lay untouched, leaving those who understood what the blight would mean there holding their breaths. But any optimism raised by this eerie pause soon vanished. In mid-September the *Irish Nation* published a chilling account of what farmers all over the country had already seen or soon would. The blight was striking with apparent caprice, despoiling one corner of a field while sparing another, or destroying all. It announced itself through livid patches covering the whole plant—root, tubers, foliage—"until the haulm [stem] becomes a putrid mass and the potatoes get soft and smell offensively as if they had been frosted." This stench of decay and death, one witness later wrote, became the tell-tale sign of the disease. When the odor permeated the air, even if the stalks looked "deceitfully luxuriant," as they sometimes did, he knew harvesting was in vain. Another hallmark, which appeared most noticeably after the smell, was a fungus growing on the stems and tubers, much like, it was said, those that attacked fruit in storerooms.

By mid-October, a *Times* (London) correspondent was reporting that "the infection seems well nigh universal." Fields that seemed healthy one day were "discovered to be irretrievably ruined" the next, "the produce being unfit food even for beasts." This was no journalistic exaggeration; various witnesses described lush fields turning black and scorched-looking within a week or even one night. The *Times* correspondent said that there was no doubt that Ireland's staple had failed completely, "which threatens consequences more disastrous than any from which Ireland has been afflicted for the last 30 years."

This warning appeared with due propriety, because potato failure was no stranger to Ireland. The three previous decades had seen food shortages strike some part of the country one year in three. Recently, the tuber had failed in Munster and Connacht in 1821–22, and more generally in 1836, 1837, 1839, and 1841. Then, too, hunger was endemic because of the meal months. Shortages had occasionally caused deaths from starvation, though the accompanying diseases, such as typhus, were bigger killers. However, severe scarcity rarely lasted more than a year, allowing the country to absorb the blow without the horrific losses that had marked the worst famines of the eighteenth century.

For a while, it looked as if the attack of 1845 would follow the brief, sharp pattern. Though the blight destroyed an estimated 40 percent of the harvest, deaths were relatively few. Probably this was because enough potatoes escaped or people sacrificed their pigs, which normally ate a third of the crop. But then ensued a series of torments that fulfilled the *Times* correspondent's prediction many times over. The blight returned in 1846, and it killed 90 percent of the potatoes, a lethal blow. By late autumn and into 1847, the death toll jumped because of starvation and diseases, chiefly dysentery and other intestinal infections; typhus and its lookalike, relapsing fever; and respiratory infections. From 1847, too, emigration increased. As a song recalling that time went: "The first downfall that Ireland got, the lumpers they were black / When I hired with Captain Murphy to work my passage to New York."

To those who stayed, Nature showed no mercy. Heavy snow fell in November 1846, leaving people who had pawned their clothes shivering before turf fires. That winter was among the harshest in memory, as it was for much of Europe. The blight receded in 1847 and potato yields increased, but the overall harvest was low because little acreage had been planted. Moreover, the respite only deceived a suffering people. The next year, 1848, the potatoes died as they had in 1846. Ireland was prostrate, but still more agony lay ahead. Cholera invaded in December and stayed until May 1849, killing thirty thousand. Its arrival was unrelated to the famine, but its destruction sharpened the miseries of those already starving.

These disasters have rightly earned the name *Great Famine*, but the description is incomplete. The first definition of "famine" in *Webster's Third New International Dictionary* is "a severe food shortage: a period of extreme scarcity of food." The second definition is "starvation." Ireland did starve, but the potato was much more than its principal food; more, even, than the sole food of perhaps 40 percent of its population. The landlord William Bence Jones thought the famine years were a time of social upheaval, when old ways were swept away, and no one knew how to cope. Naturally so, because before 1845, potatoes had been capital, wages, subsistence, and the means by which tenants diverted other resources to pay the rent. Potatoes had also been a social currency that resolved issues of land tenure and marriage settlements. Altogether, the tuber had granted a sense of security, however fragile, that life would continue.

That security was now gone, and its absence was devastating. The relief committee of the Society of Friends, the Quakers, noted that the potato's demise struck like a wave, passing the impact from one class to another. It fell with unequal force, buffeted some sooner than others, and left some untouched, but it went deep into Irish society. The first and hardest hit were conacre tenants, who had neither food nor any way to pay their rent. Next, the small holders who raised cattle or grain for cash had a cruel choice: eat the grain (assuming they could process it) and risk eviction, or sell it and starve. Servants and laborers lost their jobs because the gentry fired them to reduce expenses. Manufacturers also discharged their workers. Employment generally vanished except through government-sponsored public works, which paid pitifully little and were overwhelmed with applicants. Food prices quickly outstripped these wages, injuring not only those struggling to eat but shopkeepers, wholesalers, and merchants. Crafts and businesses suffered, as consumption dropped steeply.

The face of the countryside told the story. William Bennett, who traveled there during spring 1847, commented on the hundreds of emigrants jamming the roads to Dublin. Most journeyed on foot, carrying their belongings on their backs, though some had packed a cart with all they owned and were trying to look cheerful, "an affecting sight." In Kerry he noted the troubling absence of livestock, "almost as clean swept from the face of the county as the potato itself." The Irish landscape was nearly devoid of pigs, and even "the few dogs were poor and piteous, and had ceased to bark." A friend of Bennett's wrote from county Mayo that the land lay waste, unused for want of seeds. No trade went on in Ireland, as the English historian and critic Thomas Carlyle remarked mournfully in 1849. Whenever he saw a cart, he became hopeful, but a closer look always disappointed him. They were carrying only sacks of relief rations, "poorhouse trade."

Also striking was the number of abandoned, half-demolished houses. Since the government did its best to discourage famine relief outside workhouses, the destitute often had to seek help within them. Once they left their homes, their landlords to whom they owed back rent frequently took advantage of their absence to dismantle the houses and repossess the land. "I know not how a country looks, after the passage of an enemy through it," wrote Sidney Godolphin Osborne from the west in 1850, but he thought he was seeing an example. "Roofless gables meet your eye on every side," he added. On one estate where 482 families had lived in 1847, there were now only 2. Most land went untilled, Osborne said, and that which was planted was growing as many weeds as crops. Also from the west in 1850, Sir William Wilde reported that "we passed over miles of country without meeting the face of a human being," and rarely saw animals either. But he did happen "hot upon the smoking ruins of a recently unroofed village, with the late miserable inmates huddled together and burrowing for shelter among the crushed rafters of their cabins."

Not all of Ireland suffered this way. The Poor Inquiry had shown how prosperity could lie within a few miles of dire scarcity, and even the desert of the Great Famine had its oases. Bennett traveled a stretch in county Sligo where the cottages were decent and had more livestock than usual around them. He even noticed a drove of pigs along a road, a "novel and refreshing sight." The improvement may have been more noticeable because he was leaving the poorest parts of Connacht, where the famine hit especially hard. This in no way lessens Ireland's catastrophe, which affected every county, but not everyone fell victim or endured terrible hardships. One historian has estimated that perhaps 60 percent of the population escaped unscathed.

However, that leaves a large minority who didn't escape, and it is they especially whom history must remember. Even after one hundred and fifty years, this task is difficult and excruciating. Words seem paltry next to the agonies they are supposed to convey, yet the nightmare lives between the lines if not within them. Bennett expressed this when he wrote, "And now language utterly fails me. . . . My hand trembles while I write. The scenes of human misery and degradation we witnessed still haunt my imagination, with the vividness and power of some horrid and tyrannous delusion, rather than the features of a sober reality."

Selected examples suggest what that reality was like. In December 1846 a county Cork justice of the peace wrote to the Duke of Wellington—who was Irish-born—recounting a visit to a coastal hamlet.

> In the first [hovel] six famished and ghastly skeletons, to all appearance dead, were huddled in a corner on some filthy straw, their sole covering what seemed a ragged horse-cloth, and their wretched legs hanging about, naked above the knees. I approached in horror, and found by a low moaning they were alive, *they were in fever*—four children, a woman, and what had once been a man. It is impossible to go through the details, suffice it to say, that in a few minutes I was surrounded by at least 200 of such phantoms, such frightful spectres as no words can describe.

That same month, the Friends' famine relief workers described starvation among applicants to the workhouse at Carrick-on-Shannon, county Leitrim. "Some of these children were worn to skeletons, their features sharpened with hunger," the report said, "and their limbs wasted almost to the bone." One family consisted of a pregnant woman and two children; the husband had left to seek work. She said they had lived a week on two quarts of corn meal (a relief ration) and two head of cabbage. The observer believed that some of the people who weren't admitted to the workhouse wouldn't survive the four-mile walk home. The children's faces in particular looked "wan and haggard with hunger, and seeming like old men and women."

The Glenties, county Donegal, workhouse was so ill-equipped that on the day before the Friends inspected it, the inmates had had only one meal, of oatmeal and water. At the time of the visit, the workhouse had less than a day's supply of food. Some inmates were leaving, preferring to die in their own hovels. The only bedding was straw. Rugs were the only blankets, and as many as six people, some dying, crowded under each one. Such were conditions in December 1846. By the following March, people were so eager to get into that workhouse that they crowded around outside, waiting for those inside to die. In Ballina, county Mayo, many people went just to be sure of having a coffin. But at the Armagh facility, so many died that separate graves were no longer practical. Corpses were buried en masse, with Protestant and Catholic clergymen performing simultaneous rites.

Wherever sickness and death went, desperation rode close behind. Carlyle noted "ragged people in small force working languidly at their scantlings or peats, no other work at all; look hungry in their rags; hopeless, air as of creatures sunk beyond hope. . . ." Others hung silently about the door where a well-to-do man lived, waiting for "a word with his Honour," hoping for a job, a handout, anything. They had, Carlyle said, a tacit bargain with the house servant that neither would take notice of the other. "Sad enough to look upon," Carlyle remarked, for the answer, when it finally came, was sure to be no.

Desperate, too, were the people jamming Ireland's main roads. Elizabeth Smith saw them and told her diary, ". . . God help the people; the roads are beset with tattered skeletons that give one a shudder to look at, for how can we feed or clothe so many." Ireland's rootless included would-be emigrants, the dispossessed seeking a place to settle undisturbed, those fleeing plagues, those hoping the workhouse in the next town would take them, others just looking for a place to die. Shopkeepers were sometimes afraid to open their doors in the morning, for fear they would find corpses lying against them.

Before the famine Ireland probably counted 8.2 million people. How many died from starvation rather than disease isn't known and probably never will be. Most historians agree that the total death toll was 1 million, not including those in transit among the 1.3 million emigrants who left Ireland in those years. This was a terrible shock that numbers can't begin to measure, but one statistic suggests something of what it meant. Between these losses and the nearly five million emigrants who left over the next sixty years, Ireland's population by 1911 fell to 4.4 million, slightly more than half of what it had been in 1845.

The famine swept away cherished values as well as lives. A Friends' relief organizer, Jonathan Pim, remarked that "the bonds of natural affection were loosened," as parents neglected children, children turned out aged parents, and husbands deserted wives and families. He likened Ireland to a besieged city, rife with "tales of utter selfishness," except that it was peacetime in "the most powerful kingdom in the world." He associated most of the stories, such as those involving families fighting over food, with the west, where resources were leaner.

Mistrust also surfaced among neighbors. Traditionally, people had stored their potatoes in the open, without fear of theft. Now, Pim said, they had to "watch them constantly, or they would have been pulled up, even before they were ripe." By night, people stole potatoes and turnips, using their hands because spades made too much noise, and leaving the stalks intact to conceal the loss. Thieves speared potatoes left in barns with long poles. As countermeasures, the wary buried their food or sat up at night to guard it, sometimes lighting bonfires. To protect their cache, people might dig mantraps and cover them with bracken. Punishment for thieves varied from tying up to beatings to the occasional death, though first offenders received lenience.

Not only thieves aroused fear, but the sick did too. One of typhus's nicknames was "road fever," because so many people wandering the roads had it. Sometimes the healthy barred their doors to them, even to neighbors, but however inhumane the act, it had medical validity. The louse that carries typhus leaves a dead victim when the body cools, because it must soon find another host or die. Shunning typhus victims was more suspicion than science, because no one knew how the disease spread, but it did provide a crude check. To their credit, the charitable managed to find middle ground between self-sacrifice and avoidance. In at least one parish in county Donegal, those ministering to the sick put them in isolated huts and fed them using long-handled shovels.

All this happened in a country where hospitality had long been famous. Custom had always said that no matter how poor the home, the door remained open during meals to welcome hungry passersby. Leftovers were kept warm in the embers for the same purpose. A cottager who turned away a beggar would be thought "a bold, if not a bad man," and invite a curse. This open-handedness largely disappeared during the famine. Instead, people closed their doors to passersby, though occasionally that came from shame at what they were eating. But community feeling stayed alive in places, notably in less hard-hit eastern counties and in isolated parts of counties Mayo, Donegal, Clare, and Galway. A saying goes, "They did not eat aright unless the neighbors were thankful." Legends survive about poor folk down to almost nothing who treated visitors hospitably, and who then found after their guests departed that their larders were miraculously full.

Oral tradition also says that people fought over bodies of foxes, made soup from dogs, ate rats and diseased animals, or fish or cattle entrails. Bennett heard that on Aran Island, county Donegal, seaweed and limpets were the only food. Elsewhere, people ate dandelion roots, ferns, nuts, berries, leaves, and certain kinds of tree bark. Where people could get turnips, cabbages, peas, or beans, they ate them, but the famine was often most severe precisely where those foods hadn't been cultivated. Erris, county Mayo, was one such place. Even during the famine, people there wouldn't plant turnips for fear, unfortunately justified, that their landlords would seize the crop. For those clever enough to catch crows and seabirds, they supplied meat, as did dried snails, frogs, and hedgehogs. A county Wicklow story says that people fished the rivers clean of eels and trout.

As for marine fishing, that was a widely discussed subject, because for an island people, the Irish did little of it. Edward Wakefield thought that potato subsistence killed off any drive to go to sea, which would have required tiring labor, but he was wrong. Climate, geography, and lack of investment made fishing a dangerous and unprofitable profession. Rough seas restricted fishing, especially because the most common craft was the *curragh*, or coracle. Too small to hold a crew of more than three or four and built of wickerwork with a hide or tarred-linen covering, the *curragh* was meant for calmer coastal waters. Moreover, equipment and infrastructure were lacking, from proper tackle to curing stations to deep-water harbor facilities. Few ready markets existed, and, unlike England, Ireland had no railroads to transport the fish quickly to consumers far away. In Galway the unused portion of the catch was left to rot.

No wonder the Friends' relief committee noted that for want of proper vessels, "with food almost in sight, the people starve." Drawing a lesson from this cruel irony, the committee called it "one among many instances of the wasted industrial resources of this country, which . . . strike the eye of the stranger at every step." Most fishermen were also farmers, because few could have relied only on the sea. When the blight destroyed their crops, fishing tackle wound up in pawnshops.

A criminal waste of resources was the energy Protestant and Catholic spent hating one another. Famine-wracked Ireland had enough pain, but as tensions rose, so did bigotry. Some local relief committees excluded Catholics from their ranks, breaking the law. A few Protestant missionaries in central and western districts tried to win converts and aroused ill feeling. Efforts to proselytize under the guise of charity, though rare, included serving meat soup on Fridays. Missionaries of even meaner principle required Catholics to deny their faith or insult statues of the Virgin before receiving aid. Priests delivered sermons against "soupers," Catholics who partook, especially if they converted. Protestants who gave help were sometimes attacked, even when they offered aid without strings. The issue of who accepted what and at what price entered everyday language in words like *jumpers*, *turners*, and *soupers*, applied to those who accepted conversion or preached it. Even in the late 1950s, these terms were current, though their implication varied. In some districts, they were jokes; in others, insults.

Of course, religious feeling also appeared in more spiritual forms. Interpreting life's tragedies as divine will was a powerful concept in the mid–nineteenth century, and the famine readily evoked it. When Queen Victoria proclaimed March 24, 1847, a day of prayer, the words she ordered spoken in all houses of worship were deeply penitent. The people were to ask God "for the removal of those heavenly judgements which our manifold sins and provocations have most justly deserved," and which brought about "extreme famine and sickness." It was in that atmosphere that Charles Trevelyan, director of Britain's relief program, could invoke Providence and his policies in the same breath without getting a rock thrown through his window. Trevelyan was a stiff-necked prig even by Victorian standards, but others of suppler character also bowed their heads. How striking that almost the first words from the scientist John Lindley's pen regarding the potato blight referred to the "dispensations of Providence" and a calamity to be borne. And this was before a single soul had perished. The land agent W. Steuart Trench, who prided himself on scientific farming, wrote of "the special hand of God" that struck down his potato field. Even Alexis Soyer, bon vivant and chef, downplayed his charitable activities by saying they couldn't outreach Almighty will.

None of these people faced starvation, of course, so the feelings of those who did were likely to be keener. Peasant superstitions aside, it would be a rare person from any time or place who could take that much suffering and not wonder whether it were merited. So it was that people looked back at former days, when potatoes were so plentiful that they were thrown away, wasteful acts that had surely earned divine wrath. Testimony before the Poor Inquiry had suggested that so many Irish bore their lot stoically because they trusted that God would send them better days. To despair was therefore a mortal sin. This may help explain the emigration pattern during the famine, in which most people appeared to have waited awhile for the better days. Though almost 120,000 left in 1846, more than twice the number that had gone in 1844, 1847 saw 220,000 leave, or about 2.6 percent of the prefamine population. In that year Bennett remarked that emigrants were rarely the destitute, unless their landlords had paid their passage. Rather, they were those who "have still a little left" and were "able and calculated to do well with a fair chance and encouragement." Such people were those who dared despair of Ireland and would wait only so long.

In retrospect, the Great Famine seems inevitable. Ireland was dreadfully poor; population pressure strained subsistence to the limit; laws sapped the will and means to improve; and too many people depended on a crop known to fail. Given all that, it may appear remarkable that the crash didn't come sooner because, as many nineteenth-century observers had said, Ireland had long been heading for disaster. The only question was when.

But *inevitable* is a dangerous word. It puts a hammer in your hand and suggests that somewhere, there's got to be a nail. Those who warned about the potato's overwhelming influence were right, but the potato was their nail, and they were much safer hammering at a vegetable than at the social problems intertwined with its predominance. The Poor Inquiry followed this logic by asking whether grains could replace the potato, but the reply was what no one wanted to hear: not unless significant changes occurred. A decade later, the Devon Commission edged closer toward the truth, discussing the land tenure that made potato subsistence rampant and the peasant economy fragile and rigid. Under such conditions, the peasantry was vulnerable whenever the potato failed. The only way to remove the threat was to modify the laws, and that, Parliament would not do. So in that sense, Ireland was doomed.

But only in that famine was inevitable, not that the Great Famine was destined, or that a million people would die during four nightmarish years of it. Contemporary observers expected to hear of famine in Ireland—or "distress," as they often called it—but none could have foreseen such terrors. When Wakefield wrote in 1809 that if the potato failed, the result would be as deadly as a scarcity of rice "on the banks of the Ganges," he wasn't being eerily prophetic. He was talking about county Wexford, not all Ireland. Disasters on a medieval scale simply didn't happen in nineteenth-century Western Europe.

Not even Malthus, a great pessimist, predicted such a calamity. "It is difficult indeed to conceive a more tremendous shock to society," he wrote in 1808, "than the event of its [Ireland's population] coming at once to the limits of the means of subsistence. . . . But happily for mankind, this never is, nor ever can be the case." Much has been made of his stated wish that Ireland's excess population be "swept away," but that cruel thought was an opinion, not a prediction. Malthus foresaw Ireland's population ceasing to grow—not dying off at a stroke—when privation raised mortality and discouraged marriage. The Great Famine raised mortality, but whether even those terrible times deterred marriage is a matter of debate among demographers.

Finally, to suggest that the Great Famine was inescapable overlooks its extraordinary composition. It was many afflictions strung together in an unheard-of sequence, including a blight whose killing power and recurring ferocity were beyond anything known. The economic historian Peter Solar has compared crop losses during the Great Famine with Western European harvest patterns and concluded that the deficits of 1845 and 1848 were as bad as any in the century but not unique. The short interval between them, however, was unusual and statistically very improbable. Moreover, the losses of 1846 were beyond imagining, in themselves and because of the setbacks sandwiched around them. Factor in cereal prices rising in 1846 and the economic slump of 1847, and it's clear how the famine struck with unforeseeable force.

This isn't merely a laboratory model. The blight's repeated destruction was hardly credible at the time, despite experience that should have driven home the message. Pim commented in 1848 that, looking back, it seemed astonishing how prior attacks hadn't prepared people for the blight's virulence. He ascribed this to what had happened the previous year; when the blight came, everyone expected the worst, and yet the damage turned out to be relatively mild. Therefore, in 1848, many were hoping that reports of devastation were exaggerated, despite what they knew to be true. Even those who realized the crop was lost "could not believe the consequences would be that serious." It was as if nobody were willing to put two and two together—and indeed, Pim said that no one could "anticipate the awful reality." It should be stressed that Pim was someone who saw the famine, not an official who scribbled at a desk in London.

The question of inevitability matters because it colors what people thought and did and affects how later generations have interpreted it. Since the relief effort was (and is) notorious for penny-pinching, calling the famine inevitable implies that the government's motives were murderous and wholly conscious, a verdict with which this historian disagrees. Not to excuse or explain away negligence; but to assess it and assign blame, especially when this narrative presents the famine in the sparest outline, would also be negligent. Several books (recommended in the Notes) have recounted and analyzed the relief effort in detail. From them, the reader who wishes to may make judgments.

Rather, what this book aims to show is what the Victorians thought about the poor, why they thought it (particularly where the potato was concerned), and how their creed may have made the famine policy acceptable to them, even desirable. Moreover, this creed sounds uncomfortably familiar: that, with rare exceptions, the poor are immoral and don't deserve help, and that open-handed charity invites idleness and corruption. What stands out about the Great Famine era is that the potato reinforced such perceptions and was sometimes seized on to justify public or personal actions. But otherwise, what the Victorians said can be heard today in the United States, both in and out of government.

Britain's failure to aid Ireland more effectively resulted largely from the Poor Law of 1838, relief policy's Holy Writ. This law had created a work-house system along English lines, an advance for Ireland, but with crucial deviations. The Irish law permitted only "indoor relief," that given within the workhouse, and only to entire families. The law granted no right to re-lief, no matter how long a person had lived in the workhouse district, or union. This meant that if the workhouse were full, the union's administra-tors weren't obliged to provide an alternative. Since Ireland had one union for every sixty-three thousand people, three times the constituency of En-glish districts, indoor relief couldn't possibly assist more than a tiny minor-ity. In Erris, for instance, the nearest workhouse was forty miles away. As Elizabeth Smith remarked, the workhouses "won't contain a fourth part of the starving population"—and that was in 1841.

Moreover, all unions depended solely on local taxes, to enforce fiscal re-sponsibility and the rules on eligibility. Without that, it was thought, Ire-land would go broke. Local taxation was meant to induce landlords to em-ploy laborers and keep them off relief. This policy was unfair and arguably illegal, because under the 1801 Act of Union, Ireland was nominally an equal partner within the kingdom. Further, the Friends pointed out that the taxes eroded the landlords' capital and prevented them from hiring as many workers. As a result, landlords were paying wages and taxes, yet still had many tenants on relief. And despite grumblings that the poor were getting their livings handed to them, workhouses were grim places. The families-only rule and the Spartan atmosphere, with meals eaten in silence, were de-terrents. As Trevelyan put it, "Relief should be made so unattractive as to fur-nish no motive to ask for it, except in the absence of every other means of subsistence." Few contemporaries would have disagreed.

Certainly, sticking to laissez-faire principles was fiscally convenient. But to those footing the bill, the Great Famine was one of a tiresome string of nineteenth-century Irish crises. In 1799–1801, for example, the government bought rice, corn, and rye meal, distributed through soup kitchens or aid committees. When crops failed in 1817, the government imported oats, which it sold for seed at a subsidized price. Private relief funds received money, as did public-works projects. Afterward, in 1819, Under Secretary for Ireland William Gregory warned that the government would no longer "be the first resort when any pressure occurs." Within three years, however, famine struck again, and when the landlords couldn't or wouldn't resolve the problem, Parliament voted £400,000 for public works. Private groups did much more than that, but charity was supposed to be a private matter. Britain was getting annoyed with having to pay, especially for people who grew the lazy root and were always plotting rebellion or killing their landlords or both.

The debate over extending the Poor Law to Ireland brought the annoyance out clearly. In 1830 one observer who knew Munster firsthand wrote that a Poor Law would end the "estimable virtue" of charity, and that too much gratuitous relief would undermine the people and their prosperity. But his objection wasn't only moral; he also astutely predicted that a Poor Law would tax overburdened landowners and spur them to clear their estates. More extreme and perhaps more representative was the view of Dr. J. P. Kay-Shuttleworth, a prominent Manchester physician. Writing in 1832, he called a Poor Law "a gross and indiscriminate bounty" that bred apathy and neglect. It aroused no gratitude and killed charity among the rich, he said—and he was talking about England, where his progressive sympathies lay. As for the Irish, whom he despised, he cautioned that to supply their wants would encourage "idleness, improvidence, and dissipation." Extending the Poor Law would create a "vast infirmary" whose "endowment would swallow up the entire rental of the country." In other words, a welfare state built for potato eaters, who, Kay-Shuttleworth argued, were the people who destroyed society.

But a welfare state wasn't what George Nicholls, the expert who drafted the Poor Law of 1838, had in mind. He granted that the English system had abuses, but he thought administrators (of whom he was one) were getting rid of them. If this were copied in Ireland, with the landlords doing their part, all would be well. Extending the law was a way to help Ireland through a "transition period," when subsistence farming would yield to wage labor on the English model (implying that grain would replace potatoes). Nicholls believed that the Poor Law would relieve the urge for self-sufficiency that led to landholding at any price, permitting the peasantry to enter the labor market without fear of starving. Oddly, he thought that conacre, land hunger at its extreme, would help bring this about. Also, his system depended on landlords providing employment while paying taxes, but Irish landlords never did what theorists supposed they would or should do.

However, Nicholls wasn't reaching for paradise. He saw the Poor Law suppressing begging and land hunger, not sustaining the poor. He stated that famine was a contingency no law could deal with, and he thought it "impossible to contemplate" famine continuing to wrack the country. Nevertheless, he favored indoor relief in all circumstances, famine included. In effect, he was opening the coffers but keeping one hand on the lid—and the money inside was Irish.*

Right or wrong, prudent or selfish, this was how people thought. In mid-October 1845, when reports began to suggest that Britain would have to send help, the *Times* angrily objected. Not only was Ireland "always on the eve of a general war or a private rebellion," it was ungrateful, and its capacity to absorb aid immense. Hundreds of thousands of pounds in British charity went unremembered or got swallowed up without effect or lined greedy pockets. "The best man," the *Times* warned, "becomes at last weary of

---

* When the Great Famine came, however, Nicholls was among those who objected to the Poor Law unions having to pay for all relief.

helping those who will not help themselves, as also of undertaking for others duties of which they are still too glad to be relieved." The "others" meant Irish landlords, who would face a fierce "public gaze" should Parliament be asked to contribute while they themselves had done little. That scrutiny, the newspaper promised, would continue until their tenants became "rather less of a public nuisance and a national scandal." Strong words, but they tallied with what writers had said about the country before 1845. The outside world heard much about armies of beggars whom no help would ever restore to a state of self-support and who behaved in repellent ways. Thackeray, who thought Ireland's general miseries were so painful to see that a traveler for pleasure would "perpetually [be] made ashamed of being happy," had no compassion for the beggars. They offered "lying prayers and loathsome compliments, that make the stomach turn," he said. Worse, they didn't bother to hide that they were lies, "for, refuse them, and the wretches turn off with a laugh and joke, a miserable grinning cynicism that creates distrust and indifference. . . ." Two years later, the American missionary Asenath Nicholson thought Queen Victoria should see how her poor Irish subjects lived and so be moved to help them. Yet Nicholson too despised the beggars, whom she likened to "Pharaoh's frogs" and judged them "almost as much to be dreaded as his whole ten plagues." These weren't the sort of people whose upkeep Britain wished to pay for.

Consequently, when Trevelyan discussed his relief program in an unsigned article in the *Edinburgh Review* in 1848, he didn't justify why the government had done so little. Rather, he explained why it had done so much, to show taxpayers that their money hadn't been wasted on frivolous public works. Trevelyan admitted that not all relief recipients were deserving, and that the system was too large to permit an adequate means test. But the government wasn't to blame. It hadn't created the famine; the Irish had been foolish enough to risk their lives on the potato.

Trevelyan argued that wherever the tuber had become a "principle article of national food," it could destroy society. It impoverished populations, provided sustenance that was neither wholesome nor nutritious, and led to cutthroat land hunger, an "agrarian code which is at perpetual war with the laws of God and man." Further, since growing it required almost no effort, Irish peasants knew nothing of honest toil; and because they were self-employed on tiny plots of land, they didn't need wages. Such self-sufficient isolation lacked the mutual dependence and goodwill that knit civilized societies together.

The stolid moderate Trevelyan probably never realized he had much in common with the flaming radical Cobbett, but they saw the potato the same way: It made people lazy. Trevelyan's obsession with work was so well known that Anthony Trollope later satirized him for it in a novel. A man of particular religious conviction, Trevelyan believed that labor was meant "to obviate the evils of leisure." Where society's upper ranks had a safeguard, however imperfect, of "intellectual tastes and legitimate objects of ambition," the Irish had the tuber. Without decent food they couldn't engage in useful labor. Therefore, they would remain uncivilized unless they gave up the potato for bread and meat.

To a man of evangelical bent, the next step was obvious. An "all-wise and all-merciful Providence" had sent the blight as an opportunity to revamp Ireland, "as if this part of the case were beyond the unassisted power of man." Today, this sounds cold-blooded, but by Victorian standards, it wasn't. Contemporaries as different in outlook as the economist J. R. McCulloch, whose views tended to the reptilian, and Osborne, who wrote stirringly of Ireland's sufferings, largely agreed. Both believed the blight could accomplish good if it rid Ireland of the potato. Though neither expressed Trevelyan's religious zeal, they thought that the potato was evil—a moral plague, in Trevelyan's terms—and that a physical plague crushing it might do society a favor.

Moreover, Trevelyan depicted the tuber as the kind of moral plague that incited the lower orders to revolt. To be sure, it was a passive revolution, through which they could remove themselves from the economy and subsist in idleness. Passive or not, however, it was threatening, much as talk of "dropping out" upset mainstream American opinion during the 1960s. And there was always the chance, in both instances, that idle hands would make trouble. The year 1848 saw revolutions in France, Germany, and the Hapsburg empire, while the Chartists caused uneasiness in England. But ideas about the corrupting potato originated neither with Trevelyan nor from that time. Rather, his theory had emerged during the previous eighty or so years, born of prevailing morality, scientific thought, and anxieties about social change.

When most observers looked at Ireland, they saw rampant poverty, violence, and corruption, which they associated with the laziness almost universally assumed to be an Irish trait. Though it was often said that the Irish would work hard if oppressive laws were removed and if they could see their labor justly rewarded, it was also said that diligent labor simply wasn't in their nature. Some commentators thought laziness was inherent, part of the "national character" or the reason Ireland was poor. Quite a few, including Trevelyan, pointed out that the Irish peasant worked hard when abroad— though not all who thought so modified their views on the alleged national character. Others said the Irish preferred diversions such as fairs or comforts like "punch and a pipe" to exertion, a habit that deepened their misery. Even those who saw peasant existence with a clearer eye thought harder work would benefit the Irish. To be sure, these were foreigners, but even a few Irish contemporaries agreed, to a point. Jonathan Pim, for one, thought his countrymen lacked the "patient and persevering industry" of the English, who were more civilized. Significantly, however, he ascribed the happier circumstance to equal protection under the law.

But most observers thought that if the Irish had reasons to be indolent, they accepted their lot too easily. A familiar image from visitors is that of the peasant lounging in the doorway of his hovel while weeds overrun his potato patch. To the English, such behavior was outrageous and threatening, especially from fellow subjects. Lack of striving was unnatural and uncivilized. It meant that the Irish had no ambition, no material wants, no urge to live in any but the crudest way. As Philip Luckombe remarked in 1780, "If an Irishman feels no inconvenience from walking barefoot, he will hardly be induced to work for the price of brogues." Luckombe disapproved and called it sloth, but he said he understood it. No human being really wanted to work.

The prevailing view was much more critical. Wakefield attacked the Irish for working no more than necessary to obtain life's minimum requirements. "Such people cannot be said to live but to exist," he wrote, adding that once they supplied their "animal wants," they didn't care to do more. What encouraged this brutish way of life was potato subsistence, which tended to "depress and degrade" the "moral faculties" so that people didn't aspire to anything higher. That, in turn, led to "idleness, the worst evil that can afflict human nature."

This evil made certain thinkers worry about the risk the potato posed to England. In 1832 the Manchester physician Kay-Shuttleworth wrote a book depicting the unhealthy conditions in which many of his city's textile workers lived, and he faulted the tuber, in part. The argument followed a grim, roundabout logic. Cholera had recently struck, and Kay-Shuttleworth, like his friend Edwin Chadwick, supposed that such plagues resulted from poor sanitation. This approached the truth, but the reigning idea was that decaying organic matter released a "miasma" that was somehow toxic. Therefore, whatever allowed decaying matter to collect in homes and on streets was endangering Manchester.

But Kay-Shuttleworth was concerned with more than garbage-strewn streets and the lack of privies. Dependence on the potato was creating filth in Manchester, particularly among the Irish immigrants. In their own country, he said, they dwelled in "ignorance and pauperism," having settled for the minimum means of existence. Now, they were teaching that "pernicious lesson" to the English working classes. The English were ceasing to take pride in furnishing their homes or "multiplying the decent comforts which minister to happiness," preferring to "wallow in the unrestrained licence of animal appetite."

Since improvidence and dissipation were frequent partners and almost always led to uncleanliness, which in turn begat disease, Kay-Shuttleworth recommended teaching the poor how to live better. They should learn, in daily instruction, about the consequences of "idleness, improvidence, and moral deviations." This phrasing, a thinly veiled reference to sex, appeared beside warnings about imprudent marriage and population growth. The indictment was plain. The potato, a coarse food that subverted desires for comfort or cleanliness, stood accused of cheapening lives. Not only did it promote the ruinous cycle of poverty and population, it was partly responsible for the moral illness that helped bring about tuberculosis, typhus, and cholera.

This bizarre claim had a basis in fact. It had long been noticed that the poor suffered disproportionately from most endemic or epidemic diseases. Death rates were appalling. Demographers have estimated that life expectancy at birth in 1830s England averaged 40.5 years (and was even lower in France and Ireland). Moreover, these were national averages, whereas cities like Manchester were among England's deadliest places to live. Ten years after Kay-Shuttleworth wrote, Chadwick calculated Manchester's life expectancy at birth at a chilling 17 years. Science as most people interpreted it couldn't pinpoint why this happened, except to notice the obvious. Cities were dirtier and more crowded than the countryside. They were also less moral. Further, if it was logical to blame the poor for their poverty, it followed that they had deserved their diseases. Whatever they did that better-off, healthier people didn't do could explain where the poor went wrong. Since healthier people refused to live amid garbage (or subsist on the potato), the solution seemed evident. Drain the streets and homes, teach people to keep them clean, and both morality and mortality would improve at a stroke.

Such a view paralleled how medicine explained infection as the result of disease, not its cause. Humans could spread contagion, but it wasn't that microbes invaded a healthy host and multiplied if conditions allowed. Rather, a healthy organism, plant or animal, had to lose vigor before infection occurred. Mold or mildew, for instance, resulted from just such a weakening. Therefore, a quarter-century before Darwin, piety and natural science could still travel the same muddy road to human betterment. Attributing disease to a loss of vigor is a personal, moral approach, whereas germ theory is random and objective. A person who weakened through normal aging was, in a sense, not responsible for dying, because all creatures went that way. However, those who died before their time had apparently hastened the process. Such thinking left open the possibility of blaming the patient for being sick. Those who did not get ill could choose to say that behavior had brought on the deceased's weakness—and in certain cases, such as that of alcoholism, they might be right. However, that belief also gave comfort, because those who avoided dissipation were doing as much as they could to protect themselves from diseases known to strike the corrupt.

It may be argued that Kay-Shuttleworth's tract is an anomaly, the product of a mind that had just stared down cholera. His remarks about the Irish infecting England suggest more than mere bigotry, perhaps the xenophobia that commonly surfaces during plagues. (And Manchester had taught working-class England about the potato long before the Irish crowded the city's cellars.) Moreover, it's noteworthy that when Chadwick wrote his report, he disagreed with his friend. He said that "banishing the potatoe or discouraging its use . . . will not banish disease"—and this statement came shortly after the discussion of Manchester's life-expectancy rate.

Nevertheless, more than xenophobia circulates during times of plague. Extreme ideas that have been lurking in the air suddenly find themselves talked about, as if they too were infectious. Of course, anxieties about the potato had a long tradition. Rumors linking disease to the tuber had appeared in Western Europe in the seventeenth century and had been current as recently as the 1780s. The basic difference between what Kay-Shuttleworth said and the superstitions that Gaspard Bauhin heard about in 1620 was that, in nineteenth-century England, eating the potato was no longer said to spread contagion. Rather, living on it, what would have been unthinkable in Bauhin's day, caused the decline. With Cobbett reminding the country that the tuber was a filthy root—and filth was the issue in Manchester—Kay-Shuttleworth didn't have to stretch very far. And since Cobbett was in Parliament the year that Kay-Shuttleworth wrote, the message was flourishing elsewhere than in the doctor's mind.

If the potato could help destroy human populations, its own feebleness was no surprise. When the blight came, science ascribed the potato's collapse to weaknesses that coincided with those attributed to the people who ate it and died of plagues. The potato, after all, was a "degenerate" plant. The reader will recall from chapter 7 that "all bulbous roots" supposedly decayed over time, and that the potato suffered from a "hereditary fault," a propensity to succumb to a "latent germ of disease." This was stern moral censure in a country where wealth, social standing, landowning, and political privilege derived largely from family background. Further, suggesting that the potato lost "vitality" over generations was equally serious. England was a growing, industrializing, power-seeking nation that valued hard work, vigor, and responsibility.

Even people who didn't condemn the potato outright had to explain why it had fallen so dramatically in 1845. John Lindley, for one, fastened on the weather. July 1845 had been hotter and drier than average, followed by weeks of unseasonably heavy rains, fog, and cool temperatures. Lindley concluded that the climate changed abruptly just when the potato plants were growing rapidly and greedily soaking up nutrients. But the moisture was so heavy the plants could neither absorb nor transpire it for want of sunshine. This hastened a kind of dropsy, Lindley said, which caused the potatoes to lose their "customary vigour" and become vulnerable to decay. The decay permitted attack from "myriad of creatures whose life could only be maintained by the decomposing bodies of their neighbours." Chief among these was the fungus that smelled so rank and hastened the putrefaction but had no other role in the blight. "I am perfectly satisfied," he wrote, "that fungi do not *cause* it; though God knows they follow it fast enough." Most of the scientific world agreed.

Lindley, of course, was wrong. A fungus was the culprit, an idea the Reverend Miles J. Berkeley advanced, rather hesitantly, in 1846. Still, Lindley's theory was far more solid than what passed for wisdom in newspapers, journals, and pamphlets, which blamed, among other things, static electricity, the use of animal manure, an epidemic resembling cholera, planting cut-up tubers, and insects. Alfred Smee, a noted London surgeon, claimed in 1846 that an aphid killed the plants by sucking their juice. He christened the beast *vastator*, for its destructive power, and said it had done what Napoleon could not, having invaded Britain "in spite of all our armies, fleets and forts." Lyman Reed of Waltham, Massachusetts, also said an aphid was the cause, and, with Yankee ingenuity, he patented a cure, lugged his microscope and aphids to Washington, and convinced seventeen members of the House Committee on Agriculture that he was right.

Had Berkeley argued more firmly and publicly, he might be remembered as a pioneer of germ theory, nudging Pasteur aside an inch or so. But Berkeley couldn't prove that a healthy potato plant could contract the fungal infection and die. (No one could until Anton de Bary did so in 1861.) The theory had earth-shaking implications. Disease wasn't linked with morality, but with time and chance, which happens to all. The blight owed nothing to degeneracy, but to random conditions. The Irish hadn't brought the plague on themselves. And Trevelyan's belief that Providence was helping humankind by killing the potato was exposed for the rubbish it was.

To one scientist, however, randomness was too disturbing an idea to accept. In 1864, three years after de Bary's proof, a retired Utica, New York, clergyman passed the last weeks of his life writing an article attacking the fungus theory. The Reverend Chauncey E. Goodrich had spent sixteen years trying to breed a blight-resistant potato from imported South American stock, supposing that the plant had suffered from "diminished vitality." Goodrich diminished his own by planting some fifteen thousand seedlings, while meticulously observing the interaction between weather patterns and blight outbreaks. The results, obtained strictly through trial and error, were spectacular. Several cultivars showed some blight resistance and were the West's first long-day potatoes besides.

But what Goodrich seems to have treasured above all was scientific truth, yet one that reflected his religious faith. To the end, he insisted that the blight killed because of climate and the continued use of unfermented manure and seed tubers. He based this on faulty observation, but he had a deeper reason to argue. If fungi could attack and destroy healthy plants, that would nullify divine intent. Providence, Goodrich said, had encouraged humankind to be faithful to the soil, in return for which it "usually yield[ed] its full and beautiful fruits." If that divine law didn't exist, "there would be an end of all security of food, and of all human enterprise."

He wasn't to know, but his sort of experimention was an act that may have greatly influenced human enterprise. When European breeders imported Central and South American stock to revive the degenerate potato, they may have gotten more than they bargained for. The blight fungus, *Phytophthora infestans*, possibly reached Europe in just that way, from infected imported tubers.

Equally ironic was the treatment for it. In 1883 the French botanist Alexandre Millardet stumbled on a formula for an effective fungicide containing copper sulfate and lime. These chemicals were so common that the British population had ingested them for years in adulterated food.

Given the common attitude about the potato and the dying population that depended on it, one might suppose that Trevelyan and his partners in laissez-faire were just as happy to let them die. However, the issue wasn't so simple. Nineteenth-century thinkers were unsure about whether they should, or even could, interfere in what appeared to be a natural process—or, if they did, how. In that light, Trevelyan wrote that leaving Irish authorities to handle the famine had several virtues. First, it allowed knowledgeable people on the scene to separate false claims of poverty from real ones. Second, he averred, this policy had taught the Irish, at last, to fend for themselves.

Such smug callousness was only possible if one assumed that the poor had no right to relief, and that anything the government gave was an act of generosity that merited loyalty and gratitude. However, Trevelyan also believed the Irish deserved help; the only question was the source. When he advised subordinates who advocated a more open-handed policy to read Edmund Burke, the message was two-sided: The government must stay out, but individuals must get in. "Without all doubt," Burke wrote, "charity to the poor is a direct and obligatory duty upon all Christians," who chose the time, manner, and amount to deliver.

From Dublin in October 1847, Trevelyan, characteristically, had written the *Times* to say that the time was now (annoying his superiors by going public). And he did so because of outcries that had greeted the queen's request that churches collect money for Ireland. She had made four charitable calls within the year, two for Ireland, whereas the royal appeal had traditionally been an annual event. Moreover, since custom usually dictated that each congregation contribute unanimously, poorer parishioners were up against it, especially after the previous winter's hardships, which had left many in debt. Accordingly, Trevelyan reminded everyone of "the unhappy people in the western districts of Ireland, who will again perish by the thousands" should no help come. Since the government had recently decided not to aid them, this was twisted logic, but typical of the time and the man. Nobody knew what to do, or how.*

---

* Later in India, Trevelyan devised rules that made local famine a national responsibility. It has been said that his failure to do so for Ireland resulted partly from the policies of the government in power, which, as a civil servant, he was sworn to obey. But it is also true that he was contentious and stubborn, and he did not argue when the policy changed and became more miserly.

To be sure, starving people don't care about bureaucratic niceties or what Edmund Burke said. Just as certainly, anyone who sees famine is much more likely to rush aid than someone who stays away, like Trevelyan. When William Bennett reported hearing that people walked a dozen miles for a quart or two of corn meal, his remark somehow goes deeper than when Trevelyan said they walked twenty. Still, the two men were starting from different sides of the same basic principle. Bennett decried governmental attempts to do "positive good"—as had Burke—saying that such efforts almost always exchanged "one form of oppression for another." The only ways to bring about "active and permanent good," he said, were through "individual exertion, regeneration and development."

Bennett based his observations on a six-week tour, so his eyewitness experience was limited. However, even people who saw more than he had mixed feelings about government relief and the virtues of self-reliance. Charitable organizations were careful not to let their gifts be abused or taken for granted, or to inhibit the poor's exertions. The Society of Friends committee, whose relief credentials were beyond reproach, approved of a means test and disliked the way public works gave aid "indiscriminantly." The less charitable put this more harshly. Smith wrote in 1846 that the Irish "have got it into their heads that being in distress they are to do nothing to get out of it, but are to sit comfortably down and open their mouths to be fed." Smith disliked the Irish, about whom she made many intolerant, bigoted remarks. But weeks after this outburst, she said the well-off must do their utmost to help and wondered whether the government had acted rightly. She accepted the idea of leaving the markets to themselves but said that "one shudders at stepping over mounds of graves" just to test the principle. Carlyle, who also saw both sides, wrote in 1849 of government largesse creating "extensive *hives* for which the *bees* have not yet been found."

Morover, it wasn't only the English who asked where private charity ended and government responsibility began. In Scotland, where the potato was a staple, the blight caused terrible crop damage. Excess mortality from cholera and typhus was higher than England's, but landlords and private groups generally saw to it that people didn't starve. Relief committees sent oatmeal and subscribed public works. One church raised £11,000 just by collecting at the door. This was private charity, the way things were supposed to work in Adam Smith's native land. Of course, the famine struck on a relatively small scale; the affected population numbered about 5 percent of Ireland's. But not all was tenderness. Scottish landlords too evicted tenants from crowded estates, essentially forcing them to emigrate.

Matters were more serious in the Netherlands. Dutch land-tenure practices resembled England's, with workers renting allotments at excessive rates to supplement low wages and to enable themselves to keep pigs. Consequently, the tuber had a daily place in the diet. Unlike what happened in Ireland, the blight struck hard in 1845, more mildly the next year. But in other ways, the pattern held. Dutch wheat and rye harvests for 1846 fell short, a severe winter followed, starvation came, and then typhus and cholera broke out. Having narrowly avoided bankruptcy in 1844, the government refused to spend money for relief. It played down the misery, whose ravages the upper classes and the clergy ascribed to divine judgment anyway. Not only did the state deny subsidies to municipalities that gave relief, it warned them against the kind of charity best left to private groups or individuals. The poor, the national government said, shouldn't get the idea that they had any right to relief. Fortunately, the municipalities didn't always listen, providing the only effective aid. When the famine ended, the death toll was sixty thousand out of a population of three million, one-sixth of Ireland's rate.

Famine lies outside the American experience. It makes headlines occasionally, but always from somewhere else, in places few Americans have visited or even heard of. It's unthinkable that one-eighth the American population could starve or die of disease, or that anything close to that could happen without a massive relief effort taking place. But that's abstract, at a distance. Poverty and hunger are personal, concrete, and everyone has feelings about them. Those feelings haven't changed much, as voices from 1840s Ireland attest. Consider how Nicholson depicted a group of Galway men holding spades, waiting for an order to work that would never come. She was told they arrived every week, many having walked fifteen or twenty miles without eating.

> Their dress and their desponding looks told too well the tale of their sufferings. . . . one near me, walking slowly, picking a few shreds carelessly in his fingers, his countenance such a finished picture of despair as said, "It is done; I can do no more." . . . as soon as I met his countenance, hunger, wife, children, and despair were so visible that I turned away, and could only say, "Good God! have mercy on poor Ireland."

That despair is something Americans can comprehend, whether from having felt it or seen it. Even from the outside, it appears overwhelming, as William Bence Jones remarked in 1865 about the prefamine years.

> It was a great mass of poverty that you seemed to make no impression on, do what you would to relieve it. It appeared just to close in upon you again on all sides as if nothing had been done. . . . It was the most hopeless, dispiriting work conceivable, and looking back on it, I do not know how one faced it, and can wonder at no one who gave it up in despair.

Jones's general tone was one that would be called paternal today, yet what he says here rings true.

Along the same lines but humbler, perhaps, was the Society of Friends. In February 1848 the society's relief committee spoke of what was going on then.

> The exertions made during the past year were evidently too great to last. The sensitive had become habituated to the constant sight of misery; the energetic were wearied by the sacrifices which the distribution of relief involved; the sanguine were discouraged by the hopelessness of the task. Some who had administered relief had themselves become fit objects for receiving it.

Probably few Americans have the front-line experience that this testimony suggests, yet who can doubt the truth behind it? Not only is it easy to believe that this is what relief can mean, the fear of being sucked into poverty's vortex remains powerful even for those who are in no immediate danger.

On another, more practical level, the Great Famine evokes familiar images from political and social discourse. After the Marshall Plan, the Great Society, and the billions spent annually on welfare, we've supposedly proven how much more imaginative and compassionate we are than the Victorians who made the workhouses so unpalatable. Several historians have noted that what Britain spent to relieve the Great Famine amounted to merely 20 percent of what it spent on the Crimean War a few years later. They report this as unheard-of, cold-blooded selfishness, as if governments hadn't been choosing guns over social welfare for centuries and as if they don't do so today. High-minded declarations of war on poverty take second place to undeclared wars against foreign nations. The Great Society is only one example.

Then, too, we still wrestle with many of the social-welfare devices and issues that emerged during the Great Famine: graft, bureaucratic fumbling, public works, means tests, taxpayers' rage, conflicts over what charity is. The ongoing debate over welfare reform asks whether national or local governments should administer relief and who should pay, and a current school of thought even denies the right to relief. Political winds blow back and forth between whether government should leave matters to the private sector. President Ronald Reagan, for one, championed private charity, an ironic position given his family history. His paternal great-great-grandfather, it is said, emigrated from county Tipperary to England during the famine.

Moreover, we're still debating whether poverty results from laziness or immorality—leading to having too many children—and, if so, whether the poor deserve help. We, too, often feel that beggars are cynically taking us for a ride, and that giving them money is throwing it away. We, too, have angry taxpayers who wonder why paying a sizable portion of their income isn't enough to keep homeless people from using their doorsteps as latrines and motels. This isn't to declare one side right, because that purports to close issues that we desperately need to leave open. Rather, here's a question: Has our thinking evolved that far beyond the Victorian mindset we instinctively criticize?

10 Potatoes and Population

To treat typhus, hallowed dirt from the threshold was heated and put on the back of the neck. It was sacred because "God save all here" had been repeated so often in crossing it.
IRISH CUSTOM

THE NINETEENTH-CENTURY THINKERS who called the potato the means to a runaway population boom—and the ruin of an ordered society—based their belief partly on science that we now know to be false. But however much they misread what they saw, for whatever moral or political purposes, they correctly noted two facts: The populations of England and Ireland were growing at phenomenal rates, and the potato's influence in both places was rising. The question, then, is whether more modern science, with the benefit of hindsight, can show that observers who linked these events were right to do so, if for the wrong reasons.

The circumstantial case against the potato (or for it, depending on one's viewpoint) is striking, especially for Ireland. It's generally accepted that Ireland numbered between 2.2 million and 3.0 million people in 1732, doubled to somewhere between 4.2 million and 4.8 million by 1791, then doubled *again* by 1841, to reach 8.2 million to 8.4 million. Consecutive doublings every half-century or so would be remarkable anytime, more when they happen during the potato's rise to dominance. As for Britain, the tuber's final triumph occurred between 1800 and 1850, a period when the English and Welsh populations increased, on average, 15 percent every decade and doubled overall.

Making sense of that, however, is like looking for a black cat in a pitch-dark room. Supposing that contemporaries were right, that the potato caused more frequent marriage, and that marriage inevitably pushed up the birthrate, isn't as foolproof as it sounds. The numerical relation between marriage rates and population growth is far more complex. A comparison between, say, Britain and France suggests that from 1838 (when England and Wales first kept marriage statistics) to 1851, Britain's marriage rate was either lower than France's or about the same, whereas the British birthrate was invariably greater. Or compare the Netherlands and Britain from 1840 to 1851. During most of those years, the Dutch marriage rate was lower but the birthrate most often higher. Which is particularly interesting, because the Dutch liked potatoes as much as anyone, yet the tuber didn't always lead to the altar.

It might be less trouble, though no more certain, to try a different direction and ask what effect a potato diet—or an improved diet including the potato—had in England and Ireland. If the tuber's presence wasn't just a coincidence, then one or both of two conditions must be true. Either the diet made fertility rise by improving the health of women of childbearing age, or it helped the general population to resist infectious disease, lowering the death rate. Plausible ideas, perhaps, but science has yet to prove them. Even if it had, applying the proof would be nigh impossible because the statistics are sketchy or lacking. Accordingly, this discussion is conjecture, based more on logic than numbers. It rests largely on a well-known theory by the British demographer Thomas McKeown.

McKeown said that the population of England and Wales had gone from 5.5 million in 1702 to 8.9 million in 1801 to 17.9 million in 1851, more than trebling over 150 years. He discounted marriage as the cause, believing that marriage rates had remained relatively constant, and that early marriage would have had less effect than many people suppose. Rather, he ascribed the population increase to improved food production, which had raised the standard of living and lowered the death rate. He admitted that he couldn't prove this mathematically, because the first regular census wasn't until 1801, and deaths weren't registered until 1838. Still, he said, given a population in which both birthrates and death rates are low, if growth occurs, it will most likely come from the birthrate side. However, when both rates are high—provably the case in nineteenth-century Britain and almost surely so in the eighteenth—the opposite is true; growth likely results from lower mortality. He explained this by saying that fertility has its natural limits. Unless people have been restricting how many children they have, perhaps through contraception or by waiting to marry, they're unlikely to have significantly more. Whereas, he argued, even a slight drop in mortality will cause an appreciable population surge, with infants and children the groups gaining most visibly.

Other demographers had gone this far, wondering whether improved medical care, specifically smallpox inoculation, had lowered Britain's death rate. McKeown said no. Protecting against smallpox, he argued, couldn't have accounted for so large a rise. Besides, the dangerous eighteenth-century practice of inoculation would have had to reduce mortality to a degree that safer, more modern immunization methods would never be expected to achieve. Next, McKeown listed Britain's deadliest infectious diseases, among them tuberculosis, typhus, typhoid, cholera, scarlet fever, measles, diphtheria, and dysentery. He noted that, with rare exceptions, nineteenth-century science couldn't treat or prevent any, and in some instances, couldn't even isolate their causes. As for improved public health, that could not have reduced mortality, because efforts like Chadwick's date from the 1840s, nearly the end of the 150-year period that McKeown was studying.

Sir Arthur Conan Doyle had Sherlock Holmes say in *The Sign of Four* that if the investigator eliminated the impossible, what was left, however improbable, must be true. Demography being much like detection, the axiom fits. McKeown had ruled out marriage, a climbing birthrate, and a lower mortality rate based on medical progress or public health. Nothing was left except to say that the standard of living had risen and the diet improved—not that it was adequate, just better, and not to disregard shortages, which continued to occur. Starting in the eighteenth century, McKeown said, food production had increased, thanks partly to enclosure, crop rotations, and seed horticulture. Shipping also improved, allowing better and faster distribution. Significantly, McKeown pointed out that the potato was contributing greatly to the improved food supply.

Agricultural historians agree that British farms performed wonders, mostly without new machines or technology. They're more cautious about whether the output caused population growth or only sustained it. One historian argues that, after 1750, eighteenth-century British agriculture failed to keep the nutritional standard high enough to have lowered mortality, and that in the nineteenth century, distribution mattered more than production anyway (which rules out potato growing as an influence). Also, demographers have contested McKeown's blanket dismissal of medicine, suggesting that individual doctors and hospitals probably had some influence. Further, since nineteenth-century food packagers adulterated their wares, sometimes with poisons, one is tempted to ask whether the larger food supply always meant improvement.

Ironically, that made the potato, assuming it wasn't half green with age, safer than many foods available. It was also nutritious, though whether that sufficed to keep the death rate down remains at issue. And if the answer is yes, it's yes only sometimes. Against respiratory infections like tuberculosis and childhood diseases like measles, nutrition may provide some defense. Cholera or smallpox, however, are too virulent, while typhus prevention depends on sanitation and cleanliness. Undoubtedly, the potato's vitamin C helped against scurvy, but that disease must be very acute before it causes death.

The potato's friends believed its presence in allotments or urban markets made the difference to many who wouldn't have lived so well—or even survived—otherwise. Whether that difference was large enough by itself to help England grow so rapidly is unlikely, though the question remains intriguing.

In Ireland, the potato exerted a longer, stronger influence, yet statistics that might measure it are scarcer. As it happens, unlike the case with Britain, demographers have usually ascribed Ireland's population growth to a high birthrate. They say it resulted from any or all of the following: a high marriage rate, early marriage, and a high natural fertility rate. Concerning this theory, Joel Mokyr and Cormac Ó Gráda have offered some persuasive statistical reasoning based on the 1841 census, widely thought to be the most reliable taken before the famine. They calculated a crude birthrate and marital fertility rate (births per given number of married women of a given age) much higher than those of England and Wales. These findings, the authors say, suggest that Irish marital fertility mattered as much as the propensity to marry. In other words, the Irish either desired larger families, or women were very fertile, or both. An often-cited argument for natural fecundity is that Irish Quaker women showed consistently higher fertility rates than their coreligionist counterparts in southern rural England.

The birthrate had to be high to outstrip the mortality rate. Again from the 1841 census, Mokyr and Ó Gráda calculated a crude death rate higher than that of England and Wales—astonishing, considering that Britain was far more urban. Further, Irish infant mortality was steep, perhaps 40 percent or more higher than the typical rate for Western Europe. Nevertheless, Ireland's population grew right up until the famine, despite the loss of 1.5 million emigrants over the previous thirty years.

Using the 1841 census as a retrospective is open to question, but there's every reason to suspect that eighteenth-century trends were similar, even if the proportions differed. Accordingly, it's reasonable that the potato had an important but limited effect. It couldn't have depressed mortality, at least not immediately before 1845, because 40 percent of the country was living on the tuber, and death rates were sky-high. Rather, the potato contributed to growth in that it let people marry who otherwise might not have and made raising a family cheaper—a watered-down version of what Malthus had said. That suggests the potato was a sustainer, because growth was already happening. The potato fueled the increase, permitted further expansion, and, generally until 1845, protected the nation from famine.

Just how much the potato sustained depends on when the population began its surge. It was once thought that this happened before 1750, before the potato's rise to power. However, more recent estimates have revised this calendar, putting the greatest increase between 1753 and 1791, meaning the population about doubled in only four decades. That period coincides with the tuber's dominance and allows the chance that, however briefly, it either raised fertility or lowered the death rate. But all the theories reviewed here run along either/or lines—potato or no potato, high birthrate or low mortality. What if the Irish population boom had different causes at different times, and what if the potato's role also varied?

Every demographer agrees that the potato initially improved the diet and perhaps made the food supply more regular. Suppose that its presence lowered the death rate, but only around the 1770s and 1780s, when the potato was just reaching its dominance. This makes sense because the tuber's progress was gradual and varied by region. Its full benefit wouldn't have been felt exactly at midcentury, nor would that benefit have continued in quite the same way after 1800, when it started to displace other foods. Therefore, the nutritional issue becomes one of pure addition—what the potato added—not what it took away. No one disputes that oatmeal and the potato together offered a more solid diet than either alone.

Why eighteenth-century Ireland should have gained in this manner goes back to McKeown's theory. No doubt both the birthrate and mortality rate were high, which means change came from the mortality side of the ledger. Unfortunately, specific evidence that the potato could combat disease comes not from that time but from the Great Famine, when its absence was most clearly observed. The historian E. Margaret Crawford has calculated that in 1845–49, deaths from tuberculosis were 65 percent higher than in the previous five-year period. At the famine's height, 1847–49, tuberculosis was listed as the cause of death for almost 22,000 people a year, more than twice the prefamine average. Measles was said to have taken more than twice as many lives annually from 1847 to 1849 than it had in 1846, and more than three times as many as in the pre- or postfamine years. Dysentery and diarrheal diseases were called responsible for almost 120,000 deaths from 1846 to 1850, or nearly 24,000 a year. The total from 1843 to 1845 was about 9,000, or 3,000 per year.

These statistics are suspect, both in number and because midcentury medicine often failed to ascribe the proper cause of death. Crawford herself has cautioned about accepting them without reservation. Then, too, they pertain to extraordinary times. Nevertheless, the Great Famine shows in horrific size what might have been the long-standing relation between diet and mortality from certain diseases. Most intriguing is that they are the maladies that severely afflict the young, the group McKeown singled out as responding quickly to a fall in mortality. Adolescents are notably susceptible to tuberculosis, while measles is an infamous childhood disease. Dysentery and diarrheal ailments are especially dangerous for infants and young children.

Another disease endemic during famine was typhus. At first glance, nutrition would seem to have nothing to do with body lice, but there may have been a connection. As one historian has pointed out, people struggling to find nettles to eat lack the will, means, or strength to follow proper hygiene. Also, during food crises it was not unusual for peasants to pawn their clothes, leaving themselves more vulnerable to lice. Not only would they have changed clothes less frequently, if at all, they would have huddled closer for warmth, allowing the lice to find new hosts more easily. The story from chapter 2 about Cape Clear in 1839, when rain ruined the turf supply and more people gathered around fewer fires, shows how that could have happened.

Then there's scurvy. Crawford found that when scurvy returned during the Great Famine, Irish physicians didn't always recognize it, not having seen it before—the potato had kept it at bay. One doctor who had seen it remarked in 1847 that it was then "exceedingly prevalent." It was known to have occurred in 1817 and the following bad years, and he further suspected it was common during the famine of 1740–41. Records from the Great Famine ascribe only 167 deaths to scurvy, but Sir William Wilde, an eminent doctor (and Oscar's father) thought that misleading. Scurvy is a very debilitating disease that causes fatigue, lack of breath, depression, and, if untreated, hemorrhaging. If the hemorrhage occurs in the heart or brain, scurvy can be fatal, but Wilde supposed that such a seriously weakened victim would die of something else before then.

Consequently, it's possible that once the potato improved the Irish diet, mortality may have receded, particularly among the young, who would then have had a better chance of raising children themselves. But when the diet began to erode again, the protective edge eroded with it, and perhaps mortality went back up. A possible starting date for this might be around 1809, when Wakefield saw that foods like oatmeal and milk were becoming less common. At that time, too, the lumper had just arrived from Scotland. As land hunger sharpened and rents increased, the heavier-yielding but poorer-keeping lumper displaced the Apple, bringing the hardships associated with the meal months to a larger proportion of people. Also, when milk disappeared, it robbed the lower-class Irish diet of calcium and vitamin A, with untold results to health. Those observers who marked the difference between people who had milk and those who didn't may have said more than they realized. As for conacre, it was supposed to have increased the population. But a quarter-acre plot supplies meager food for a large family, even when it's planted in lumpers. What if the households that wouldn't have existed except for conacre were more liable than others to lose members to sickness?

Further, if mortality returned once the diet regressed, that might help explain why the nineteenth-century growth rate slowed. Since the diet declined gradually, sooner for certain social classes, much as it had improved the previous century, mortality wouldn't have appeared catastrophic, except during famines. Admittedly, this link would be hard to prove. Measuring early-nineteenth-century mortality at all, let alone among particular classes, is probably impossible. Also, why the population should have doubled a second time *after* the potato achieved dominance is hard to explain, unless, when mortality rose, the birthrate rose to compensate. That isn't unheard of, and Irish fertility was apparently more than mere legend.

Probably no one will ever prove what made Ireland's population increase, or exactly how the potato was involved. What's curious, however, is that the terms of the debate have changed little. Contemporary observers saw the potato as the creator of unwanted mouths through sinful behavior, which also led to their destruction. Demographers have stripped this moral baggage away, but in birthrates and mortality, they are still talking about creating and destroying. Their work shows how enormously intricate these basic activities are, so much so that trying to reduce either to a single cause is hopeless. What may be said is that no matter which population theory is correct, contemporaries accorded the tuber too much power. Neither a maker nor unmaker of society, it may have been a sustainer. It may have preserved, or helped to preserve, existing laws and customs, but it made none. After all, it was only a vegetable.

11 Women's Work

O**N FEBRUARY 15, 1877**, the Grinnell, Iowa, farm wife Lydia Moxley told her diary that she churned thirteen pounds of butter and baked five loaves of bread, five pies, three fruit cakes, and, for supper, spare ribs. She was sick that day, too. On another day, when her husband was ill, she "did housework"—a laconic phrase that could mean any or all of pulling up and beating the carpets to whitewashing the kitchen to mopping and waxing the floors to cleaning the windows to washing and hanging up and ironing clothes—and churned butter, and welcomed more than half a dozen visitors. "Have my hands full," she remarked.

Why this twenty-five-year-old woman of the Great Plains should have chosen that particular day for editorial comment isn't clear. She might have settled on the day that, beyond "doing up work," she made soap and ink and sowed garden seeds. Or the time she did up work, then baked six pies, four loaves of bread, and cooked supper for seven guests. But Lydia wasted few words on interpretation. Her laconic diary, which she kept for one year, suggests little about herself beyond pride at her talent and energy, and annoyed weariness at having to stretch them constantly. Maybe, too, she wasn't sure she should complain, least of all to leave a permanent record of it.

However, her diary does say more about nineteenth-century American farm life and how people like her and her husband, Anson, met its demands. For instance, sales of Lydia's butter helped support the household. That she had to churn regardless of her health or other chores surely went without saying. Then, too, amid all else, visitors might come, and she had to entertain and feed them without dropping anything. During harvest season she also had to cook for the temporary help: "Had 9 men here to dinner and 5 to supper," she wrote in early September. But though their presence was an unquestioned necessity, when it came to Lydia's work, assistance was less forthcoming. When three dinner guests offered to sell Anson a sewing machine for thirty dollars, he refused. Whatever feelings lay behind Lydia's comment—"Anson would not buy it"—she didn't confide to paper.

Anson wasn't exactly a slouch, though. The Moxleys' farm produced corn, wheat, oats, and vegetables, and chickens, cattle, and pigs. One July day when the mercury stood at 108 degrees, Anson plowed until late afternoon, then dug potatoes until dark. Moreover, he sold them for a much higher price than a neighbor got, which may mean he had some hustle. One day he also kept house and got lunch together so that she could go visiting. But the question isn't whether the American farmer pulled his weight. Rather, it's that his burden was respected in a way that accorded him help as a right, not a privilege. His wife's wasn't.

Not that daily household pressures were unique to the United States; Victoire, in *The Life of a Simple Man*, comes readily to mind. However, what separated this country's rural domestic society from its European counterparts was that America lived on a larger scale. The Homestead Act of 1862 offered 160-acre tracts, the size of holding no English, Irish, or French peasant could have rented, let alone bought. And what Americans built on their land was similarly impressive. When, in *All Around the House* (1878), Mrs. Henry Ward Beecher considered how big a middle-class kitchen should be, she named dimensions that would have dwarfed many European cottages. Equally large was the volume of food the kitchen produced. Lydia Moxley's pies and breads, no doubt sturdily reinforced with butter, might have outweighed the average English tenant-farm diet by themselves. They would also have overwhelmed any tenant-farmer's wife who had to bake them without a decent oven or the fuel to fire it.

It bears repeating that farm size didn't always imply affluence, and that not everyone ate well or occupied roomy houses on grand spreads. But where the domestic workload was concerned, affluence didn't matter. In fact, it probably made things worse. Lydia Moxley lived better in 1877 than she would have in 1857 or 1827, but she earned it. For instance, before she could even mix her pie or bread dough, she had to make yeast, churn butter, cut sugar off a block and pound it, grind spices, shell nuts, sift flour (likely to be heavy or coarse), pump water, and load, light, and regulate a temperamental stove. Everything she cooked, if its recipe was the least complex, involved time-consuming, exacting toil. In a way, culinary self-reliance was only wise, because food packagers shamelessly adulterated their products. Mrs. Beecher advised, "Learn what constitutes a pure article, and, as far as in your power, manufacture it yourself."

But that placed an extraordinary burden on the housewife, leaving her no corners to cut. That was where the potato served her, as a labor-saving device. Its presence didn't stop Lydia from wanting that sewing machine, but without the tuber, she and her sisters would have been up against it more than they were. The potato supplied bulk, feeding the farmhand horde without fuss or expense. No Sunday dinner would have been complete without it, yet its preparation took far less time or bother than, say, plucking and roasting the chicken it accompanied. On ordinary days, potatoes furnished rib-sticking fuel for heavy labor, which meant they were even welcome at breakfast. Yet despite the plain utility, they were also a delicacy in high society and low.

For these reasons, among others, the potato easily became a powerful fixture in American domestic life, one that needed no explanation or excuse and invited no political attack.

A plentiful, varied table was an American legend to which many nineteenth-century voices paid homage, including William Cobbett's, remarking that all it took to set a copious table were sobriety and diligence. The memoirs of Rebecca Burlend, an Englishwoman who emigrated to western Illinois in 1831, the year Abe Lincoln started keeping store and studying law, said that "generally speaking, everybody has plenty of plain good food." Frederick Julius Gustorf, a German visitor to Illinois in 1835, met settlers who had been "dependent laborers" in Europe. Now they were landowners, "well-to-do, considering their former circumstances," and had "plenty to eat and drink." Catharine Beecher and Harriet Beecher Stowe—Mrs. Henry Ward Beecher's sisters-in-law—wrote in 1869, "There is no country where an ample, well-furnished table is more easily spread, . . ." though they disliked how often people abused the abundance. The next year, an adventuresome Pennsylvania woman named Abbie Bright went to Kansas to teach school and keep house for her brother in a twelve-by-twelve cabin. For twenty miles west, she wrote, she saw "open prairie and not a building of any kind—and only one lone tree." Yet she could get chocolate, nutmeg, cakes, and sugar from Wichita, also twenty miles away, because a friend walked there.

Nevertheless, these comments don't tell the whole story. Cobbett was writing about the Northeast, and he had odd notions about what made a good diet. Both Burlend and Gustorf were careful to mention that some Illinois settlers, especially those who had been there longer, lived better than others. Burlend's memoirs say that the less well off ate a liberal but monotonous diet: eggs, milk, butter, bread, coffee, and bacon. Despite her pretense otherwise, most of these foods would have been luxuries to peasants in her native Yorkshire, but if the comparison suggests a prosperous America, advertisements to potential immigrants had promised more. One contemporary Englishman said of Ohio's Western Reserve that every settler had orchards whose fruit was so plentiful it was free for the taking. Accordingly, when the Beecher sisters spoke of the relative ease with which Americans spread a good table, they hit the mark exactly. The possibility lay within broader reach, remarkable by any standard known. But not everyone could take advantage or bothered to.

This was especially true looking back a few decades from 1869. Before midcentury the rural diet, particularly on the frontier, revolved around two foods, corn and pork. Corn reached the table as hominy, mush, breads, biscuits, and griddle cakes. North and south, it was the most important crop, said to be more valuable than gold because it fed everyone and everything. However, it may have been a food that wanted getting used to. Frances Trollope wrote in 1832 that she knew of at least a dozen kinds of corn cakes, all bad, though she thought bread made of wheat and corn was the best she had ever tasted. Charles Dickens, who liked the country more but the food even less, said in 1842 that hot cornbread was "almost as good for the digestion as a kneaded pin-cushion." Whether that was true or not, corn was the keystone of what could be a very simple existence. For the humblest Illinois settlers, Gustorf said, "Food is very plain—nothing but coffee, tea, bacon, potatoes, and corn bread year-round."

What added sameness to prairie living was that, as Gustorf implied, the pork was rarely fresh. The same climate that favored corn spoiled anything that wasn't dried, canned, or salted, and before 1840, refrigeration was the exception, not the rule. Salt pork and bacon, then, were the staple meats. Elisabeth Koren, who left Norway for wild Iowa in 1853, ate salt pork three times a day and liked the routine at first. Five months later, she was complaining that the only way to get fresh meat was to kill a rooster or shoot a wild bird. Salt pork's most famous hour, perhaps, was as the Civil War's principal meat ration, fried or broiled and eaten with hardtack. It was, wrote one Union veteran, often "musty and rancid," edible only because "we ignored the existence of such a thing as a stomach in the army." Salt pork, presumably of better quality, was the staple of mining and logging camps both before and after the war, and won an ardent following. During the 1880s one group of Maine lumberjacks refused the fresh meat their employer offered them because it was "too fancy, and hain't got strength into it."

The potato lodged right beside the pork. Many settlers' memoirs and diaries say that potatoes figured among their few possessions when they set up house and farm. A newly married Ohioan who moved to Missouri in 1860 found space for a half-bushel of them in his trunk. For others, too, the tuber was among the first crops planted, and it formed a vital part of the diet, especially before the land began producing much else. Elisabeth Koren, at her wits' end over what to cook besides salt pork, pined for potatoes. "It is really boring, this constant puzzling over tiresome food," she told her diary.

The San Francisco of 1851, wrote a British miner, had few vegetables, so "Potatoes and onions, as fine as any in the world, were the great stand-by." When gold was discovered in Idaho in 1860, much of the potato crop—modest, at that time—went to feed the miners. From mining camps to army camps, the potato was a sought-after item. During the war, lobscouse, the old Lancashire stew, was a popular Army of the Potomac dish; it was amazing what miracles you could work with moldy hardtack. Daily rations for every hundred men supposedly included a half-bushel of fresh potatoes, "when practicable," but often it wasn't, and the troops received a dried preparation instead. The Ohioan who had moved to Missouri, now a cavalryman, wasn't satisfied with that. He was willing to pay a sutler two dollars for forty pounds of the real article when a private's pay was thirteen dollars a month. (But the southerners had it worse. As one Army of Northern Virginia veteran wrote, rations were much slimmer, when delivered at all, and there were no sutlers.) Northern soldiers requesting packages from home asked for potatoes (along with turkey, onions, chocolate, condensed milk, and the like), and their loved ones learned to use a spud or apple, rather than paper, to fill unused space. "I think the art of box-packing must have culminated during the war," remarked one veteran.

If the potato was everywhere during the first half of the nineteenth century, green vegetables were nowhere. Raw vegetables met the deepest mistrust. Only the rich had green salads, though the middle class ate salads of potatoes, cabbage, and tomatoes, the last escaping solitary confinement in the ketchup bottle during the 1830s. The most acceptable raw vegetable was celery, the crunching of which punctuated a meal from start to finish. That was still true in 1906, when an appalled French visitor reported that New Yorkers indulged in this singular habit. For much of the nineteenth century, the culinary ethic followed a simple rule that worked against raw vegetables: If it fit in a frying pan, it was worth eating. Most food reached the table cooked in butter, lard, or bacon grease. Fresh green vegetables, raw or cooked, had too little respect, particularly in cities. Until around 1840 the urban diet leaned on salt pork, blood pudding, and starches: potatoes, crackers, and bread. Those who didn't keep house for themselves—that is, they lived in boardinghouses—began around then to enjoy fresher food, but only in a relative sense. The dietary emphasis remained much the same.

Boardinghouses were an essential feature of urban life. They provided food and lodging for people who had left home to seek city wages and who couldn't have bought or rented their own housing. Occasionally, the houses also furnished a social and cultural life. Dickens was amazed to find, among the textile mill towns of eastern Massachusetts, boardinghouses that had pianos, lending libraries, and workers' periodicals. But they didn't exist only to keep single (in this case) female operatives busy during breaks in a twelve-hour workday. Walt Whitman wrote of New York in 1856 that rents, which he said absorbed at least one-fourth of a worker's salary, forced lower-middle-class married couples to become landlords. Unable to find suitable, affordable housing—has anything changed?—they rented larger dwellings and sublet what they didn't use. The strategy wasn't unique to that time or place. In 1910, a study of Homestead, Pennsylvania, a working-class Pittsburgh suburb, cited it as a common way to try to get by. One couple and their baby shared two-room lodgings with twenty men, each of whom earned $1.65 a day.

Maintaining an arrangement like that took sharp management if it was to succeed and a crushing amount of labor whether it did or not. It was as if a platoon of hired hands showed up at mealtime and never left. No wonder that boardinghouse food involved large quantities of potatoes, beets, and cabbage—cheap, filling, and easily cooked. However, mill workers, like most Americans, wanted meat on the table too. Dickens said of a house in Boston that "breakfast would have been no breakfast" without "a deformed beef-steak with a great flat bone in the center" as a main dish. More than thirty years later, that tradition lived. John Leng, a British visitor to the nation's centennial celebration of 1876, remarked on the feasts in a Lawrence, Massachusetts, mill company boardinghouse. The workers, mostly women, had meat twice a day (breakfast included), with potatoes, cabbage, and other vegetables, and bread, rolls, pies, coffee, and tea. "This will be thought very luxurious living," Leng said, but he believed most American workers ate as well.

Luxurious, maybe, but hard on the system. The American passion for bread, meat, and butter fat, washed down with coffee and tea, all likely consumed in haste, led to "dyspepsia," how the nineteenth century termed indigestion. The Beecher sisters wrote that the country was "proverbial" for a "gross and luxuriant diet," and that the nation's health would improve if people traded meat for modest helpings of fruit, vegetables, bread, and milk. They quoted a doctor who said that "for every reeling drunkard that disgraces our country, it contains one hundred gluttons." From daughters of a famous temperance lecturer, these were no idle words. They used their own pulpit to advise readers to avoid serving too many tempting dishes at one meal. Further, they warned that "stimulating condiments" excited the body so that people lived faster than nature intended.

This was making dinner into a morality play of a few short acts whose underlying theme sounds remarkably like seventeenth-century herbalism. But their ideas weren't based on fancy. Americans did add mustard and hot pepper to whatever they ate (another habit that repelled the French tourist in 1906). Moreover, the urban working-class diet had always focused on fats and starches, and did so past 1900. Sample menus from a popular cookbook of 1906 suggested serving potatoes alongside macaroni, puddings, and corn cakes. In 1909, a study of 391 New York workers' families showed that bread, rolls, butter, eggs, milk, crackers, and coffee or tea were the mainstays, with meat, potatoes, and occasionally soup for supper. Sunday brought a roast and, sometimes, cake for dessert. The Homestead diet was similar, except that breakfast sometimes included bacon. Potatoes, the most important vegetable, appeared once a day, every day.

The Beecher sisters would have approved of that, at least. Potatoes, like rice and other grains, were nutritious, digestible "farinaceous articles." What they didn't realize was that, as in Europe, the potato was substituting for fresh fruit, a commodity that formed even less a part of the diet than green vegetables. Not that Americans disliked fruit; they simply couldn't get it fresh except in season and if they lived near an orchard. Starting in the late 1860s, refrigeration and railroads did much to change that, but most fruit was preserved and remained a treat. Accordingly, at the time of the centennial, America probably got more vitamin C from fresh potatoes than from any other single source (and was still doing so when the next centennial rolled around).

Potatoes were also cheap. As in England, the tuber marked urban life partly because it stretched a budget that had almost no elasticity. It was fashionable to blame that on extravagance—shades of England again—but the author of the Homestead study disagreed. Daily necessities were so expensive, she said, that buying on credit was the only way to get them, which meant chronic debt. This old song had a familiar refrain in that Homestead women accused the merchants of gouging. Accordingly, getting by required the housewife's "constant, intelligent watchfulness" or the family's doing without "some of the essentials of a normal, healthy life." An often-used economy measure was leaving most of the house unheated, which forced everyone to gather around the kitchen table. However delightful that may have seemed, the author remarked, no one had quiet or privacy for school-work, intimate conversation, courting, reading, or any spiritual or intellectual pursuit.

In other words, those who criticized the Homestead housewife for mis-management or lack of imagination didn't realize that her choice of what to feed her family was quite limited. Whatever it cost to set the table marked domestic life between meals as much as during them, in ways that wouldn't have affected people who had more money. To the extent that the potato, with bread and cereals, made the urban dollar go farther, the tuber acted much as it did in England and France. It was bulk, thrift, and sustenance all in one, the housewife's staunch ally even if she wasn't accustomed to singing its praises that way.

Rather, people were more likely to commend it as good food, especially "new" potatoes. Diaries suggest that their presence at dinner was something to remark on, a mundane event that still brightened the spirit. It might be a treat that leavened a hard day's work, or a luxury that softened a soldier's life on campaign. Or it might be a welcome sign of variety, a hint that life in the new settlement wouldn't be drab forever. So it was that without a struggle, the potato earned universal acclaim, what one food writer in 1913 called an "almost instinctive" liking. The only apparent challenge was the charge that the potato was overused, an accusation that, in 1892, *American Kitchen Magazine* saw fit to rebut. However, cookbook writers took the hint and began including recipes for potato leftovers. In 1906, one author offered seventeen recipes—more than for fresh—and urged her readers to practice the art of disguising the twice-cooked tuber. This was wise, because a competing cookbook writer offered year-round sample menus in which potatoes appeared twice a day most days, and in almost half the meals overall.

With the potato so popular, it readily took its place among the country's most important crops. The census of 1860 calculated output at 100 million bushels, 90 percent of that coming from the northern states. New York was the single largest producer, followed by Pennsylvania, Ohio, and Maine. The Reverend Chauncey E. Goodrich, as if to explain why he had bothered raising all those seedlings, noted in 1864 that the tuber ranked fourth among edibles after wheat, corn, and oats, and ahead of peas, beans, buckwheat, and rice. This was well before Idaho was heard from—the state didn't enter the Union until 1890. But the events that brought Idaho its most famous potato progeny were already at work, and, indirectly, Goodrich played a part.

In 1853 he bred a potato he called Garnet Chile, honoring the land where he thought his tuber stock had come from. Eight years later, in someone else's nurturing hands, Garnet Chile begat Early Rose. Early Rose, besides having the most poetic name ever given a spud, was the English-speaking world's best-known potato cultivar. At home equally in Oxfordshire and in California's San Joaquin Valley, it remained popular at least until the Great Depression, far longer than the twenty-five years a commercial cultivar was supposed to last. Both Garnet Chile and Early Rose were true long-day types, and they passed on that desirable trait to countless descendants. Virtually every potato in the United States today can claim them as ancestors.

Accidental meetings can decide which way any family tree grows, and so it was with the potato. In 1872 Early Rose met Luther Burbank. Or, rather, an Early Rose specimen happened to choose Burbank's New England garden as the scene for freakish behavior. No one had known Early Rose to produce a seedball, but it was Burbank's luck to find one. He was luckier still when he bred plants from it whose tubers were much larger than Early Rose's and whose yield sometimes doubled or tripled its noble parent's. Burbank sold his prize for practically nothing, but he was allowed to keep ten tubers, and when he moved to California, that was how he introduced the Burbank potato to the West Coast. A few decades later, probably in Denver, it mutated again. The result was the russet Burbank, what the country knows as an Idaho, a superb baking and frying potato, the one that fast-food chains use today in record tonnage. Incidentally, Burbank never bred another successful spud, despite raising a half-million more seedlings.

It was fitting that the United States would breed heavy potatoes, because the tuber provided a great deal of heft on the table. The diet's weight was partly by design because there was work to do, which required proper nourishment. That began with breakfast, whose proportions would have staggered a European. An English visitor to Ohio in the early 1830s was astonished to be treated to "fried pork steaks, boiled potatoes, toast saturated with cream, coffee, & c. & c." What he didn't know was that he got off easily. Throughout the century, breakfast in farmhouse, boardinghouse, or hotel often meant that menu plus eggs, breads or biscuits (or both), whatever variety of hotcake was popular, doughnuts, milk, and sometimes fruit pie. In cold weather there was porridge and, from the 1870s, dry cereals like those Dr. John Kellogg and his brother, Will, made a household word. So strong was the tradition of the morning stoking-up that in 1929 a sociological study of Muncie, Indiana, reported that meat, potatoes, and hot bread still furnished the breakfast table.

As with Dickens and the "deformed" steak, the copious quantity of meat at breakfast was what struck most observers. But the potato's appearance was equally remarkable; in Europe, that simply wasn't done. Cobbett, of course, waxed apoplectic at the thought. Even in Ireland, until well into the nineteenth century, oatmeal porridge was the preferred morning food, at least where people could get it. A breakfast composed largely or entirely of potatoes was a sign of poverty. But the objection also derived from taste. In 1825, an English visitor to Connacht remarked, "A person unused to live entirely on potatoes finds them unpalatable in the morning, but when custom has once overcome this disgust, I really believe there is no food more wholesome and nutritious."

Americans never hesitated. Boiled or fried potatoes were a breakfast by-word. Cookbooks and magazines published recipes for various potato cakes, the ancestors of today's hash browns or home fries, recommending them without a blush as morning fare. In 1876 John Leng noted that when he crossed the Atlantic the chef of his luxury liner served potatoes daily at breakfast and dinner. (Ironically, the ship's name was the *Celtic*.) Moreover, Leng said that American hotels offered five kinds of potatoes for break-fast—boiled, baked, stewed, fried, and Lyonnaise—and these were fine establishments. This was clear proof that the homely, humble tuber could grace anyone's plate anytime without evoking the class consciousness that surrounded the vegetable in Europe. In America the potato had found a socially comfortable home.

Perhaps nowhere was that more evident than at Saratoga Springs, New York, where, as Leng said, the "Hotel Life of the United States reaches its height." During the early 1850s the town's Half Moon Hotel had a chef named George Crum, whose canvasback duck was deemed pure artistry. But artists can be temperamental, and the story goes that when a disgruntled patron sent back his fried potatoes, saying they were too thick, Crum figured to teach him a lesson. He sliced the potatoes paper thin, fried them in deep fat, and salted them heavily. Much to his surprise, the patron was delighted. Enter the potato chip.

Legend, almost certainly false, says that the patron was Cornelius Vanderbilt, but what the nation called Saratoga chips didn't need the Commodore's blessing. Right after the Civil War, no less a fashion arbiter than *Godey's Lady's Book* advised on the best way to prepare them. Thanks to the mass production of cheap cooking oils (an innovation that also ushered in the french fry), chips could come from modest home kitchens as well as those of restaurants or grocery-store suppliers. However, Saratoga chips were a labor-intensive treat, so it was only logical that someone would open a factory, which a Cleveland entrepreneur did in 1895. The factory chip arrived at stores in barrels, were displayed in glass cases, and dispensed in paper bags. The cracker-barrel packaging didn't give way to individual waxed, sealed bags until the 1930s.

Before the potato chip became a popular treat, the tuber in its more usual forms was also a fast food, though in an older sense. America is supposed to be the place where ingenuity subdues drudgery, but if that conquest has ever transformed the kitchen, it didn't during the nineteenth century. According to one historian, the only labor-saving devices that reached enough homes to change American cooking were the eggbeater and the cast-iron stove. Consequently, as in Europe, one of the potato's culinary functions was to reduce the amount of elbow grease that mealtime required.

As in Europe, what the houses looked like inside and what the kitchens possessed suggest that cooking was a rudimentary affair, if not a battle. Such was the case, for example, in Rebecca Burlend's Illinois of 1831. Her memoirs describe log houses, usually windowless, with two sixteen-foot-square rooms, and the fire on the floor at one end. The only light and ventilation came via one door, during summer. Almost the only kind of oven ever seen, "vulgarly called a skellit," was a "shallow flat-bottomed iron pan, with a cover to it." When Elisabeth Koren and her pastor husband arrived in midcentury Iowa, they lived in a series of borrowed houses, all made of finished boards and better appointed than the Burlends'. But none was much larger than fourteen by sixteen, and one was so cramped, the pantry was a shelf opposite the bed, so they had to put their clothes in the loft. Koren was delighted when she got a stove, kept in a shed outside, but her enthusiasm waned when she discovered that the shed leaked. "It is raining so hard today," she wrote, "that I do not know how I shall prepare dinner; my stove will no doubt be full of water." Abbie Bright spent her year in a tiny Kansas cabin cooking over a fireplace armed with only a skillet and a Dutch oven.

The oven fit no more than either a single loaf of bread or five cookies. Each loaf took her three hours because she couldn't keep the oven hot enough. And until a guest made her a rolling pin, she rolled her cookie dough with a tin can.

This was the frontier, but the city wasn't much different, at least for the lower classes. Tenements were cramped and so poorly lit, plumbed, and furnished that cooking had to be makeshift and unpleasant. Midcentury New Yorkers lived in rooms not much bigger than cupboards, without much light, water, or air. In 1909 the poorest tenement dwellers were likely to have no more furniture than a bed, a few chairs, a table, and perhaps a sofa. Kerosene provided light, while coal or gas fueled the stove, but many families also burned wood they gathered, usually boxes that merchants threw out or scraps from building sites. Partly for want of storage space (and cash), they bought food in small, uneconomical quantities. A woman who grew up in a Midwestern Jewish ghetto in the 1890s recalled how happy she was when her family left a one-room cellar for luxury quarters: two bedrooms and a kitchen. To afford it, they kept the bedrooms unlit. But then, her aunts came from Europe, and the breathing space vanished. During the same time in Muncie, Indiana, perhaps one family in six or eight had running water, meaning a backyard pump or, if they were lucky, a tap at the kitchen sink. Twenty years later, even Homestead workers who occupied four- or five-room houses, complete with large kitchens and excellent coal- or gas-burning stoves, rarely had running water inside.

Housekeeping was a Herculean labor, whether the place was a tenement, prairie shack, or middle-class brick-and-clapboard castle. Sometimes the effort was heroic. When Burlend's husband cut his leg so severely he almost died, she reaped, gathered, bound, and stacked three acres of wheat, helped only by her ten-year-old son, while nursing the invalid and caring for house and family. That was an extraordinary circumstance, but the usual was trying enough. Koren marveled at a friend who spent one day baking bread, sawing wood to make household repairs, washing clothes, and scrubbing the floor with lye water, a substance Koren hated.

Her Norwegian countrywoman and sister Iowan Gro Svendsen shared that dislike. Preparing lye involved much extra work on washday, but without it, the water would have been too hard to use. The housework burden added up so much that, Svendsen said, a woman needed to be a cook, maid, and housekeeper, and do all three jobs better than an upper-class servant would have done any one of them. "We are told that the women of America have much leisure time," she wrote in 1862, "but I haven't yet met any woman who thought so!"

The novelist Hamlin Garland, who grew up in Wisconsin and Iowa in the 1860s and 1870s, recalled that his mother's duties were as "relentless as a treadmill." Besides the usual cooking and cleaning, she made almost every stitch of clothing in the house, sewed rugs and quilts, churned butter for sale, tended the children, and nursed the sick. While machinery made the fieldwork lighter, Garland said, adding farmhands to operate it increased her load. "I doubt if the women—any of them—got out into the fields or meadows long enough to enjoy the birds and the breezes," he wrote. "Even on Sunday as they rode away to church, they were too tired and too worried to react to the beauties of the landscape." Not everyone, of course, thought that was so bad. An immigrant who settled in Ellensburg, Washington, around the 1880s said that he "had wrestled with the skillet and sour dough" six years and didn't realize he was tired of it until he met the woman who was later to marry him. Their cabin was spare: A box nailed to a log was a cupboard, the furniture was split pine, and they had no stove. But, he said, his wife "was not lonesome. Her three children were both care and company. . . . Seasons and crops and babies filled all her time and mind."

Part of the trouble with housework, critics said, was that men designed what women used. Mrs. Henry Ward Beecher complained that when it came to planning a kitchen, architects, usually the "most obstinate" men and "not always the wisest," were even harder to deal with than husbands. A dozen years later in 1890, *The Home-Maker* magazine went much farther, attacking "the sinful amount of drudgery" that housewives bore and implied that architects and engineers were partly to blame. Why were water pumps in the backyard, subject to all weather? Why should women still "be lifting about the old, unmerciful, iron kettles weighing some part of a ton"? These were good questions, but the willingness to design furnishings intelligently wasn't the only issue. The cast-iron stove, a deservedly popular invention, had earned almost a thousand patents by 1881, and 220 manufacturers competed in the marketplace. However, none solved a serious social and domestic problem: the heavy labor of tending and stoking a fire. In 1899, Boston's School of Housekeeping measured a stove's coal consumption over six days at almost three hundred pounds. Ministering to the metal beast absorbed an hour a day.

To be sure, moving thirty- or forty-pound kettles on and off a stove was easier than hauling them in and out of a fireplace. Stoves were also easier to regulate, demanded less bending and stooping, and were far less likely to burn the house down. They did have drawbacks; the cook could still burn herself, and, as the Beecher sisters warned, leaky stoves emitted dangerous fumes. But it was a blessing when, by midcentury or shortly afterward, cast-iron stoves cost little enough so that all but the poorest could afford them. The blessing, however, was mixed. As the historian Ruth Schwartz Cowan has pointed out, the stove probably created work. Whereas it was nearly impossible to bake, boil, and simmer different dishes over the same fireplace flame, a skilled cook could do so on a cast-iron stove. That greatly expanded the menu, a welcome advance, but at a price. Cooking became more complex, demanding more time, ingenuity, and muscle power. The housewife was the one who supplied them.

Unfortunately, her sacrifice commanded only just so much respect and attention. By all accounts, the expense of buying a stove aroused no opposition, perhaps because no one could reasonably expect the cook to do without one. Besides, her pies and breads tasted good. But paying for household help was another story. When nine men showed up to harvest the Svendsens' grain, they had a mechanical reaper, but Gro's letters said nothing about help for her to feed and house them. The outraged writer in *The Home-Maker* said that men could buy cigars or club memberships or spend freely on machinery or hired hands while begrudging their wives money for a servant's wages, a far lesser sum. This raised the question of whether all household drudgery belonged to a woman, whether married or hired, but the 1890s wasn't ready to consider this. Those used to wondering why it should be so could sound weary and pained. "Marriage," remarked a Muncie advice columnist in the late 1920s, "brings a woman a life sentence of hard labor in her home. Her work is the most monotonous in the world and she has no escape from it."

The besieged housewife, then, had to find her remedies where she could. The potato was one. She did have to buy it or dig it, wash it, and (most always) peel it, but whatever else she put on the table required that much labor or more. The potato was something she could throw in a pot and forget about a while. When the family charged in, bent on that search-and-destroy mission known as eating, the tuber afforded stopping power. Garland remembered noon lunch on plowing day, when the menfolk ate "like dragons," devouring so much salt pork and potatoes that his mother said, "Boys! Boys! Don't 'founder' yourselves!" The potato was also the cook's friend when company came. Lydia Moxley dug a bushel (and baked three pumpkin pies) the week harvesting started. Two other housewives' diaries, one from Arkansas and the other from Nevada, suggest that the potato was a useful standby when time was short or unexpected guests arrived. And in some places, time was always short. The Homestead steel workers, many of whom had no regular meal break and whose shifts changed often, expected to eat when they felt like it. Quickness and convenience mattered to diner and cook, so it was no wonder that potatoes made the menu so frequently.

Convenience and fast foods have infused American culture so much that neither the pace of living they imply nor the energy spent maintaining it seems striking unless one steps back to reflect. During the nineteenth and early twentieth centuries, however, many observers, most of them foreign but not all, noticed the way Americans approached food and eating. More than a few linked that with what they thought was the American attitude. It wasn't so much that Americans were *what* they ate, though that drew comment, but that *how* they ate suggested who they were. In part this concerned manners, but the observers were talking about more than that. They were asking what purpose food served, if any, beyond satisfying hunger. Concerning the potato, that suggests another, unasked question: What, then, was the point of a food that helped society move faster?

The way a person eats is such a personal matter that summing up how a nation approached it is difficult if not misleading. Nevertheless, so many people noticed a particular fashion that it couldn't have been an accident. Americans, wrote Cobbett in 1818, ate quickly, seemed not to care what was on their plates, and never talked about it. He found this carelessness "very amiable," but others objected. About a decade later, Mrs. Trollope decried the habit she saw in boardinghouses and taverns of eating "with the greatest possible rapidity, and in total silence." Gustorf spent two years traveling the Midwest in the mid-1830s before he saw, at a St. Louis hotel, "people eating decently," without shoveling the food down. He thought that singular exception had to do with the European-style service and the proprietor enforcing a tacit decorum.

Dickens observed in 1842 that Americans looked "dull and languid" at the table, as if meals "were necessities of nature never to be coupled with recreation or enjoyment." Considering what they were eating, maybe that was apt. The British miner in San Francisco in 1851 thought that since eating interrupted work, consuming food was a necessity to be "despatched as quickly as possible." Once, he saw a dining room where, after a bell rang, fifty or sixty men rushed to a table where they demolished a mountainous feast in minutes. Good humor reigned, but no conversation took place except to ask a neighbor to pass something—and while one hand obliged, the other continued to wield a fork. A Hungarian politician who saw Indianapolis the following year depicted a similar scene: a bell, a mad scramble, a meal in which not a word could be heard above the workings of forks and knives. Eating, the politician commented, was a serious business.

Indeed, that was how Europeans described the United States—all business. Dickens was especially adamant, referring to "that vast counting-house which lies beyond the Atlantic" and saying that Americans were so serious and sad that they "rejected the graces of life as undeserving of attention." He later apologized for his harsh judgments, but the difference between his remarks and others' was mostly tone. The San Francisco miner said, "They [Americans] make the voyage through life under a full head of steam all the time; they live more in a given time than other people. . . ." This was why mealtime brought no rest, he said. When Leng came for the centennial, he said of New York and Chicago that "everything seems to be done at full speed." Banks and offices kept a rapid pace, clerks and storekeepers were constantly busy, pedestrians walked as fast as they could, and newspapers appeared "at almost every hour of the day." He thought Americans worked harder than the British, were paid more, and had more enjoyments, but had less leisure. It showed, Leng believed, in "careworn, haggard, languid countenances" among all classes, more than in Europe. Significantly, however, he wrote that he saw none of "the bolting of food which was formerly said to be universal," except at train stations. At late dinners, he said that "time seemed to be no object," and that the food was the main concern. But he was probably basing that on what he saw in expensive hotels. Meanwhile, Garland was having harvest lunches: "At noon we returned to the house, surrounded the kitchen table and fell upon our boiled beef and potatoes with such ferocity that in fifteen minutes our meal was over."

From so many of these descriptions, then, it seems Americans didn't live to eat but ate to live. The ethic went deep, even among those who argued against it. In 1889 Helen Nitsch, a popular writer in *The Home-Maker*, begged her readers not to neglect cooking. Nitsch said that health was at stake; it was "fifty times better the windows should grow dull, the carpets be unswept" than meals suffer. The misplaced emphasis came, she said, from a "fatal keeping up appearances." Secondly, Nitsch believed it was better for women who did paid labor to sacrifice an hour's wages (presumably for piecework), than stint on kitchen time, especially if their wages were low. Besides, she said, an attentive cook need not hover around the stove, and to prove her point offered recipes that demanded only sporadic care. Nitsch's plea is remarkable not only for its passion, but for its accent, which was entirely practical. There was nothing about taste, culinary artistry, or the graciousness of a well-cooked meal. Whether this was because Nitsch knew her audience or was treading around delicate social issues doesn't matter. Her reasoning wouldn't have been possible or even necessary had food commanded, not so much a higher, but a different sort, of respect.

For instance, it would be hard to imagine that Nitsch's appeal would have been necessary in France, and not because of the fabled French love of gastronomic pleasure. If peasants ate in silence, which they did in many places, that was partly out of deference. In Berry, custom dictated eating slowly, and in Brittany, the table itself was so sacred that bumping one's derrière against it was cause for apology. The respect that one Cévennes memoirist recalled when her family ate bread and bacon was probably not unusual. This isn't to say that the French had thoroughly enviable dining habits; in many places, women served at table but couldn't eat there. Moreover, the French, too, sometimes rushed through their food. In 1888 a Parisian observer of manners complained about "knocking off our meals at top speed," thanks partly to life's bustling pace. A chef writing in 1892 addressed the trouble of eating well when "the demands of life are imperious." His solution was to cook with gas, the fastest method available. But even these complaints suggest that the speed felt jarring, and that a slower pace would be normal.

Which perhaps explains why the Frenchman who visited New York in 1906 was horrified that Americans "ate like horses," without caring what they put in their mouths, or how. To be sure, he was unready to admit that American civilization offered anything worth eating, but regardless of his snobbery, he had pegged the style right. The following year a New York waitress bore out what he said in an article for *McClure's* that likened the lunchtime rush to "panic in the theater." On a typical day, before she had served ten customers, all men, others were standing in line waiting for seats. When one got up, another took his place, shoving aside the dishes and eating on top of the mess. "When it was over," she wrote, "some of the girls would be almost shivering with fatigue." If this sounds vaguely familiar, it should. A pale version of it might still happen in an overcrowded American city, but not, *mon Dieu*, in Paris.

It remains to ask what all that utility in the American kitchen was for. It certainly wasn't to save time for leisure, epicurean or otherwise. Rather, it allowed bursts of dyspepsia-inviting energy. Whatever let the cook keep pace with modern life—the potato, for instance—was permitting a peculiar sort of thrift. Not only did the tuber expand the diet and stretch resources, as it did in France, it also fit a get-up-and-go rhythm. Speed created time for work, which created affluence, which created more work, demanding more speed. This is all very dreary, but if there was—or is—a break in the chain, it's that time spent eating a meal need not be as short as time spent preparing it. It's worth thinking about, anyway.

12   The Good Companions

An' besides, my young man, 'e say, ef you gives me that
stinkin' mess, I'll throw it at yer.
LONDON HOMEMAKER

IN HIS BOOK *Frying Tonight*, the English historian Gerald Priestland
fondly recalled the times during his childhood when his mother took
him to a fish-and-chips shop. It was during the Second World War, and they
bicycled to their destination because they didn't have gas for the car. "The
smell that came out of the shop was delicious," Priestland wrote, "but it
stood in a poor part of town near the chemical works, and it was quite clear
to me that these picnics were exceptional, taken only because of wartime exi-
gencies." Sure enough, when the war ended and gas was available once
more, they never went to the shop again. From that, young Priestland got
an early lesson about food and social class. However wonderful the fish and
chips tasted, doubtless all the better after a bicycling adventure, they came
from the wrong side of the tracks. As Priestland wryly observed, the issue
remains so strong it has even divided Britain's political parties. When
Labour convenes its party conferences, the rank-and-file crowd the shops;
when Conservatives hobnob, they wouldn't dream of it.

    This is true even though Churchill, the century's most famous Conserva-
tive, called fish and chips "the good companions." The phrase is apt, not

only because fried fish and potatoes are meant for one another, but because, from the late nineteenth century onward, they were good company for the urban working class. Without them, the diet would have been poorer, the homemaker harder pressed, and the factory worker leaving the late shift hungrier in soul if not in body. Life in those "smoke-fouled streets" was drab, especially in winter, when laborers trudged to work before sunup and returned home after dark, living their workdays by gaslight. It was these turn-of-the-century towns where a worker who had "been through the mill" had spent childhood years toiling hard on little sleep and so in adulthood "looked sunken and white-faced." Without visits to the fish-and-chips shop, one of life's few pleasures, daily existence would have been even drearier.

As only one of the good companions, the fried potato from cart or shop wasn't providing all this support alone. But at home, the tuber in its other forms continued to do its job. As a turn-of-the-century Yorkshireman remarked, "It's no dinner without there's potatoes." Of London's Lambeth district, it was said in 1914 that people would have rather done without greens, butter, or nearly all their meat than forgo spuds. By the late nineteenth century, the potato was a national institution—in 1881, the per capita weekly consumption was estimated at six pounds. The snobbery that fish and chips elicited wasn't about the potato but about fast food, which polite society called improper, immoral, and a bad influence on the poor. Still, that these names had once applied to the potato isn't entirely coincidental.

Before their union, both fried fish and chips had reached the street separately. No one knows exactly when or how, but it's certain that fish came first, by at least three decades. Dickens mentioned a fried-fish warehouse in *Oliver Twist* as if they were common in London, which dates the trade no later than 1837–39, when Oliver's adventures appeared in serial. Within a few years afterward, Alexis Soyer reportedly liked to walk the streets of his adopted city eating twopenny worth of fried fish in a paper bag. If a contemporary description was at all accurate, the great chef may have sought his treats where others feared to tread. "A gin-drinking neighbourhood suits best," Henry Mayhew was told of the fish sellers in 1851, "for people hasn't [sic] their smell so correct there." He had reason to say so, because fishmongers didn't use enough ice, especially in poorer areas. The fish fryers lived in secluded alleys and garrets, Mayhew reported, because even the poorest slum-dwellers objected to the odor, even when the fryers' rapeseed oil was fresh. Frying disguised spoilage and whether the fish came of a desirable breed, which made the operation wholly disreputable. But gibes about smell went much deeper than rancid frying fat. Critics were still putting their noses in the air well past 1900, after improved methods had removed most cause for complaint.

As for the deep-fried potato, its origins are obscure. A few years ago, *The Economist* reported that Thomas Jefferson brought it back from Paris in the mid-1780s, following his tenure as ambassador to France. Charming as this story is, Jefferson never mentioned his find, and though around then the potato and chic Parisian society did have a brief liaison, it's very unlikely the attraction included deep frying. Moreover, if Jefferson did bring home the secret, it remained just that. Not only are American cookbooks silent on the topic, George Crum's midcentury Saratoga trick suggests that culinary sensibilities traveled a different path. Crum was trying to chasten a pesky customer, after all, and maybe he chose deep frying because it was unorthodox.

In England, by the 1840s at least, cookbooks were offering recipes for fried potatoes, but not in deep fat. In 1846, Charles Elmé Francatelli suggested a garnish of potatoes "cut or turned in the form of olives, and fried in a little clarified butter." Savory morsels, perhaps, but neither they nor their dainty bath could have survived in the streetside rough-and-tumble, let alone most kitchens. The same year, the fifth edition of Eliza Acton's *Modern Cookery* recommended shaving potatoes or slicing them less than a quarter-inch thick and frying them to a light brown in boiling butter or pure, clarified dripping. Though this closely resembled the Saratoga recipe, it wasn't the French *pomme frite*, and anyway, Acton thought her dish much less common in England than on the Continent. Soyer's *Shilling Cookery*, which came out around 1854, included a recipe for very thinly sliced potatoes, fried in two inches of fat. That sounds more like the real thing, but it still wasn't quite.

By then, the baked-potato trade had been proving for several decades that people would buy potatoes as fast food. Frying them was an obvious step, but it didn't happen until the 1860s. The date coincides roughly with the deep-fried potato's arrival on French streets and in American restaurants, which suggests that something occurred everywhere at once to make frying possible. That something may have been the appearance of cheaper cooking fats, such as cottonseed oil. Why the potato fryers couldn't have used rapeseed oil like their fishmongering brethren is a mystery. But if a new oil was the key ingredient, it granted the fryers a kind of monopoly. The average working-class kitchen could barely manage "frizzling in a very tiny amount of half-boiling grease." People couldn't prepare deep-fried fast food themselves, so it was that much more seductive.

Curiously, chips first won fame not on London's streets, but Lancashire's. This was because Oldham, an industrial city outside Manchester, had a baked-potato tradition like London's, and some of its purveyors branched into frying. But London wasn't far behind, and the demand grew such that, during the 1870s and 1880s, manufacturers in both places began producing equipment to support the business.

The fryers needed it. The iron caldrons and brick furnaces with which they started out were inefficient and dangerous, so several foundries cast stoves especially for their use. Automatic potato-peelers were another boon, because fryers had only makeshift ways to peel potatoes in bulk. Some dumped the spuds in a barrel, threw in broken bricks, and stirred with a broom handle until the potato skins had been scoured off. Or there was "Owen's dolly," a five-legged stool that worked like a crude washtub agitator. Each leg had nutmeg graters attached. Then, during the 1870s, came the Wonder Potato Peeler, which had a drum lined with abrasive material. It held thirty pounds but ran on muscle power. The next decade saw more automated gadgets that resembled foundry machinery. Collins's Patent Potato Peeler, for example, rotated a potato against a cutting edge, like a lathe. But not every fryer had such conveniences, and those who didn't either labored mightily or cut corners. It was a selling point when the potatoes were perfectly peeled, and as late as the First World War, a shop could still advertise the fact.

As with the London baked-potato sellers who fashioned themselves older or more original than their competitors, London and Lancashire have vied for the right to call themselves the place where fish first joined chips. Whatever evidence that could settle the debate has probably slipped forever into the historical deep, but what's certain is that the trade took off during the 1880s, thanks to yet another industrial advance. The steam trawler could go farther faster than any fishing boat before it, permitting fresher catches—now preserved in enough ice and sped to inland markets via railroad—and exploitation of more distant fishing grounds. The trawler's range was especially important, because established grounds were yielding less, and England's North Sea ports faced decline. Steam vessels changed that. By 1891, fishing fleets were going as far as Iceland.

What they brought back led to a revival, and then some. The catches of cod and hake alone nearly doubled during the century's final decade, and eastern and western ports expanded. The fish-and-chip industry grew with them. In 1888 there may have been ten thousand or twelve thousand shops in the United Kingdom. By 1905 Oldham and Leeds, cities of about 140,000 and 430,000 people respectively, reportedly had one shop for every four hundred souls. By 1910 the kingdom boasted perhaps twenty-five thousand shops in all. For the trawlermen, this was a bonanza market, absorbing the cheaper, less well-liked fish such as haddock or plaice, species they would have otherwise sold for fertilizer, discarded, or even given away. In some eyes, of course, that was a mark against the fryers, but the bottom line was inarguable. By the First World War they were buying between 100,000 and 150,000 tons of fish annually, or one-fifth to one-quarter of the nation's catch. (They were also consuming half a million tons of potatoes, as much as 10 percent of a small crop.) Most working-class people ate no other fresh fish. Sad as that was, it represented progress over the 1860s, when Dr. Edward Smith found that fish rarely made it to the laborer's table, and then usually as dried herring, the cheapest variety. Perhaps the industry truly came of age during the 1921 coal strike, when fryers, like bakers, got preferential treatment on fuel deliveries. Snobbery be damned.

The turn-of-the-century urban working-class diet needed all the help it could get, partly because wages flattened or declined from 1900 to just before the war. A 1902 study of York said the poorest lived on a "dreary succession of bread, dripping, and tea," with bacon, coffee, and only a little butcher's meat. There was nothing to add interest or variety. Five years later, a survey of a north Yorkshire steel town revealed weekly diets that, except for sugar and tea, would have lasted a family in "better circumstances" only two days. Condensed milk replaced fresh because it went farther, but it was sweet, skimmed, and less wholesome. Some workers did have a daily hot meal of meat and potatoes, and perhaps cold meat another meal—more substance but also repetitive. Maud Pember Reeves said of 1914 Lambeth that bread topped the food budget, potatoes were a distant second, and meat and fish followed. Meat went into Sunday dinner, whose leftovers supplied a second meal; into a stew; a suet pudding; and perhaps cheap sausages a fourth night. Pickles were ever-present. Breakfast was tea and bread and butter, jam, or margarine. Children never tasted milk once they finished nursing.

No wonder a national survey in 1904 uncovered widespread chronic digestive troubles, bad teeth, anemia, and general debility among the working classes. Particularly hard-hit were nursing mothers, too poorly nourished to feed their infants, and the infants themselves. The babies got condensed milk, which contained too little fat or vitamins A or D, and consequently couldn't prevent rickets. In 1900, one in six babies of working-class parents died in their first year; in York, among the poorest class, it was one child in four. To be sure, this appalling mortality rate resulted from more than inadequate diet, but still, much of the English population was underfed. During the Boer War, the rejection rate of recruits ran as high as 60 percent in places, nearly 40 percent countrywide. Accordingly, in 1902, the military had to reduce the minimum height requirement to five feet from five foot three, the second such lowering in less than twenty years.

Fish and chips bolstered the diet in vital ways, especially if the dinner included the peas or beans many fryers offered as side dishes. To other social classes looking down, however, the shops were anything but healthy places. This came partly from ignorance, because even by 1914, most general practitioners had hardly heard of proteins, and vitamins were too recent a discovery to mean much. Government medical officers were always trying to show that fried fish and enteric fever were connected. One dissenting voice spoke in 1910, when a well-known brain surgeon (and believer in red meat) praised fish eating as an escape from "monotonous rounds of bread, dripping, and tea" and said the fryers furnished "wholesome, acceptable meals." But the shops' social tone was such that nutritional knowledge really wasn't the issue. A campaign promoting fish and chips would have almost surely sounded like seventeenth- and eighteenth-century pamphlets advocating the potato as food someone else should eat.

This was because, for the higher classes, the shops had many distasteful associations. Cottonseed oil, a byproduct of textile manufacture, smelled vile, and the odor clung to a person's clothes. Just after the century turned, an extra process added to the refining removed the smell, but the perception of frying as hazardous and foul lived on. When the trade began, this charge bore some truth, because equipment was primitive, and a few shops were prosecuted for selling spoiled fish. However, the industry often found itself snubbed, as when a government agency in 1907 classified frying as "offensive," lumping it with gut scraping and tallow melting. The judgment stuck until 1940.

Moreover, what went on in the shops appeared common and altogether too democratic. Ownership was ethnically diverse, with Jews and Italians participating in the trade during the nineteenth century, and Cypriots and Chinese in the twentieth.* Women found employment there, otherwise scarce for them in mining and metalworking districts, and ran many shops, especially during the war. It should have counted more in the shops' favor that women and children could visit them freely, unlike pubs, but fish and chips had a bad reputation nevertheless. Depending on the hour, the atmosphere could be rowdy, as in one establishment where the owner kept a sawed-off chair leg under the counter, just in case. Shops became hangouts for the young, particularly those who wanted to do their courting away from parental eyes. In 1912, concerned parents in Scotland protested shops keeping late hours, particularly on Saturday nights, which all too easily became the wee hours of Sunday, the Lord's day. Then, too, eating in the street, out of a newspaper, and with the hands offended finer sensibilities. It suggested dirt, poor hygiene, and disregard for privacy and domesticity. These were, of course, the same accusations the potato had faced, but the link between the two wasn't the vegetable. It was the speed and ease with which people fed themselves, and their acting as if those advantages outweighed other considerations.

Which were expense, propriety, and pride in domestic skills. In other words, to critics, the working-class habit for fish and chips implied the ignorance, immorality, and extravagance for which the poor had long been blamed. In 1913 sixpence or seven-pence bought peas, chips, and two pieces of fish, a very cheap meal, but the willingness to spend it created unease. It

---

* There were other "foreign influences" as well. The cottonseed oil came from Egypt, beef dripping from Australia, and potatoes sometimes from Germany, Belgium, and Holland. Some of the peas and beans were imported too.

was still gospel that "the lives of the lowest class are in every way wasteful," and that "what they earn is badly spent." So engrained was this notion that several social surveyors analyzed working-class budgets to the penny, showing that any extra expense, whether for new shoes or a doctor, would put a household in debt. Why the poor should have been cited for excess about sixpence is hard to figure. Certainly, sixpence mattered in the twenty-two-shilling-a-week salaries that Reeves heard about in Lambeth. But perhaps what caused ill feeling was the thought that the poor, heaven forbid, were using that tiny sum to enjoy themselves.

What they should have been doing with it, apparently, was to cook proper meals at home. Visiting the fish-and-chips shop was shirking responsibility. Behind this charge lurks the ghost of J. P. Kay-Shuttleworth, pointing a finger at the moral degradation born of slothful housekeeping. However, a closer look at the kitchen told a different story. Not only could the purchase of adequate pots and pans take food off the table, fuel spent on cooking could mean sacrifices elsewhere. Many homes had coin-operated gas systems, and each penny in the slot implied a choice, much as the Homestead, Pennsylvania, families had to choose between a warm house and a richer diet. A penny's worth of gas would cook two batches of steaks or chops *or* light a room eight hours. Many ovens were so fuel-hungry that lengthy cooking was too costly to indulge in more than once a week, on Sunday. Where people lacked ovens altogether, having to make do with old-fashioned ranges or coal grates, housewives got Sunday dinner ready-made. The rest of the week, they used their few beat-up pots on the stovetop or served cold food. Reeves told of a home where, one week, a bandage on the baby needed a small object inside to supply pressure, so they put a penny in. The next week, that penny was the only one in the house, so they unwrapped the bandage to cook the dinner. To reinforce the bandage, the interviewer gave them a lead weight from her coattail.

The belief that the poor were extravagant cooks came partly from their habit of buying small, uneconomical quantities. Reeves wondered, astutely, whether the lack of storage, especially that secure from dirt, mice, or insects, led women to shop every day. However, it was much easier to assume, as Edwin Chadwick had done, that waste or poor management resulted from ignorance. George Gissing's 1889 novel, *The Nether World*, depicts a good-hearted but inept young London woman named Pennyloaf throwing her money away on unwholesome snacks. "Like all women of her class," runs Gissing's description, "utterly ignorant and helpless in the matter of preparing food, she abandoned the attempt to cook anything, and expended her few pence daily on whatever happened to tempt her in a shop. . . ." The author of the York study, though less absolute, wrote that the poor lacked the knowledge that could have let them choose a nutritious, economical diet.

Cooking skills were undeniably meager. Most millhands' wives in the north Yorkshire steel town didn't "know how to cook at all, or at any rate do not wish to do so," though some did and said they took trouble to. Reeves commented that a woman rearing a family on twenty-two shillings would be even more discouraged than she was if she knew more about cooking and nutrition.

What the Lambeth woman did know, Reeves said, was her kitchen and its limitations. Consequently, when Reeves urged the housewives she met to make porridge for breakfast—porridge was thought a great asset in social evolution—she got nowhere. Not because, she realized, the women were stubborn or ignorant, but because the husbands and children hated it. It had no milk or sugar, burned easily in old pots, and absorbed whatever taste had last touched the metal. No one would eat it. The women couldn't bear to watch food going to waste, so they bowed to custom and served what their families liked. Said one woman, "An' besides, my young man 'e say, ef you gives me that stinkin' mess, I'll throw it at yer."

Again like their American counterparts, women also had to contend with their husbands' work schedules. Arranging family meals and the lunchpail was so complicated, said one observer, that the lunch was "often of a sketchy and rather unsatisfactory kind." Part of the trouble was finding the time to cook, especially in between other chores. However good porridge might be, remarked the author of the York study, it took more time than tea and bread and butter, while broths and healthful vegetable dishes required "considerable pains." And cooking wasn't the only pain. Bathing was another, Reeves said, demanding considerable labor. The copper tub—sometimes portable only in the loosest sense—might be one floor away from the nearest tap. But even if baths were just weekly, the normal routine was pressured enough without tending a meal. The housewife had to leave the cooking pot to itself while she nursed a baby, washed clothes, or cleaned the room. When the older children were home from school, she had to mind them too, and at mealtime, she didn't even try to eat with her family, and perhaps didn't even sit down. Wrote Reeves, "The Lambeth woman has no joy in cooking for its own sake."

Accordingly, fish and chips became a lunch standby, especially for workers who lived far from home and didn't or couldn't pack anything substantial with them. Some workshops sent the apprentices out to bring back the lunch order. A trade newspaper recounted a case, reportedly "but one of hundreds," of a four-person family, all workers, who left home at 6:00 A.M. and had only an hour for lunch. Four days out of six, they bought fish and chips. The anecdote was self-serving, coming from a fryer, but if he exaggerated, it was in stressing his heroism as family savior. Fish and chips was a great social convenience. During the 1930s, miners and tinplate workers in south Wales used to buy when coming off the late shift at 11:00 P.M. so they wouldn't bother their wives, who'd have to get up early to make breakfast for the rest of the family. In hot weather the shops did particularly well, because the tenements were too stifling to cook in, and people spent a lot of time outside anyway.

Perhaps it was fitting that industry, having moved life into a higher gear, would devise a culinary institution that kept pace. How ironic that this institution rested partly on a vegetable whose cultivation predated Western civilization and came from a rural society whose most important piece of equipment was a spade. How ironic too that the world's most technologically advanced nation had managed to re-create in its largest, busiest cities the domestic conditions that made the potato so valuable on the Andean altiplano. Britain's mines and refineries produced fuel that helped build an empire far richer than the Incas', but the laborers who made this possible might enjoy a warm home only once a week. Their stoves, if they had them, weren't modern enough to cook their food properly, but it was they who cast iron and steel in the metalworks.

The potato had been the so-called lazy root, supposedly allowing a farmer to subsist in idleness. Yet it wound up sustaining a hard-working urban population, freeing time that was mostly spent at labor. Throughout the nineteenth and early twentieth centuries, critics were always worrying that the working classes weren't working enough or earning whatever they got, as if the capacity to loaf were theirs alone and explained their plight. Perhaps the critics expected life to be a tussle and that if the poor weren't struggling visibly (or in the approved manner), they were getting away with murder. Consequently, what they ate and how they cooked it came under fine scrutiny. The potato was an easy target no matter how they looked at it. It started the nineteenth century being too cheap and therefore encouraging irresponsible behavior; much later, in its fried form, it encouraged irresponsibility because it was too expensive. But the potato had its day. By 1914 British farmers raised only half the meat the nation consumed and less than one-fourth of the wheat. When war came and German submarines began sinking British merchantmen, the tuber's value became that much more apparent. So much rode on it that when the autumn 1916 crop failed, shortages brought on scurvy outbreaks. Incidentally, the fryers, forever defending themselves, were quick to say what they and their product meant to the country.

That the defense was necessary seems silly today, especially to Americans, but the moral indignation about fish and chips—really about fast food—had a point. This concerned eating with the hands, largely a question of manners but also one of social outlook, as Cobbett and others had said. If people ate with their hands, that meant they weren't sitting at table properly, devoting their time and attention solely to their meal and, perhaps, to the people with whom they shared it. As this narrative has argued, many circumstances made that necessary or even desirable, but something was lost nevertheless. Fast food allows the freedom to pursue other activities while eating, but that's trading whatever happens around the dinner table for a different experience, perhaps a less companionable one. As the world spins faster, it becomes less possible for people to follow parallel or even intersecting paths. Speed can create connection, but it can also create disconnection. Perhaps the stuffy Edwardians who wrinkled their noses at fish and chips sensed that.

13 Good Breeding

OVER THE LAST FOUR CENTURIES, the West's attitude toward the potato has gone through different shades of disrespect. In the seventeenth century, the tuber was exotic and fearsome, feeding only those who couldn't afford anything better or were too uncivilized to care. During the eighteenth century and into the nineteenth, the potato lost its ominous qualities but kept its lower-class label because of its cheapness and ease of preparation. Now, in the late twentieth century, the potato is no longer beneath contempt. Rather, it's almost beneath notice.

One measure of the tuber's place is that potato experts have always arrived at their skill by accident. Parmentier did because he was a prisoner of war. Goodrich did because he left the active ministry while still young and took up market gardening to occupy his spare time. R. N. Salaman, who gave up his medical practice because of ill health, studied genetics while he convalesced. Five years later, in 1911, he bred a blight-resistant potato. In the late 1940s Austin Bourke was the first to analyze weather patterns and correlate them correctly with *Phytophthora* outbreaks. He would never have done so except that his employers, the Irish weather service, needed to justify their operating budget and thought that figuring out such a connection would be a worthwhile way.

Which means the potato is either so laughable or commonplace that no one ever grows up dreaming of building a better one. This itself might be funny but for the context. Each potato expert mentioned above was working to save a food supply at risk. Parmentier was lobbying to protect France against grain failure. Goodrich was looking for a way to prevent late blight; so was Salaman. Bourke was trying to help potato farmers by telling them when they needed to treat their fields with fungicides.

Today, more than one hundred countries grow the potato. Annual production represents more than 290 million tons of food, placing the tuber alongside wheat, corn, and rice in importance. If the security of that human investment rested solely on a few people who just happened to think it was worth protecting, we would be in deep trouble, as Western Europe was in 1845. The comparison isn't far-fetched, either, because late blight may now be more virulent than ever. Since 1990 fungicide-resistant strains have struck fields in various parts of North America, causing heavy damage. This is particularly worrisome because North American potato farmers rely largely on six standard cultivars, and the lack of biodiversity makes the crop more vulnerable. Fortunately, the International Potato Center in Lima, Peru, and the United States Department of Agriculture have succeeded in breeding blight-resistant germ plasm, which may provide more resistant stock. Someone, at least, takes the tuber seriously.

With starvation or nourishment at stake, it's remarkable the European potato should have made so many enemies, especially in Britain, where the fear of poison faded sooner than in France. But shortly after mid-eighteenth-century science had chased away the nightshade bugbear, another fear replaced it: that unsettling events and the tuber's rise were connected. In a way, they were. Between 1750 and 1850, the population of England and Wales roughly tripled, which wouldn't have happened unless the food supply also expanded. The potato counted in that, particularly after Waterloo, but not everyone approved. The nation was rapidly becoming crowded and urban, and the ranks of the poor seemed to grow faster than any other. Critics wondered whether the potato always caused or accompanied poverty—specifically, that more potatoes meant less bread and meat. In other words, sacred traditions were dying, and the potato looked like the killer.

What happened on the land seemed to argue that way. Enclosure prompted laborers to raise the potato (or, as critics said, condemned them to it). As larger farms and wage labor replaced small, independent cottager farmers or farmer-craftspeople, the potato became vital to domestic life, particularly in allotments. When people left the land for industry, either because farms no longer supported them or higher wages were seductive, the tuber was waiting for them in city or town. Sometimes it entered their lives through urban allotments, but more often as a cheap shop purchase that made a quick meal. Accordingly, those who abhorred what later generations called the industrial and agricultural revolutions hated the potato too, because it represented the loss of freedom to be self-supporting. Not only were the lower classes no longer working for themselves, they were ceasing to supply their wants, especially bread, from their own produce and domestic labor. Cobbett's was the most eloquent voice crying that the potato robbed people of their independence.

In fact, the tuber offered laborers their best chance to keep their freedom, let alone to survive. An anecdote in the memoirs of Alexander Somerville, a Scottish political activist, speaks to what the potato meant. His father was a limestone quarrier but rented enough land to raise a few cattle and turnips to feed them, plus a potato patch. The patch was significant, because Somerville recalled that in 1816, when he was five, potatoes were almost the only food. That dire situation worsened when the turnip crop failed, and a hunger-crazed ox broke into the pantry. Somerville and his two sisters watched their mother hit the beast with fireplace tongs, trying to drive him out. "His hide and hair were so thick," Somerville wrote, "that he cared nothing for all the blows which our mother could give him. He kicked out with his hind feet, and kept eating." By the time she persuaded the ox to leave, most of the potatoes were gone.

The story vividly conveys the terror of want that makes the most prettily crafted political theory seem irrelevant. But Somerville's account also contains other suggestive details. It wasn't his family's intention, but their potatoes fed both humans and animals, a condition the tuber's critics deplored. However, the Somervilles had also done what the theorists liked, living on a craftsman's wage and on the soil, not surrendering their hold on the land and what it yielded. Had it not been for a cow that gave milk copiously—another asset the theorists would have praised—the family might have starved. To the Somervilles, then, self-sufficiency had many components (quarry wages, livestock, allotment crops that furnished both fodder and human food). Even at that, they lived close to the edge. Without the potato, they would have gone over it.

Consequently, the question of whether the potato encouraged or stifled self-sufficiency was more complex than it appeared. Moreover, people differed over whether self-sufficiency was even desirable, especially for certain classes. A telling sign was how some farmers refused to grant their tenants allotments, fearing that their hold over them would weaken. Most agricultural experts disapproved, but only so far. They might grumble about farmers playing Scrooge and hurting their own best interests, but interfering legally or in any other way would have violated the laws of laissez-faire. Also, no one wanted to see the lower classes become entirely independent, and the potato's apparent (but fictive) power to make them so caused uneasiness. The proof was Ireland, where allotments existed in their extreme form as subsistence acreage or conacre. The Irish were criticized for insulating themselves from civilization and natural law, and for teaching the English lower classes to do likewise. Fingers itched to dismantle potato subsistence, but once more, laissez-faire barred the way. However, the reaction to the Great Famine suggests that divine power was going where Parliament would have liked to tread. That feeling surely influenced the relief effort in spirit if not in deed.

Whether the potato stole self-sufficiency or granted too much of it left the tuber a pariah once more, tainting whomever it touched, no matter which direction they were heading on the independence continuum. An unfair judgment, but it sprang from a human fear that the means of living might vanish amid social and economic upheaval. Cobbett was afraid the lazy root would displace bread and meat and therefore ruin the yeomanry, re-creating Ireland in England. The laissez-faire economists he detested worried it would wreck agriculture and with it, society, likewise re-creating Ireland. Each opinion supposed that it wasn't enough that people earned their livings by the sweat of their brow; they had to sweat enough to erase their sins. Potato culture was too easy. What this viewpoint forgot or discounted was that the Irish clung to the potato not because they were sinful but because they, too, were intensely worried that their sustenance would evaporate.

For the French, this argument took place on strictly practical, not moral, grounds. French peasants feared what disasters might happen if they committed meager land and labor to a plant that lacked tradition and whose behavior and character were either suspect or unproven. Their experience was famine, and wasting resources was inviting want. Once they realized that the potato was safe to eat, didn't fail, didn't displace their beloved grains, and fit their self-sufficient, home-centered economy, they adopted it wholeheartedly. Anything that sustained their bodies couldn't wreck their society, especially if it let them worship bread all the more. Accordingly, they suffered few if any pangs over which hell the potato led to, which suggests they knew how to separate their stomachs from their souls. Perhaps that ability was what led Philip Thicknesse, an Englishman who visited France in 1775, to wish he had been born French. He said that Frenchmen "live as if they were never to die," whereas "Englishmen die all their lives. . . ."

The potato came of age when the world began moving faster. This century has seen so much rapid movement that stories about the first railroads or cars chugging along at a few miles an hour seem quaintly prosaic. Picturing what the world was like before computers is hard enough these days, let alone imagining life before the telephone or the turnpike. But that's because we are inured to a more crowded planet in which more must be produced in the same amount of time. When the potato began its march to power, these pressures were measured on a smaller but no less meaningful scale. The Edinburgh-London summer journey that took ten days in 1754 and four in 1776 was a sign of things to come. In 1785, William Thomson wrote of Birmingham that, fifty years earlier, the city had had only three main streets. Now Birmingham was "so crowded, and at the same time so extensive a town," showing just how quickly the steel and iron industries had burgeoned. Growth had happened so fast that only within the past three years had the streets been paved with flagstones.

Within another fifty years, the railroad would begin to push England to an even faster pace. In 1830, England and Wales had 875 miles of track; in 1860, almost 7,600. A traveler wishing to go from London to Birmingham in 1836 could figure on an eleven-hour journey by road. By 1854, the trip was a three-hour train ride. Even those who seldom or never traveled by rail saw their lives touched in profound ways. In 1856 an observer remarked how Birmingham, before the railroad, had had few fishmongers, and fish was scarce and expensive. Now, however, every evening the city enjoyed fish caught that morning on both coasts, although Birmingham stood at England's geographic center, a hundred miles from the nearest seaport. This far outdid Daniel Defoe marveling in 1725 that turnpikes allowed fish to reach the city in two days instead of six.

As daily life sped up, it was bound to leave traditions behind. One was home baking. Those who mourned its death had a point, not about self-sufficiency, but about the art of living. Baking has always been a craft. Even with conveniences unknown in past centuries like quick-firing ovens, bread baking requires patience and skill. The return is commensurate. The interaction of leavening and flour is one of life's great miracles, a domestic drama that has never failed to express hope and promise. Nothing smells or tastes like freshly baked bread. That European peasantries made inedible bread from bad flour and impure yeast, then ate the result after it was long stale, in no way lessens the magic. A dish of boiled potatoes was cheaper, faster, more digestible, and maybe healthier. But it demanded no skill, possessed no mystery, no richness, no link to the past. As the Western religions have said, bread feeds the soul as well as the body. It may be centuries before the tuber does the same.

Not that this demeans the potato or suggests that we have surrendered to it out of expedience. Rather, we are less concerned with breeding than our eighteenth- and nineteenth-century forebears, which is a good thing. Also, as time and space keep shrinking in a more populous world, we have redefined what miracles mean and what value we place on them. Which is also a good thing, because however ugly and prosaic the potato might be, hunger is far worse.

Notes

ABBREVIATIONS

IN Irish Nation
LH Leicester Herald
LT Times (London)
BPP/HCSP British Parliamentary
   Papers, House of Commons
   Sessional Papers

BOARD OF AGRICULTURE SERIES

In the mid-1790s Britain's Board of Agriculture and Internal Improvement commissioned county-by-county agricultural surveys. I have drawn on sixteen: Bedford, Berkshire, Buckingham, Chester, Cumberland, Durham, Gloucester, Lincoln, Middlesex, Norfolk, Nottingham, Rutland, Shropshire, Somerset, Worcester, and Yorkshire (North Riding). All had virtually the same title: *General View of the Agriculture of the County of _____: With Observations on the Means of Its Improvement.* All were published in London in 1794, except for the Lincoln study, which appeared in 1799. All have named authors, except for Lincoln, attributed to the board. The Notes cite them by the author and the county: Foot, *Middlesex*. The Bibliography does not list them.

Introduction

"I have always thought": Parmentier, 2.
Change of heart in a generation: Roze, 191.
"So banal a subject": Salaman, ix.

Chapter One: Treasure of the Andes

Plowing at La Raya: Bingham, 121–22.
Potato's age: wild: Hawkes, *Potato*, 19;
   cultivated: Hawkes and Francisco-
   Ortega, 86.
Plowing: woodcut: reproduced in
   Hawkes, *Potato*, 23; Cobo's description:
   Cobo, *Religion*, 214.
Spanish see potatoes in 1537: Hawkes,
   Potato, 10.
Altiplano environment: Paul T. Baker and
   Michael A. Little, eds., *Man in the
   Andes: A Multidisciplinary Study of High-
   Altitude Quecha*, United States/International Biological Program Synthesis Series (Stroudsburg, PA, 1976), I,
   25–31; Bingham, 102–3; Salaman, 37.
Potato's advantages: drought resistance:
   J. G. Hawkes et al., eds., *Solanaceae III:
   Taxonomy, Chemistry, Evolution* (London, 1991), 350; 230 species: letter from
   J. G. Hawkes to the author, Aug. 6,

1993; choosing species: Hawkes, *Potato*, 60–61; Salaman, 10.

Scarcity of fuel: Bingham, 51, 103, 145; J. J. von Tschudi, *Travels in Peru*, trans. Thomasina Ross (New York, 1865), 213; Clements R. Markham, *Travels in Peru and India* (London, 1862), 104.

Chuño: Cieza, 164, 271; Vasquez de Espinosa, 613; Salaman, 40–41.

Seville hospital: Hawkes and Francisco-Ortega, 97.

Potato a richer haul: Donovan S. Correll, *The Potato and Its Wild Relatives* (Renner, TX, 1962), 7.

Spanish praise the potato: "good food": Cieza, 44; boiled chestnuts: ibid., 317; "floury roots": q. Hawkes, *Potato*, 22; "repulsive vermin": Cobo, *History*, 27; "delicious fritters": q. Salaman, 103.

Chuño and the miners: Cieza, 271.

"Dainty dish": q. Hawkes, *Potato*, 22; similar remark: Vasquez de Espinosa, 368.

Sweet potato: Columbus: Salaman, 71; Henry VIII: Waverly Root and Richard de Rochemont, *Eating in America: A History* (New York, 1976), 62; "venerous roots": Harrison, 92; "Let the sky": William Shakespeare, *The Merry Wives of Windsor*, act 5, scene 5.

Altiplano's barrenness: José de Acosta, *The Natural and Moral History of the Indies* [1591], trans. Edward Grimston [1604], ed. Clements R. Markham (London, 1880), III, 132, 161; Cieza, 270; Cobo, *History*, 5; Vasquez de Espinosa, 493, 606.

Taste for sweet flavors: "the most delicate root": q. Safford, 512; vanilla, chocolate: Gottschalk, II, 12; "confections": Harrison, 92; sweet pie: Woolley, 288.

French expressions: Desnoues, 16.

Botanists' description of the potato: q. Roze, 86–93.

Mandrake: Rachel, Leah: Genesis 30:14–16; herbalists: Boorde, 281; Coles, 35, 72; Culpeper, 223; Lovell, 262; Parkinson, *Theatrum*, 345; Salmon, 678; Westmacott, 108; "drowsy syrups": Shakespeare, *Othello*, act 3, scene 3.

Henbane: smoking it: Lovell, 204; warnings: Coles, 36; Culpeper, 239; Parkinson, *Theatrum*, 364; Salmon, 515.

Warnings about deadly nightshade: Coles, 97; Culpeper, 128; Parkinson, *Theatrum*, 349; Salmon, 781.

Belladonna like the potato: Parkinson, *Theatrum*, 347.

Steroidal alkaloids: William G. D'Arcy, ed., *Solanaceae* (New York, 1986), 85, 202–3.

Solanine: ibid., 204; bitter potatoes: Thouvenot, 50.

Recommendations on use: University of California, Berkeley, "The Great Potato Skin Debate," *Berkeley Wellness Letter* 9, 8 (May 1993), 2–3.

Tobacco: and belladonna: Parkinson, *Paradisi*, 516; "Natures Extreams": Tryon, 124; medical uses: Culpeper 177–78; Lovell, 424; Parkinson, *Theatrum*, 712.

"Scarcely innocent": John Ruskin, *Queen*

of the Air (London, 1869), 106; "natural curse": ibid.

Roots' powers: Boorde, 279; Culpeper 130, 132, 224, 225; G. Markham, 131; Lovell, 18, 445; Parkinson, *Paradisi*, 506, *Theatrum*, 873–74; Salmon, 794, 906.

Health hazards: onion and leek: Coles, 75; Culpeper, 220, 225; poisoned blood: Boorde, 287; Culpeper, 218; Westmacott, 79.

Theory of infection: G. Markham, 10.

Leprosy: reported of France: q. Roze, 122; in England: John Gerard, *The Herball; or Generall Historie of Plantes*, ed. Thomas Johnson [1633](New York, 1975), 928; Lovell, 347.

Appearance and disease: Coles 94, 95; Lovell, 16; G. Markham, 27.

Chapter Two:
The Solace of Miserable Mortals

The "sauce of the poor man": McKay, 92.

"The meanest cottager": Luckombe, xxi.

"The most inattentive observer": Young, *Ireland*, I, 79.

A large population: Malthus, 47.

Raleigh: McIntosh, 12; Plumtre, 368; Wakefield, I, 442.

Romantic tale: untrue: Safford, 516; *Newsweek* gaffe: *Newsweek*, Fall/Winter 1991, 60.

Unknown Spanish sailor: William H. McNeill, "The Introduction of the Potato into Ireland," *Journal of Modern History* 21, 3 (1949), 218. I am indebted

to Professor McNeill for bringing this to my attention.

County Wicklow: Cullen, 159.

Irish diet: oats: Cullen, 142; buttermilk: ibid., 143; tuber graduates: ibid., 144; famine relief: Bourke, 12; wheaten bread: Wakefield, II, 741.

Climate: rainfall: Salaman, 189; wetness: Young, *Ireland*, II, 8; Thackeray, 169; Irish words: O'Sullivan, 39; rain causes shortages: Wakefield, I, 217.

Curl: advent: Bourke, 27; effects: Salaman, 179; words for wind: O'Sullivan, 66.

Temperature: mildness: McCulloch, I, 360; Safford, 525; snow and frost: Wakefield, I, 216; temperatures: Salaman, 189; solar season: J. E. Van der Plank, "Origin of the First European Potatoes and Their Reaction to Length of Day," *Nature* (London) 157, 3990 (April 20, 1946), 504.

Maine potato farming: Bret Wallach, "The Potato Landscape: Aroostook County, Maine," *Landscape* 23, 1 (1979), 20.

Short-day subspecies: Hawkes, *Potato*, 38; Salaman, 67.

The potato emerging as a field crop: Langer, 53.

Young praised the Irish: Young, *Ireland*, II, 47.

"Vegetate": "Reflections on the State of Ireland," 94.

"It would be fairer to ask": BPP/HCSP, *First Report of Commissioners for Inquiring into the Condition of the Poorer Classes*

in Ireland, 1836 (hereafter Poor In-
quiry), XXXII, Appendix E, 69.
"Naked, bleak dreary view": Young,
Ireland II, 85.
"Thousands of women and children":
Pim, 115.
Feared the trees would fall: Society of
Friends, 199.
Kilkenny "marvelous": Pococke, 129. By
1812, Edward Wakefield was complain-
ing about smog: Wakefield, I, 615.
Coal imports increased: Foster, 201.
Turf: "kneaded": O'Sullivan, 26; attrib-
utes: Wakefield, I, 622–23; crucial
chore: ibid., 622; bribe agents: Reid,
225–27; Cape Clear: Kohl, 102; Wicklow
rain: Smith, 200.
Lack of chimneys: "it is true": Young,
Ireland I, 35; other writers: Inglis, I, 30;
Kohl, 48; Luckombe, 19.
Cabins: Poor Inquiry, App. E, 40, 41, 42,
44, 48, 56; "acrid fumes": ibid., 44.
Comments on cabins: De Beaumont, I,
266; Kohl, 48; Luckombe, 154; Wood,
29, 33.
Smoke: escaping: Bicheno, 31; who suf-
fered: Nicholson, 213; Wakefield, I, 88;
"smoked ham": Young, *Ireland*, II, 48;
low stool: Luckombe, 154; other sto-
ries: Pococke, 87; Wood, 29.
"Children eat": Young, *Ireland*, I, 79. See
also Ó Gráda, 22.
More open-handed practice: Young,
Ireland, II, 42.
Furnishings: ibid., 48; Wakefield, II, 782;
Poor Inquiry, App. E, 69, 73.
Eating habits unvaried: Nicholson, 98.

The inn at Kerry: ibid., 330.
Kettle: "vessel of honour": Bicheno, 31;
inverting: Poor Inquiry, App. F, 69;
Reid, 153.
Currency rare: Swift, 2099; Thackeray, 74;
Wakefield, I, 512.
Forks: advent: Gottschalk, II, 66; little
used: Fenton and Kisban, 45; Sherrill,
106; Weber, *Modern Europe*, 591.
Plows: cost: Gailey and Fenton, 51;
scarcity: Poor Inquiry, App. E, 40; F, 4;
W. Jones, 20; Wakefield, I, 501.
Description of loy: ibid., 504.
Waiting for horse: Reid, 155.
Description of hopeful laborers: Wood,
70.
Workers crossing to England: Kalm, 82.
Lazy beds: described: Edwards and
Williams, 101–2; Trench, 81; labor for:
Young, *Ireland*, I, 346; term derived:
Bourke, 66; drainage: McCulloch, I,
516; drainage late: Gailey and Fenton,
51; frost: K. H. Connell, "The History
of the Potato," *Economic History
Review*, 2d ser., 3 (1951), 389.
Yields: Poor Inquiry, App. E, 2; App. F, 4,
8, 20, 28.
Wakefield's 5.5 pounds: Wakefield, II, 714.
The Poor Inquiry said it was that or
more. See App. E, 1, 2, 16, 18, 28.
One farmer's abundance: Wakefield,
I, 450.
Potatoes vs. meat: debilitating food:
Wakefield, I, 519; "good beef": ibid.,
579; meat seldom eaten: Luckombe,
19; Young's dissent: Young, *Ireland* II,
43.

Irish Apple: ibid., I, 38, 63; Edwards and
Williams, 103;

Salaman, 162.

The rich ate them hot: Plumtre, 47; Wakefield, II, 782.

Colcannon: stolen ingredients: Wood,
212; Young, *Ireland* I, 64; in the United
States: Leslie, 187.

Cobbledy: O'Sullivan, 46; "by no means":
Inglis, II, 195.

Boiled potatoes an Irish specialty: Acton,
301.

By the 1740s: Connell, *Population*, 128–29.

Pigs didn't eat them: Cullen, 152.

Famine of 1729: Salaman, 252; Swift:
Swift, 2094–95; Wakefield, II, 6.

Famine of 1741: freeze: Wakefield, I, 222;
villages gone: J. C. Beckett, *The Making
of Modern Ireland 1603–1923* (New York,
1966), 174; death toll: Grigg, 117.

Late-ripening oats: Cullen, 171.

Young heard the Apple lasted: Young,
Ireland, I, 63.

Diet in Mayo: Pococke, 87; Young, *Ireland*,
I, 247, 256.

"Increased 20 fold": Young, *Ireland*, I, 53.

Stirabout: Plumtre, 368; Young, *Ireland*,
I, 151.

Meat in Ireland: in diet: Young, *Ireland*,
I, 92; "common Irish": Luckombe, 19;
exports: Cullen, 157; inferior pig:
Edwards and Williams, 109; exports
rose: Foster, 201; cottagers' pigs:
Young, *Ireland*, I, 64, 79, 91, 294;
"haven't they": Bicheno, 32; Inglis,
I, 39; clergyman in bed: Pococke, 7;
docile hogs: Wakefield, I, 354; European custom: Babeau, 25; Caird, 389;
Chevalier, 484; Nadaud, 32; welcome
sight: Inglis, I, 79.

Argument for prosperity: See, for example, Foster, 197–205.

Emigration: summer 1727: Wakefield, II,
6; pattern, figures: Foster, 216; uneasiness: Young, *Ireland*, II, 56; "linen
trade": ibid., I, 120; so many ships:
M'Robert, 146.

Rundale: described: Edwards and
Williams, 110–11; Wakefield, I, 260;
advantages: Connell, *Population*, 77;
"little children: BPP/HCSP, *Report
from Her Majesty's Commissioners of
Inquiry into the State of the Law and
Practice in Respect to the Occupation of
Land in Ireland*, 1845 (hereafter Devon
Commission), XIX, Part I, 140; vanish-
ing by 1845: Edwards and Williams,
113; "barbarous": Trevelyan, 240.

Potatoes and fertility: Wales: G.
Markham, 254, note 24; "and an heir":
q. Bourke, 17; "it's the praties": de la
Tocnaye, 145; Malthus: Malthus, 36.

Wedding fees: ibid., 64; Wakefield, II, 579,
690; clerics objected: Connell, *Population*, 80–81.

Attitude to children: desired: Young,
Ireland, II, 120; "noble trait": Wakefield, II, 804; "extreme love": Thackeray, 228; economics: Wakefield, II,
691.

"A landlord in Ireland": Young, *Ireland*,
II, 54.

Four-fifths of the population: ibid., I, 159.

Penal Laws: William Butler, *Sir William*

Butler: An Autobiography (London, 1911), 8; Connell, *Population*, 84; "Reflections on the State of Ireland," 65; evasion: Foster, 205.

Whiteboys: "lawless ruffians": Luckombe, 83–84; before 1800: Beames, 26.

Rural Ireland's influence: Goldstrom and Clarkson, 32.

Marriage: "solace": Luckombe, 154; Kerry: Wakefield, II, 764; "humiliated Catholic": Malthus, 63; other cases: Inglis, I, 217.

Early marriages unusual: See, for example, Michael Drake, "Marriage and Population Growth in Ireland, 1750–1845," *Economic History Review* 16, 2 (Dec. 1963), 311; Grigg, 138; Mokyr and Ó Gráda, 477.

Marriage and population: opinion not uniform: McKeown, 38; "expedient and proper": "Reflections on the State of Ireland," 108; "such a pair": Smith, 90; "respectable societies": Luckombe, xxii; Malthus: Malthus, 36–42.

Chapter Three:
The Better Sort of People

Covent Garden opened: Burton, 73.

Meat eating: "God may send": Boorde, 260; "pottage": ibid., 262; salads: Harrison, 26, 106; recipes: G. Markham, 64; summer feast: Woolley, 315; vegetables healthier: Tryon 23, 158; lettuce, onions: ibid., 153; pepper: Kitchiner, 188; "little nourishment": Graham, 33.

Backyard foraging: G. Markham, 8; "nature:" Harrison, 26.

Praise for artichoke: Bonnefons, 112.

Asparagus liked: Culpeper, 218; Parkinson, *Paradisi*, 468.

Turnip "esteemed": Parkinson, *Paradisi*, 509; introduction: Chambers and Mingay, 56.

Hierarchy among roots: Tryon, 158, 159.

Potato boosters: Royal Society: Salaman, 447; Forster: Safford, 526; "vulgar potadoes": q. Salaman, 448; "many servants": q. ibid., 445.

London mob: Foster, 132.

"Poorer parts": q. Drummond and Wilbraham, 216.

John Hill's herbal: John Hill, *The British Herbal: An History of Plants and Trees . . . Cultivated for Use or Raised for Beauty* (London, 1756), 327.

Meat eating: not like Spain: Defoe, II, 140; Smollett: Smollett, 35, 52; Kalm: Kalm, 14, 85.

Roots as fodder: "no reason": Defoe, I, 48; "good for none": q. Salaman, 478; used: Bailey and Culley, *Cumberland*, 26; Foot, *Middlesex*, 67; endorsed: Wedge, *Chester*, 19.

Young's advice: Arthur Young, *A Six Months Tour Through the North of England* (London, 1770), IV, 147, 158–59.

Middlesex dairy trade: Foot, 83–85.

Ruins soil: Billingsley, *Somerset*, 85; Tuke, *North Riding*, 23.

London-Edinburgh: Pawson, 289; Weber, *Modern Europe*, 448.

Population: Mitchell, *British Statistics*, 26; Pawson, 123.

Britain, Belgium, and the Netherlands: Grigg, 42.

Transportation: "state of Nature": Marshall, II, 131; large wagons: Kalm, 12; "mud and filth": q. Copeland, 11; London mutton: Defoe, III, 251; fish: ibid., 253–54.

Lancashire: "inestimable root": Aikin, 18–19; by 1680: J. Burton, 75; lobscouse: Salaman, 454; roads: John Francis, *A History of the English Railway, Its Social Relations and Revelations, 1820–1845* (London, 1851), I, 27; pack-horses: Copeland, 12; canal building: Aikin, 112; canal barges: Pawson, 22; Frodsham: Aikin, 46; Wedge, *Chester*, 19–20; second crop: ibid., 18.

London and Cornwall: *LH*, Feb. 27, 1795.

Curl: Lancashire: Salaman, 179; pushes breeders: ibid., 161; experts suspected: Granger, *Durham*, 49; Parmentier, 63.

Work hours: Birmingham: W. Thomson, 16; general: Holyoake, I, 8; Rule, 56, 60.

"Offensive, dark, damp": Aikin, 192.

Hiring ovens: Holyoake, I, 16; Wells, 29.

Nottinghamshire garden plots: Wells, 21.

"A most important auxiliary": Aikin, 204.

Scurvy: Budd: Drummond and Wilbraham, 268; Smollett's thoughts: Smollett, 242; Admiralty: Chadwick, 12; potato not accepted: Drummond and Wilbraham, 470.

Bread: and geography: W. Stern, 183; Londoners: Kalm, 88; praised: Boorde, 261; Tryon, 145; who ate what: Harrison, 96; laws: Garnier, *Landed*, 322.

Shortage: harvests: J. M. Stratton, *Agricultural Records A.D. 220–1968*, Ralph Whitlock, ed. (London, 1969), 91–97; meat prices: Chambers and Mingay, 113; famine argument: Wells, 1; violence: *LH*, April 10, 24, 1795; "indiscreet tampering": Burke, 120; free market: ibid., 135–37; Board's "Hints": *LH*, Feb. 27, 1795; potato subsidy: Wells, 202.

Times (London) and: recipes: July 11, 13, 1795; "most noble": July 19, 1795; "God forbid": Aug. 30, 1795; barley: Jan. 7, 1796; mixed loaf: July 31, 1795; not cheaper: Aug. 13, 1795; bakers: Jan. 7, 1796; king cuts back: July 22, 1795; upper classes: July 28, 30, 1795; refusal to legislate: Dec. 14, 1795; March 2, 1796; "less rigour": July 19, 1795; advises readers: July 16, 1795; stretching meat: Oct. 20, 1795.

Workhouses and hospitals: W. Stern, 182.

Glasse's recipes: Glasse, 30, 227, 231, 232, 241, 258.

French potatoes sometimes bitter: Roze, 128.

Certain districts: Board of Agriculture, *Lincoln*, 144.

Claim about most farmers: Garnier, *Landed*, 253.

Chapter Four: *Vive la Pomme de Terre*

Harvest yields: Goubert, 130.

Figures on famines: Braudel, 384; Weber, *Modern*, 194.

Cause and result of famines: Goubert, 129–31.

De Serres's mistake: Salaman, 129–30.

Early potato: "vile and gross": Roze, 123; "silk intestines": Gottschalk, II, 4; improved yields: Roze, 97; *pomme de terre*: Salaman, 134; reached Paris: Roze, 121.

Diet of rich: Gottschalk, II, 2–3, 6; asparagus: ibid., 5.

De Combles's views: q. Roze, 128, 130.

Ways of cooking potatoes: ibid., 130.

Opposition: Irish merchants: Cullen, 159; late dates: Labbé, 26–27; Roze, 159–61, 194–96.

Not enough cultivars: Braudel, 271.

"A rule to be well observed": Bonnefons, 137.

Twelve cultivars: Parmentier, 38–44.

Rumors: Turgot: Roze, 160; Faculté de Paris: ibid., 147; Parmentier: Parmentier, iii, 15, 297.

Others object: Diderot: Denis Diderot, ed., *Grande Encyclopédie* [1765] (Stuttgart, 1966), XIII, 4; digestion: Gottschalk, II, 269; animal food: Michel Morineau, "The Potato in the Eighteenth Century," in *Selections from the Annales: Économies, Sociétés, Civilisations*, Robert Forster and Orest Ranum, eds. Elborg Forster and Patricia M. Ranum, trans. (Baltimore, 1979), V, 24; gourmet objects: Gottschalk, II, 196; agriculturist: Roze, 131.

Bread: color: Baroli, 174; Bouet and Perrin, 32; Chevalier, 215; Brittany: Bouet and Perrin, 32; cross: Chaleil, 147; Guérin, 140; Vincenot, 351; crumbs: Cressot, 63; Vincenot, 348; proverbs: Weber, *Peasants*, 135; baking: Deffontaines, 79; Weber, *Peasants*, 136; "the knife": q. Poitou, 176; "like tile": Mayaud, 161; *tremper*: Nadaud, 93; "soup makes the man": Weber, *Peasants*, 131.

Bouillie: vogue: Gottschalk, II, 20; moderation: Thicknesse, II, 98, 165; Brittany: Bouet and Perrin, 268; Norman view: Guérin, 135; Mâconnais: Tardieu, 97–98.

Climate in the Pyrenees: Chevalier, 239.

Dauphiné: deserted hamlets: Deffontaines, 78; brush, dung: Weber, *Peasants*, 136; *veillées*: Deffontaines, 79; hardscrabble: Garavel, 82.

Potatoes said to sap the soil: Parmentier, iii.

Meaning behind recipe names: Desnoues, 17.

Dauphiné wheat thought inferior: Gottschalk, II, 17.

Potato in the Pyrenees: Chevalier, 214–216, 237, 240.

Fuel scarcity: ibid., 525–26; Thicknesse, I, 292.

Not every area: The Champagne lacked fuel but wasn't known for potatoes, whereas the heavily forested Ardennes had them, maybe by 1750. See Deffontaines, 79; Labbé, 27.

Famine in Naples: Salaman, 446.

Potato and scrofula: Roze, 146.

Prussians resisted: "neither smell nor

taste": q. Salaman, 115; servants near the Elbe: Braudel, 270.

Russian peasants resisted: Langer, 54.

Parmentier: "perpetual object": Parmentier, 21; in army: Cuvier, 166; 40 years: ibid., 176; personal passion: Parmentier, 5, 12; 15,000 pages: Desnoues, 48; "fire": Young, *France*, 90; 20 dishes: Parmentier, 285; Louis's flower: Cuvier, 175; Parmentier's ruse: Parmentier, 12; too much theory: Young, *France*, 137.

Commission listens: France, *Commission des subsistances*, 187–91.

"He'll make us eat potatoes": Cuvier, 177.

The medal caused trouble: Desnoues, 48.

The Republican Cook: Christian Guy, *Histoire de la gastronomie en France* (Paris, 1985), 58.

Napoleonic era: Benoiston de Châteauneuf, 42; rose fifteenfold: Jean-Claude Toutain, *Le produit de l'agriculture française de 1700 à 1958* (Paris, 1961), Part I, 94.

Chapter Five: The Democratic Table

"Let us eat potatoes": John Adams, *Familiar Letters of John Adams and His Wife Abigail Adams During the Revolution* (New York, 1876), 40.

Washington and Jefferson: Wilson, 342.

Bermuda handed on the potato: Hawkes, *Potato*, 39.

Penn: William Penn, "A Further Account of the Province of Pennsylvania and Its Improvements for the Satisfaction of Those That Are Adventurers, and Inclined to Be So," *Pennsylvania Magazine of History and Biography* 9, 1 (1885), 69; "brave increase": ibid., 74.

Londonderry legend: Edward L. Parker, *The History of Londonderry: Comprising the Towns of Derry and Londonderry, N.H.* (Boston, 1851), 37, 48.

Permanent crop: Wilson, 334. Though I differ with Wilson here, her research has strongly informed my own.

Dreaming of potatoes: Chandlee, 111.

Potato's spread: Chester: "Original Letters and Documents," *Pennsylvania Magazine of History and Biography* 5, 3 (1881), 350; coastal Maine: Robert Hale, "Journal of a Voyage to Nova Scotia Made in 1731 by Robert Hale of Beverly," Essex Institute, *Historical Collections* 42, 3 (1906), 222; Poughkeepsie, NY: Filkin, 2; Salem, MA: John Preston, "Extracts from the Diary of Lieut. John Preston, of Salem Village," Essex Institute, *Historical Collections* 9 (1872), 257; Narragansett clergyman: Wilson, 337; New Sweden: Israel Acrelius, *A History of New Sweden or the Settlements on the River Delaware*, William M. Reynolds, ed., Historical Society of Pennsylvania, *Memoirs* (Philadelphia, 1874), XI, 150; Kittery, ME: Wilson, 340; Portland, ME: ibid., 337.

"Of so rank a taste": q. ibid., 335.

"Table potatoes" and "hog potatoes": ibid., 336.

"Spanish Petatoes": Lane, 77.

Potato's influence: overstated: William Douglass, *A Summary, Historical and Political . . . the British Settlements in North-America* (London, 1760), I, 123; Hechtlinger, 31; Virginia: *Virginia Gazette* (Williamsburg), Dec. 8, 1752; "tators": William Calk, "The Journal of William Calk, Kentucky Pioneer," Lewis H. Kilpatrick, ed., *Mississippi Valley Historical Review* 7, 4 (1920–21), 366; *tater*: Salaman, 139; Dartmouth: Wilson, 343; *Boston Gazette*: Mar. 13, 1775, 4; rations: Samuel Bixby, "Diary of Samuel Bixby," Massachusetts Historical Society, *Proceedings* (Boston, 1876), 286; Rhode Island: Rhode Island, *Records of the Colony of Rhode Island and Providence Plantations in New England*, John Russell Bartlett, ed. (Providence, 1862), VII, 531; "daily proportion": Library of Congress, *Journals of the Continental Congress, 1774–1789* (Washington, 1905), III, 383.

Deane and Eliot: Samuel Deane, *The New-England Farmer; or Geographical Dictionary*, 3rd ed. (Boston, 1822), 345; Jared Eliot, *Essays Upon Field Husbandry in New England and Other Papers, 1748–1762*, Harry J. Carman and Rexford G. Tugwell, eds. (New York, 1934), 113.

Potato barter: Filkin, 5; Maine Historical Society, *Collections*, 2nd ser., *Documentary History of the State of Maine*, James Phinney, ed. (Portland, 1910), XIV, 285; see also: Griffith, 59; Bradbury Jewell, *The Fishbasket Papers: The Diaries, 1768–1823, of Bradbury Jewell . . .* , Marjory Jane Harkness, ed. (Peterborough, NH, 1963), 105, 230.

"Universal use": A. Simmons, 10; garnish: ibid., 17.

Irish population figure: Foster, 216.

Reverence for meat: Cummings, 14; "fashion": Hulbert, 63; Saint-Méry: Moreau de Saint Méry, *Moreau de St. Méry's American Journey, 1793–1798*, Kenneth Roberts and Anna M. Roberts, trans. and eds. (New York, 1947), 155; Philadelphia diet: ibid., 265.

"Hardly to be expected": Hulbert, 137.

Digestibility of corn: M. Duhamel-Dumonceau, *A Practical Treatise on Husbandry . . . Valuable Observations*, John Mills, trans. (London, 1759), 285.

"The blast": Cummings, 14; Wilson, 338; wheat black: L. Jones, 58.

Potassium carbonate: A. Simmons, xiii.

Sweet potato: Cummings 11; Joe Gray Taylor, *Eating, Drinking and Visiting in the South* (New Orleans, 1982), 38.

Lane's shortages: Lane, 64, 68.

Not for trough: Buck, 113; Griffith, 72; William Thiel, "Diary of William Thiel of Oregon," *Umpqua Trapper* 13, 2 (1977), 45.

Population densities: Bureau of the Census, *Historical Statistics of the United States* (Washington, D.C., 1975), I, 8; Mitchell, *British Statistics*, 8–9.

Abundance: "scarce an house": "Original Letters," 350; James Birket: q. Hechtlinger, 31.

Simmons: A. Simmons, 11–15.

Glasse: "lower sort": Glasse, iii; role for vegetables: 205.

For "all Grades of Life": A. Simmons, xiii.

English visitors: Mair, 83; M'Robert, 146, 166.

Cobbett's views: Cobbett, *Year's Residence*, 38, 148–49.

Day laborers ate well: q. Sherrill, 80.

"Plain, coarse and primitive": L. Jones, 40.

"An ugly weed": Mair, 81; leeks in milk: L. Jones, 58.

Young Philadelphian: Chandlee, 112; iron pot: ibid., 58.

Forks only for carving: Sherrill, 106.

People who lacked forks: Fenton and Kisban, 45–46.

Mrs. Trollope's observations: F. Trollope, 18.

Garlic better medicine than food: A. Simmons, 12.

"Overworked condition": q. Hechtlinger, 229.

Chapter Six:
He Would Rather Be Hanged

Cobbett's attacks: "the fashion": *Year's Residence*, 124; "slovenliness": *Cottage Economy*, 58; well-being: *Rural Rides*, I, 18; *Year's Residence*, 130, 131; Raleigh: *Rural Rides*, II, 40; "be hanged": ibid., 285.

"I despise the man": Cobbett, *Cottage Economy*, 7.

Enclosure: described: Chambers and Mingay, 49–50; a fourth of land: Mingay, *Rural Life*, 12; wheat imports:

Garnier, *Landed*, 236; open fields: Chambers and Mingay, 49–50; food prices: ibid., 79; rents double: J. Bright, 58; Garnier, *Landed*, 403; 2,000 acts: Mingay, *Rural Life*, 12; advantages: ibid., 12–13; drawbacks: Chambers and Mingay, 97–98; Caird on rates: Caird, 514.

Allotments: "angles and corners": *LH*, Feb. 27, 1795; Norfolk, Bedford, Rutland: Crutchley, *Rutland*, 19; Kent, Norfolk, 46; Stone, *Bedford*, 69; north vs. south: Burnett, in Mingay, ed., 557; "steal": *Sixth Report of the Medical Officer of the Privy Council, Appendix No. 6: Report by Dr. Edward Smith on the Food of the Labouring Classes, 1863* (hereafter *Sixth Report*), 235; Dorsetshire: Caird, 72; Oxfordshire: ibid., 29.

Bread consumption: *Sixth Report*, 241.

Corn Laws: theory: Chambers and Mingay, 123; Garnier, *Landed*, 403; effect unclear: Burnett, *Plenty and Want*, 6; Mingay, *Rural Life*, 26–27.

Farmers allow grain: *Sixth Report*, 240.

Food in shops: Wells, 21.

"Perfectly tormenting": Cobbett, *Cottage Economy*, 127.

Cost of bread: Salaman, 540.

"One week under another": Arch, 78.

Employer owned the shop: Hawker, 2.

More frequent pay: *Sixth Report*, 264.

"No hope": Arch, 13; Corn Laws: ibid., 10.

Oxfordshire allotments: Thompson, 7, 14, 16.

Potatoes and relief: Chambers and Mingay, 97.

Healthiest diets: ibid., 137; Burnett, in Mingay, ed., 557.

Issues of life: Burnett in Mingay, ed., 554.

Wiltshire diet, 1843: ibid., 556.

Smith's survey: parameters: *Sixth Report*, 291; potato consumption: ibid., 242; importance: ibid., 242–43; meat a luxury: ibid., 246; laborer's meat: ibid., 249.

"Half a pig": Thompson, 11.

Old practice: Burnett, in Mingay, ed., 557; Mingay, *Rural Life*, 85.

Fuel, oven lacking: Burnett, *Plenty and Want*, 2; baking lasted: Burnett, in Mingay, ed., 557; *Sixth Report*, 239.

Fuel: expense: Thompson, 19; colder houses: Mingay, *Rural Life*, 84; free coals: Arch, 8; "expensive": Caird, 85.

Game Code: critics: ibid., 408–9; J. Cobbett, 240; Kalm, 143; La Rochefoucauld, 212; Tuke, *North Riding*, 96; Sherwood Forest: Christopher Thomson, *The Autobiography of an Artisan* (London, 1847), 301; poaching: Chambers and Mingay, 138; "foragers": Cobbett, *Rural Rides*, I, 26; Reading: Chadwick, 338; wood chips: Arch, 148; two sticks: ibid., 150–51; "Old widow": Hawker, 20.

Women not baking: Cobbett, *Cottage Economy*, 64; *Sixth Report*, 239.

"The worst thing": La Rochefoucauld, 43.

Housing design: ventilation: Chadwick, 85, 86, 97; model cottages: ibid., 327; "garnished hovels": Arch, 41; Thompson's houses: Thompson, 2–3, 14.

Boarding in: fading before 1750: Kalm,

206; Smith saw: *Sixth Report*, 254; "abundant nutriment": Burke, 125; sold more: Burnett, in Mingay, ed., 555; no bargaining power: Grigg, 174; Norfolk farmer: Kent, *Norfolk*, 54; Devon farm: *Sixth Report*, 254; farmers object: Garnier, *Annals*, 312; social pretensions: Chambers and Mingay, 19; in Darbyshire: Caird, 395; Lancashire: Grigg, 174.

Potato supports family: Billingsley, *Somerset*, 81–82.

"Not only acquiesced in": *Sixth Report*, 249.

Gissing's version: Gissing, 364.

Naysayers: "considerable scorn": q. Garnier, *Annals*, 306; "potato-fed": q. J. Bright, 66; Buckinghamshire: Caird, 9, 14; Francatelli: Francatelli, 187, 196, 269, 281.

Tuber's rise: "invaluable root": Graham, 34; "wholesome": Plumtre, 368; "prudent families": William Stuart, *The Potato: Its Culture, Uses, History and Classification* (Philadelphia, 1923), q. 379; "two million": q. Burnett, *Plenty and Want*, 8; London consumption: Dodd, 376; London trade: ibid., 387.

Farm healthier: Woods and Woodward, 54.

"The dissolute": Marshall, I, 50.

"Neatness, cleanliness": Aikin, 220.

"A great error to suppose": Cobbett, *Rural Rides*, II, 31.

England more urban: McKeown, 82; Mennell, 223.

A quarter of working males: Mennell, 222.

"Air of discomfort": Kay-Shuttleworth, 28.

"Meanest comforts": *Conditions of Work and Living*, 14, 51.

Engels on Manchester: Engels, 54, 55, 60, 63.

Evangelical slant: Chadwick, 29–30.

Cheap building materials: Hartwell, 50.

Liverpool health code: Woodham-Smith, 273.

"Scanty culinary apparatus": Kay-Shuttleworth, 29.

"A saucepan or cup": William Lovett, *The Life and Struggles of William Lovett, in His Pursuit of Bread, Knowledge and Freedom* (London, 1876), 71.

Mayhew on Spitalfields: Mayhew, *Chronicle*, I, 53, 96.

A "respectable butcher": Chadwick, 197.

Manchester butchers and diseased meat: Engels, 68.

People toured: Christian Guy, *La vie quotidienne de la société gourmande au XIXe siècle* (Paris, 1971), 73.

"Chemical laboratory": Dodd, 512.

Five pounds for utensils: Burnett, *Plenty and Want*, 143.

Wages rose 60 percent: Mingay, *Rural Life*, 22.

"One kettle, one frying-pan": Reeves, 56.

Saturday nights at coalyard: Holyoake, I, 22.

York coal dealer: Rowntree, 109.

Lambeth rich spent less: Reeves, 22.

London dwellings crowded: Booth, XVII, 9.

"Coarse food": Kay-Shuttleworth, 25.

Birmingham doctors: Chadwick, 205; "ignorance": ibid., 309.

"Want of discretion": q. Burnett in Mingay, ed., 556.

Soyer's advice: Morris, 80; "black saucepans": ibid., 51.

Forty-four thousand cooks: Burnett, *Annals of Labour*, 138.

Bouillabaisse and pot-au-feu: Burnett, *Plenty and Want*, 144.

Until ten o'clock at night: Hawker, 1.

Young pottery worker: Burnett, *Annals of Labour*, 302.

Home manufactures of Birmingham: Holyoake, I, 10–11.

Power weavers more numerous: Burnett, *Annals of Labour*, 234.

Mill hours: Rule, 57.

Female workers: Burnett, *Annals of Labour*, 34, 68.

Bread: budget: Johnston, 20; London preference: Dodd, 167, 204; white bread: Johnston, 26; per capita: ibid., 22.

Manchester workers' lunch: Kay-Shuttleworth, 23.

Engels notes diet: Engels, 72.

"Animal food": Mayhew, *Chronicle*, I, 62; "never taste": ibid., 58.

London diet around 1900: Booth, IX, 428.

"Thoughtless extravagance": Chadwick, 205.

Sunday soup or roast: Burnett, *Plenty and Want*, 21.

Rushed shopping: Burnett, *Annals of Labour*, 303; Chadwick, 313; Engels, 68; Holyoake, I, 22.

Leeds manufacturer: Chadwick, 311–12; paying groups: ibid.

"Rolls and cheese": q. Burnett, *Annals of Labour*, 303; children eating: ibid.

"Little savoury knick-knacks": Dodd, 517–18.

Baked potato trade: "'tato man": ibid., 517–18; 300 vendors: Mayhew, *London Labour*, 173–74; renting oven: Holyoake, 16; Wells, 29; potato cans: Mayhew, *London Labour*, 173; "improvement": ibid., 174; "great brown": Salaman, 597.

Chapter Seven: A Fortress Besieged

"Landlords first get": Luckombe, 19.

"The great object": Senior, I, 1.

Eight thousand landlords: Mokyr, 16.

No laborer could refuse: Young, *Ireland*, II, 54.

"Less ceremony": Wakefield, II, 773.

"Poor below the law": Bourke, 72.

Landlords' neglect: "pest of society": Young, *Ireland*, II, 155; "been spoiled": Bicheno, 137; lavish hospitality: Inglis, II, 82; receivership: Goldstrom and Clarkson, 135; "intellect, knowledge": Smith, 56 (italics orig.); Jones: W. Jones, 8, 18–19, 112; "requires alteration": BPP/HCSP, *Report from Her Majesty's Commissioners of Inquiry into the State of the Law and Practice in Respect to the Occupation of Land in Ireland*, 1845 (hereafter Devon Commission), XIX, Part I, 15; country houses: Inglis, I, 13, 185.

Style copied: avoid wages: Pim, 61; better off: Devon Commission, XX, Part II, 60, 86, 161, 185; XXI, Part III, 12; "a horror": ibid., XIX, Part I, 181; inheritance: W. Jones, 18–19; "permanent interest": McCulloch, I, 517; "lowest ranks": Smith, 142.

Middlemen the middle class: Inglis, I, 57, 82.

"The traveller in Ireland": de Beaumont, I, 262. See also Senior, II, 9; Thackeray, 344.

The peasant without land: de Beaumont, I, 299.

"The poor would rather lose their lives": BPP/HCSP, *First Report of Commissioners for Inquiring into the Condition of the Poorer Classes in Ireland*, 1836 (hereafter Poor Inquiry), XXXIII, Appendix F, 56.

"In my neighborhood": Devon Commission, XX, Part II, 229.

Spalpeen: "pigstie": Young, *Ireland*, II, 40; county Tyrone: Reid, 201; derivation: Thomas Crofton Croker, ed., *Popular Songs of Ireland*, coll. Henry Morley (London and New York, 1886), 17.

"No bribe will tempt": Wood, 244.

Marriage, land: "few men": Poor Inquiry, XXXIII, App. F, 35; county Waterford: ibid., 28; showed leases: Devon Commission, XX, Part II, 224; "if I now" ibid., 35; "how they exist": ibid., 38.

Fortress under siege: de Beaumont, I, 299.

"If a man thinks": Devon Commission, XX, Part II, 266.

Subdivision and misery: Poor Inquiry, XXXIII, App. F, 43.

Rack-renting middlemen: Devon Commission, XIX, Part II, 139; XX, Part II, 60, 122, 128.

Population density: per square mile: Edwards and Williams, 89; Connacht: Mokyr, 19; Leinster: ibid.; average: Edwards and Williams, 89.

Wiggins on high rents: Devon Commission, XX, Part II, 36–37.

Whiteboys: Beames, 197, 211–13.

"Working for a dead horse": Wakefield, I, 253.

Famines: 1817, 1822: Crawford, 17, 19; work for food: Reid, 239; "heaven only knows": ibid., 264; seaweed: Royle, 45; death tolls: Ó Gráda, 12; less severe: Stuart Daultrey, David Dickson, and Cormac Ó Gráda, "Eighteenth-Century Irish Population: New Perspectives from Old Sources," *Journal of Economic History* 41, 3 (1981), 628; Ó Gráda, 121; Mokyr, 7; "enormous price": Wood, 45; autumn rains: Royle, 45.

Tendency to degenerate: Berkeley, 18; Goodrich, 108; McCulloch, II, 514; Trevelyan, 278; Wakefield, I, 446.

Seed balls: Parmentier, 127.

"Latent germ of disease": Osborne, 224.

Estimated 65,000 farms: Edwards and Williams, 92.

Bourke's calculations: Bourke, 52–53.

"Potatoes in the morning": q. Ó Gráda, 14.

"It frequently happens": Poor Inquiry, XXXII, App. E, 8.

Same or similar conditions: ibid., 3; App. F, 4, 10, 11, 29.

The Apple kept one year: Ó Gráda, 15.

Lumper: wider use: Poor Inquiry, XXXII, App. E, 7; from Scotland: Bourke, 25; relative yield: Poor Inquiry, XXXIII, App. F, 8; outperformed others: Ó Gráda, 87; less manure: Bicheno, 142; "coarsest": Trevelyan, 232; disliked: Ó Gráda, 87; "our gentry": q. Edwards and Williams, 103; "never believe them": Poor Inquiry, XXXII, App. E, 3; Apples would help: ibid., 7.

Meal months: potatoes bad: ibid., 28; Bicheno, 21; "yellow month": O'Sullivan, 92; mustard seed: Poor Inquiry, XXXII, App. E, 9; shortages: ibid., 23, 28; county Wicklow: ibid., 23; other hardships, 3, 17, 18, 19, 20.

Gombeen system: described: Bennett, 7; excesses: Poor Inquiry, XXXII, App. E, 10, 20, 23, 28, 29; agents Catholic: Bourke, 72.

Potato-and-milk diet: Luckombe, 19; de la Tocnaye, 117; Young, *Ireland*, I, 213, 256, 294, 369; ridiculed: Cullen, 158; McKay, 92.

Peas and beans disappear: O'Sullivan, 53.

Wakefield on Connacht: Wakefield, II, 751; Wexford: ibid., I, 408; bread: ibid., I, 622, II, 766; salted herring: ibid., II, 766; "leaving the bone": ibid., I, 450.

Even a casual observer: Malthus, 65. Malthus was a casual observer in that he got his information secondhand.

Oatmeal and buttermilk: Plumtre, 368. Plumtre was a casual observer in the more conventional sense.

"Bull's milk" and hard praties: Reid, 204.

"Sour milk" and cheese as luxury: Bicheno, 17, 19.

Buttermilk as affluence: Inglis, I, 33, II, 297.

Farmers not "rolling in plenty": ibid., I, 47.

Consumption: Poor Inquiry, XXXII, App. E., 1, 2, 16, 18, 28.

Meat and eggs: ibid., 1, 2, 8, 10, 18, 20, 23, 28; buttermilk "a treat": ibid., 1; milk lacking: ibid., 28.

"In many districts": Devon Commission, XIX, Part I, 35; testimony: XX, Part II, 288, 380; XXI, Part III, 67, 178; potatoes and salt fish: XX, Part II, 152, 161.

Milk expensive: Cullen, 149.

County Donegal cows: Young, *Ireland*, I, 174.

Cow in dowries: Devon Commission, XX, Part II, 266.

Pigs: shipped overseas: Inglis, I, 130; pork-potato link: Wood, 51; statistics: Grigg, 125; prosperity: Bennett, 6; de Beaumont, I, 267; Whiteboys spared: Beames, 79.

Dietary habits: two meals: de Beaumont, I, 267; Devon Commission, XXI, Part III, 67; nicknames: Edwards and Williams, 392; "I am happy": Nicholson, 30.

For the well-off: meat: Cullen, 147; more bread: Inglis, I, 63; O'Sullivans' diet: O'Sullivan, 93; meat-buying: ibid., 47, 68; see also Inglis, II, 314.

Potato as investment capital and money: Pim, 124.

Jones describes truck system: William Jones, 5–6.

Working off the rent: Devon Commission, XX, Part II, 171; Malthus, 38; Poor Inquiry, XXXIII, App. F, 10; Wakefield, I, 245, 507.

Wages lower with food: Devon Commission, XX, Part II, 106; XXI, Part II, 67.

Unemployment: rate: ibid., XIX, Part I, 9; would-be workers: W. Jones, 31; Nicholson, 192; Reid, 239; Thackeray, 39; Wood, 70; regular work desired: Devon Commission, XIX, Part I, 12; Inglis, I, 33; Thackeray: Thackeray, 30–31.

"A commercial speculator": Society of Friends, 9.

Conacre: described: Poor Inquiry, XXXIII, App. F, 8; Wood, 54; rents: Devon Commission, XX, Part II, 34, 83, 106; lower for cash: XXI, Part III, 67; competition: Poor Inquiry, XXXIII, App. F, 30; "life and death": Pim, 54; high offers: Devon Commission, XIX, Part I, 15, 146; XX, Part II, 60; Inglis, I, 58; de la Tocnaye, 127; "worse off": Devon Commission, XX, Part I, 182.

Reckless marriage: Poor Inquiry, XXXIII, App. F, 10, 20, 28.

"Unmitigated evil": Devon Commission, XX, Part II, 344.

"Species of savings bank": Poor Inquiry, XXXIII, App. F, 20.

"Take the country": Reid, 158.

Conacre's advantages: ibid., 9, 11, 20, 29, 30.

Farmer pays labor: ibid., 10; servants profit: ibid., 9, 10.

Grain never a staple: ibid., XXXII, App. E.,

5, 8, 18, 20.; "a rood": ibid., 8; storing meal: ibid., 28; lack kiln: ibid., 9; rickstand: ibid., 17; granaries: ibid., 19; oven, ibid., 28.

More enlightened critics: Society of Friends, 9.

Queen Victoria's charge: Devon Commission, XIX, Part I, 3.

Insecurity discouraging: ibid., XX, Part II, 61, 117, 288, 380; XXI, Part III, 64; an excuse: XIX, Part I, 129, 182; XX, Part II, 152; urges remedy: XIX, Part I, 17; English custom: ibid., XX, Part II, 253.

Unscrupulous agents: ibid., XIX, Part I, 22.

Estate steward anecdote: Poor Inquiry, XXXII, App. E, 20.

Racking the tenantry: ibid., XXXIII, App. F, 38, 43, 70.

County Cork middleman: Devon Commission, XXI, Part III, 14.

Absenteeism: turmoil: ibid., XX, Part II, 61; good agent: ibid., 370; high absenteeism: Ó Gráda, 124; difference to laborer: Bourke, 70.

Examples of profligate landlords: Ó Gráda, 29.

Estates legally frozen: Devon Commission, XIX, Part I, 102.

Jones's absentee forbears: W. Jones, 97; obstacles to improvement: ibid., 20; friend lost: ibid., 30.

"Certainly as wild": Devon Commission, XX, Part II, 24.

Lord Monteagle: q. Edwards and Williams, 92.

Backward habits: division: Devon Commission, XIX, Part I, 139–40; XX, Part

II, 122; turnips: Smith, 50–51; green crops: Devon Commission, XIX, Part I, 267; XX, Part II, 152, 167, 195; paring and burning: Ó Gráda, 122.

Whiteboys: classic victim: Beames, 130, 138; stop improvement: Devon Commission, XX, Part II, 117; witnesses diverge: Poor Inquiry, XXXIII, App. F., 40, 47; condemn violence: Devon Commission, XIX, Part I, 42.

English manufacturers: Mokyr, 259. I am indebted to Joel Mokyr for this argument.

Property insurance rates: Ó Gráda, 333.

"A landlord who should attempt": McCulloch, I, 378.

Violent, fractious, unruly: Boorde, 132. Boorde's remarks in 1549 are merely old examples of a common stereotype.

John Wiggins's testimony: The relevant portions are Devon Commission, XX, Part II, 32–37.

Chapter Eight: A Passion for Thrift

Gascar's memoirs: Gascar, 92, 94, 96, 97, 98, 108–9.

Farm employment, 1906: Dupâquier, et al., 255; Mennell, 222.

"Solidity": Vidal de la Blache, 386.

Famine stories: Haute-Marne: Cressot, 75; Gard: Chaleil, 91; Mâconnais: Weber, *Peasants*, 130.

Young on sharecroppers: Young, *France*, 297.

Sharecropping covenants: Guillaumin, 95.

Selling grain cheap and buying dear: Houssel et al., 193.

Nivernais inquiry: G. Thuillier, 515.

Living on credit all winter: Grafteux, 14.

"Worked almost like serfs": Grenadou and Prevost, 10–11.

Land let you live: Cressot, 11.

Census of farm wages: Block, 38.

Mazières wages, prices: Thabault, 57; cattle price: ibid.

French leases: Houssel et al., 167.

Lack of care: Young, *France*, 21, 286.

Sickle yields to scythe: Houssel et al., 174.

"It's a principle of mine": Guillaumin, 95.

Peasant ownership: Babeau, 27; Houssel et al., 124.

Young's views on buying land: Young, *France*, 284, 297.

Héritage: Vidal de la Blache, 384.

"A few feet of vineyard": Jules Michelet, *The People*, trans. John P. McKay (Urbana, IL, 1973), 31.

"Nourishing mother": Vidal de la Blache, 386.

Movable goods, real estate: Houssel et al., 104.

Home ownership: Weber, *Peasants*, 156.

Land ownership: Block, 23–24.

Trading labor: Houssel et al., 151.

Ownership concentration, 1826: ibid., 144.

Farm sizes in France, England: Block, 29, 31.

Tiennon and Victoire: Guillaumin, 70.

Wedding customs: Limousin: Corbin, I, 63; Mâconnais: Tardieu, III; Mazières:

Thabault, 116; Puy-de-Dôme: Sylvère, 5; Gard: Chaleil, 94.

Victoire's duties: Guillaumin, 106; women's work: ibid., 72.

Breton women like baking: Bouet and Perrin, 172.

Cottages dark: lack windows: Young, 31; Breton homes: Bouet and Perrin, 138; clasps poor: Weber, *Peasants*, 157–59; (see Smollett, 43, about 18th-century Boulogne); hard to see: Bouet and Perrin, 138; Mayaud, 168; Poitou, 172; A. Thuillier, 401.

Hemp oil cheaper: Weber, *Peasants*, 161.

Hollowed-out potato lamp: Sylvère, 4.

First saw electricity: Chalon, 47.

Hearths light, heat: Chalon, 11; Poitou, 174; Tardieu, 74.

Hearth in Nord: Pierrard, *Nord*, 51.

Fuel: peat: J. Cobbett, 240; coal, marl: Pierrard, *Nord*, 51; smelled like death: Grafteux, 19; precious: Cressot, 71, 78; Mistral, 61; lice in Gard: Chaleil, 92–93.

Animals in houses: Babeau, 25; Chaleil, 84; Chevalier, 484; Nadaud, 32; Pierrard, *Nord*, 48.

Fire: woman's first task: Chaleil, 85; damping: Cressot, 73; borrowing embers: Chaleil, 93; hard to light: Cressot, 73; sign of competence: ibid., 71.

Home size: upper floor: Pierrard, *Nord*, 48; large room: Poitou, 174; Sion, 472; see also Guillaumin 92–93; Thabault, 46; Solognat ceilings: Poitou, 172; Breton ceilings: Bouet and Perrin, 138; *la maison*: Grenadou and Prevost, 11–12.

Marriage: Young, *France*, 278; work ethic: ibid., 299.

Eating one's fill: Rey, 25.

No scorn for poor: Chaleil, 94.

Peas, beans: Houssel, et al., 175; Mazières: Thabault, 174.

Famine of 1812–13 in Morvan: G. Thuillier, 53.

Contemporary comments: Benoiston de Châteauneuf, 42; France, *Commission des subsistances*, 393, 680–99.

Potato production statistics: Block, 60–61.

Reclaiming land: France, *Commission des subsistances*, 190.

Proverbs about appetite: q. Weber, *Peasants*, 131, 135.

Home economies: sweeteners: Chaleil, 95; vinegar: Thabault, 56; purchases: Rey, 69; matches taxed: Tardieu, 75; coffee: Pierrard, *Nord*, 65; Grafteux, 10; farm tools wooden: Thabault, 57.

Clothes: from the land: Chaleil, 95; Cressot, 209; Garavel, 82; Poitou, 180; Thabault, 54; colors: Grenadou and Prevost, 12; hempen clothes: Cressot, 209; wedding shawl: Nadaud, 123; different Masses: Guillaumin, 39.

Kitchen equipment in a cupboard: Sylvère, 5.

Tables in the Gard: Chaleil, 95.

Communal *marmite*: ibid., 89; dishes scarce: Thabault, 54.

Forks in Finistère: Weber, *Peasants*, 164.

Soup: Mâconnais diet: Tardieu, 101; Brittany breakfast: Bouet and Perrin, 50; spoons: Brékilien, 81; Berry breakfast: J. Cobbett, 141; Limousin breakfast: Corbin, I, 61; Tiennon's breakfast: Guillaumin, 7; Puy: Sylvère, 95; couldn't make soup: Weber, *Peasants*, 131.

Potato in soup: Brittany: Brékilien, 83; Gard: Chaleil, 89; Vaucluse: Chalon, 44; Cévennes: Rey, 21; Mâconnais: Tardieu, 101.

Cheese, eggs: Limousin omelet: Corbin, I, 59; Nivernais butter: G. Thuillier, 52; egg in coffee: Grafteux, 10, 12; Gard, Vaucluse: Chaleil, 89; Chalon, 42; homemade cheese: Cressot, 63; Rey, 69; Mâconnais eggs: Tardieu, 104–5.

Meat: rendered beef fat: Guérin, 133; Rouen laborers: Sion, 457; Flaubert: Gustave Flaubert, *Madame Bovary* (Paris, 1971), 31; Tiennon and Victoire: Guillaumin, 7, 32; Martin Nadaud: Nadaud, 67; Creusois masons: Armengaud, 27; Franche-Comté: Mayaud, 161; Sologne: Poitou, 177; Mazières: Thabault, 169; Cévennes: Rey, 20, 52; Haute-Marne: Cressot, 53–54.

Bread: Brittany: Bouet and Perrin, 172; Tiennon's ruse: Guillaumin, 113–14; "devourers": Cressot, 77 locking cupboard: Chevalier, 215; rationing: Chaleil, 90; Gascar: Gascar, 94, 96.

Potato feeds the pig: Parmentier, 6.

Forest foraging fees: Alexandre Tollemer, *Un sire de Gouberville: gentilhomme campagnard au Cotentin de 1553 à 1562* [1872] (Paris, 1972), 393–95.

Pig husbandry declines: Braudel, 273.

Viard's recipes: André Viard, *Le cuisinier impérial*, 15th ed. [1837] (Paris, 1975), 384–87; Urbain Dubois and Emile Bernard, *La cuisine classique* (Paris, 1856).

Lower-class recipes: Chaleil, 89; Chalon, 42; Corbin, I, 55, 65; Parmentier, 234; Pierrard, *Nord*, 68; Tardieu, 105; Thouvenot, 55; G. Thuillier, 52.

Inviting a guest: Chaleil, 147.

Bucket of potatoes: Weber, *Peasants*, 134.

"By means of cookery": Young, *France*, 262–63.

How Lille workers lived: Pierrard, *Lille*, 84, 85, 87, 204.

Parisian diet: Benoiston de Châteauneuf, 41, 42.

Coffee in Lille: Pierrard, *Lille*, 87, 206; rest of diet: ibid., 204, 207, 208.

Diet in Nord: Pierrard, *Nord*, 68, 69, 74, 98.

Census of textile workers: Block, 141.

Girls and home work: Nord: Grafteux, 12–15; Cévennes: Rey, 14, 47.

France that spoke no French: Weber, *Peasants*, 67.

James Cobbett's conclusions: J. Cobbett, 87, 177.

Potato production: in 1817: Benoiston de Châteauneuf, 67–68; fraction of arable: Houssel et al., 177; largest yield: Block, 60–61.

Crisis of late 1840s: rural violence: Agulhon et al., 78; potato losses: Block, 60; reliance on grain: Agulhon et al., 140;

price rises: Houssel et al., 232; Morvan: A. Thuillier, 98; corn, buckwheat: Baroli, 177; Agulhon et al., 141; demography: Armengaud, 28, 31.

Chapter Nine:
The Lumpers They Were Black

Potato blight: rapid pace: Large, 13–14; Lindley: q. ibid.; symptoms: *IN*, Sept. 13, 1845; smell: Trench, 83–84.

Correspondent's report: *LT*, Oct. 16, 1845; similar reports: q. Woodham-Smith, 91.

Shortages one year in three: Royle, 44.

How people survived 1845: Ó Gráda, 189.

Blight potato toll in 1846: Bourke, 174.

"The first downfall": q. Edwards and Williams, 393.

Snow and harsh winter: Woodham-Smith, 142–43.

Cholera: Edwards and Williams, 306.

Jones on upheaval: W. Jones, 5.

Ripple effect: Society of Friends, 52–53.

Food prices: ibid., 145; Nicholls, 349; Smith, 108.

Bennett's descriptions: roads to Dublin: Bennett, 5; livestock in Kerry: ibid., 122; pigs and dogs: ibid., 6, 31; no seeds: ibid., 94.

Carlyle on lack of trade: Carlyle, 114.

Desolation: "I know not": Osborne, 22; 482 families: ibid., 23; land untilled: ibid., 35; "smoking ruins": Wilde, 73. See also Senior, I, 321–22; Smith, 204.

"Novel and refreshing sight": Bennett, 52.

Percent who escaped: Crawford, 233.

"Language utterly fails": Bennett, 26.

Letter to Wellington: James Carty, ed., *Ireland: A Documentary Record*, vol. 2, *Ireland from Grattan's Parliament to the Great Famine* (Dublin, 1949), q. 172.

Workhouse scenes: Leitrim: Society of Friends, 146; Glenties without food: ibid., 150; following March: Bennett, 62; Ballina: Society of Friends, 198; Armagh: Bennett, 89.

Carlyle on crowds: Carlyle, 145; "sad enough": ibid., 176.

Smith on travelers: Smith, 246.

Shopkeepers and corpses: Trench, 95.

Death toll: Phelim P. Boyle and Cormac Ó Gráda, "Fertility Trends, Excess Mortality, and the Great Irish Famine," *Demography* 23, 4 (1986), 555.

Emigration and 1911 population: Grigg, 132.

Social ties weaken: "natural affection": Pim, 72; west: ibid., 73; watch crop: ibid., 120; thievery, countermeasures: Edwards and Williams, 402; good samaritans: ibid., 306.

Hospitality: open door: Nicholls, 206; Wakefield, II, 776; leftovers saved: Edwards and Williams, 393; "a bold" man: Nicholls, 182; inviting curse: Bicheno, 251; door shut: Edwards and Williams, 399; "did not eat aright": ibid., 402; legends of charity rewarded: ibid., 405.

Desperate measures: dead animals: ibid., 402; Aran limpets: Bennett, 72; roots and nuts: Edwards and Williams, 399; other vegetables: ibid.; Erris turnips: Trevelyan, 272; no fish in Wicklow: Edwards and Williams, 401.

Fishing and potato subsistence: Wakefield, II, 129.

Rough seas: BPP/HCSP, *Report from Her Majesty's Commissioners of Inquiry into the State of the Law and Practice in Respect to the Occupation of Land in Ireland*, 1845, XIX, Part I, 221.

Curragh: construction: Pococke, 64; Wood, 354; calm waters: Society of Friends, 148.

Infrastructure lacked: Ó Gráda, 148; railroads: Woodham-Smith, 290.

"With food almost in sight": Society of Friends, 148.

Religious strife: committees: Edwards and Williams, 240; missionaries: ibid., 258; insults: ibid., 410; sermons: ibid.; slang: ibid., 411.

Victoria's prayer: q. Salaman, 314.

"Special hand of God": Trench, 84; Soyer: Morris, 80.

Wasteful acts earn wrath: Edwards and Williams, 395.

Despair a mortal sin: BPP/HCSP, *First Report of Commissioners for Inquiring into the Condition of the Poorer Classes in Ireland*, 1836 (hereafter Poor Inquiry), XXXII, Appendix E, 8.

Emigration: numbers: Kinealy, 298; "able and calculated": Bennett, 53.

"Banks of the Ganges": Wakefield, I, 408.

"It is difficult indeed": Malthus, 42.

Famine didn't discourage marriage: Ó Gráda, 216.

Solar's study: Crawford, 117.

Famine's severity unexpected: Ó Gráda, 189.

Hoping reports were exaggerated: Pim, 67.

Books on the famine: See the relevant essays in Edwards and Williams (1957); for entire works, see Kinealy (1995); Mokyr (1983); and Woodham-Smith (1962).

Poor Law: differs from England's: Crawford, 158; larger unions: Society of Friends, 16; capacity: Smith, 38.

Thought Ireland would go broke: Crawford, 159.

Landlords paying two ways: Society of Friends, 17.

"Relief should be made": Trevelyan, 314.

Famine relief history: 1799–1801: Royle, 44; Gregory's warning: ibid., 45; public works: ibid., 46.

Opinions on Poor Law: Munster observer: Bicheno, 253, 261, 268; Kay-Shuttleworth: Kay-Shuttleworth, 45, 83; Nicholls: 163, 166, 167, 177.

Times (London) broadside: Oct. 18, 1845.

Beggars: Thackeray, 36; Nicholson, 46, 49.

Trevelyan's article: on public works: Trevelyan, 255–56; "principle article": ibid., 233; caused poverty: 310; "agrarian code": 232; not civilized: ibid., 231.

Obsessed by work: Trollope: Anthony Trollope, *The Three Clerks* [1858] (London, 1907), 60; "obviate the evils":

Trevelyan, 231; work and Ireland: ibid., 318.

"All-wise and all-merciful Providence": ibid., 320.

McCulloch, Osborne agree: McCulloch, II, 514; Osborne, 224. See also Smith, 102.

Ideas not new: Even Alfred Smee, a surgeon, had described Ireland in much the same terms in 1846. Smee, 160.

Oppression held back effort: Bicheno, 21; Society of Friends, 47; Inglis, I, 343; "Reflections on the State of Ireland," 95; Wakefield, I, 85.

Presumed laziness: "national character:" W. Jones, 14; explains poverty: McCulloch, I, 514; worked abroad: Bennett, 142; Caird, 284; de la Tocnaye, 117; Senior, I, 46; Trevelyan, 317; preferred diversions: Nicholls, 163; "punch and a pipe": Smith, 21; work would benefit: Kohl, 96; "patient and persevering": Pim, 28.

A familiar image: Inglis I, 41, and Senior I, 47.

"If an Irishman feels": Luckombe, 153.

"Animal wants": Wakefield, I, 262; "finer feelings": II, 67.

"Miasma" theory: Chadwick, 62.

Kay-Shuttleworth: attacks Irish: Kay-Shuttleworth, 21, 28–29; cause of disease: ibid., 29; teach poor: ibid., 98. Life expectancy: Ó Gráda, 22; in Manchester: Chadwick, 247.

Theory of infection: Large, 17.

"Banishing the potatoe": Chadwick, 247.

"All bulbous roots": Wakefield, I, 446.

"Hereditary fault": Osborne, 224.

Lindley's theory: moisture: Large, 14–15; "perfectly satisfied": q. Berkeley, 8.

Competing theories: electricity, manure, etc.: Berkeley, 18; Smee's aphid: Smee, 91; Reed's aphid: A.G. Wheeler, Jr., "The Tarnished Plant Bug: Cause of Potato Rot?" *Journal of the History of Biology* 14, 2 (1981), 326.

Goodrich: "diminished vitality": Goodrich, 108; explains blight: ibid., 115, 116, 119; divine plan: ibid., 127.

Infected tubers and blight: Bourke, 30.

Trevelyan and laissez-faire: famine a local concern: Trevelyan, 312–13; self-reliance: ibid., 319.

Burke on charity: Burke, 129.

Trevelyan's letter: *LT*, Oct. 12, 1847; out-cry: *LT*, Oct. 13, 1847.

Trevelyan as policymaker: India: Wood-ham-Smith, 415; serving government: Bourke, 173.

Walking miles for meal: Bennett, 34; Trevelyan, 254.

Bennett's views: Bennett, 146.

Friends dislike public works: Society of Friends, 14.

Smith's ambivalence: Smith, 105, 108.

Carlyle's views: Carlyle, 179.

Scotland: excess mortality: Ó Gráda, 180; small scale: Salaman, 375.

Famine in the Netherlands: M. Bergman, "The Potato Blight in the Netherlands and Its Social Consequences (1845–1847)," *International Review of Social History* 12, 3 (1967), 391, 399, 413, 417, 422, 425; Ó Gráda, 180.

Nicholson on hopelessness: Nicholson, 182.

Jones on poverty: W. Jones, 31.

Friends on relief work: Society of Friends, 68.

Famine spending vs. Crimean War: Kinealy, 295, 351; Mokyr, 292; Ó Gráda, 176. Mokyr was the first to raise this.

Reagan's family history: Associated Press, Nov. 1, 1980.

Chapter Ten: Potatoes and Population

To treat typhus: Wilde, 103.

Fifteen percent every decade: Mitchell, 8.

Irish population estimates: q. Mokyr and Ó Gráda, 475.

Comparing marriage rates: Mitchell, 4, 8, 92, 93, 95, 99.

McKeown's theory: low mortality: McKeown, 35–38; smallpox: ibid., 12; other diseases: ibid., 92, 97–110; diet: ibid., 129–32; potato: ibid., 132.

Farm output: J. V. Beckett, *The Agricultural Revolution* (Oxford, 1990), 67; Chambers and Mingay, 3; Hartwell, 76.

Nutrition didn't lower mortality: Grigg, 63, 166.

Medicine played role: Woods and Woodward, 34, 66.

Food adulterations: Arthur Hill Hassall, *Food: Its Adulterations, and the Methods for Their Detection* (London, 1876), 248, 325, 348, 453.

Nutrition versus disease: Crawford, 205.

High-birthrate theories: See Connell, *Population*; Daultrey et al. (cited in chapter two); Joseph Lee, "Marriage and Population in Pre-Famine Ireland," *Economic History Review* 21, 2 (1968), 283–95; Goldstrom and Clarkson; and Mokyr and Ó Gráda. The latter two authors have also discussed the subject in their own books.

Mokyr and Ó Gráda on birthrate: Mokyr and Ó Gráda, 479; on death rate: ibid., 483–84.

Potato as sustainer: See Connell, *Population*, 242.

Low mortality: See Drake (cited in chapter two).

Crawford's mortality statistics: Crawford, 206.

Unreliability of cause of death: McKeown, 50.

Osborne reported deaths from dysentery: Osborne, 53.

Typhus and food: lack strength for hygiene: Edwards and Williams, 271; pawning clothes: Bicheno, 36; Reid, 264; Cape Clear: Kohl, 102.

"Exceedingly prevalent": q. Crawford, 207–8; deaths from scurvy: ibid., 209.

Chapter Eleven: Women's Work

Lydia Moxley: daily chores: Moxley, 277, 280, 286; butter sales: 278; hired hands: 286; Anson's chores: 277, 284.

Beecher on kitchens: Mrs. H. W. Beecher, 94; "learn what constitutes": ibid., 320.

The table: Cobbett: Cobbett, *Year's Residence*, 38; "plain good food": Burlend and Burlend, 60; "dependent laborers": Gustorf, 49; "no country": C. Beecher and Stowe, 167; Abbie Bright: A. Bright, 237, 414. See also F. Trollope, 116.

Orchards with plentiful fruit: Griffith, 67.

Corn: importance: Cummings, 15; Thomas K. Wharton, "From England to Ohio, 1830–1832: The Journal of Thomas K. Wharton," James H. Rodabaugh, ed., *The Ohio Historical Quarterly* 65, 2 (1956), 123; corn cakes: F. Trollope, 298; "kneaded pin-cushion": Dickens, 158; Illinois diet: Gustorf, 48.

Salt pork: Koren's diet: Koren, 100, 228; "musty and rancid": Billings, 137; mining camps: Borthwick, 169; "hain't got strength": q. Cummings, 16.

Potato a standby: in trunk: Cormany and Cormany, 85; vital: A. Bright, 409; Burlend and Burlend, 86; Cormany and Cormany, 89; Joseph Heath, *Memoirs of Nisqually*, Lucille McDonald, ed. (Fairfield, WA, 1979), 37, 50; Mitchell Young Jackson, "Making a Farm on the Frontier: Extracts from the Diaries of Mitchell Young Jackson," comp. Solon J. Buck, *Agricultural History* 4, 3 (1930), 106; Koren, 239; Works Project Administration (hereafter WPA), I, 7, 111, 189; III, 150.

Mining camps: "Potatoes and onions": Borthwick, 57; gold in Idaho: Davis and Stillwell, 12.

Civil War ration: lobscouse: Billings, 118; rations: ibid., 111; from sutler: Cormany and Cormany, 276; Army of Northern Virginia: Carlton McCarthy, *Detailed Minutiae of Soldier Life in the Army of Northern Virginia 1861–65* (Richmond, 1882), 57, 63; packing: Billings, 234, 238.

Green vegetables: salads: Sutherland, 71; tomatoes: Cummings, 36; French visitor: Huard, 153; rarity: Cummings, 20; urban diet: Strasser, 16.

Boardinghouses: Dickens: Dickens, 68; Whitman: Whitman, 96, 99; Homestead example: Byington, 138; "deformed beefsteak": Dickens, 61; "luxurious living": Leng, 243.

Beechers on diet: C. Beecher and Stowe, 127, 130, 132; "condiments": 131. See also Kitchiner, 223.

Mustard, hot pepper: Huard, 153; McCord, 235.

Sample menus: q. Hechtlinger, 62–64, 106–8, 183–85, 254–55.

Urban diet: New York: Chapin, 274–75; Homestead: Byington, 63–64.

"Farinaceous articles": C. Beecher and Stowe, 133.

Homestead budget: overcharging: Byington, 75; getting by: ibid., 79; forgoing heat: ibid., 86. There were similar problems in New York; see Chapin, 132, 248.

Liking for potatoes: Bolsterli, 48; Cormany and Cormany, 458; Koren, 293; Haskell, 93; Moxley, 283; "almost instinctive": Arnold Lorand, *Health and Longevity Through Rational Diet* (Philadelphia, 1913), 234; not overused: q. Hechtlinger, 228; leftovers: Isabel Gordon Curtis, *Mrs. Curtis's Cook Book* (New York, 1909), 163; menus: q. Hechtlinger, 62–64, 106–8, 183–85, 254–55.

Potato production statistics: Goodrich, 104.

Early Rose: popularity: Mary Cone, *Two Years in California* (Chicago, 1876), 111; Thompson, 58; longevity: McIntosh, 17; and Burbank: Davis and Stillwell, 20, 24.

Breakfast: "pork steaks": Griffith, 90; other foods: Cormany and Cormany, 139; Leng, 243; Hechtlinger, 130; McCord, 235; Sutherland, 55: Muncie: Lynd and Lynd, 158.

Potatoes at breakfast: Cobbett: Cobbett, *Rural Rides*, I, 179; sign of poverty: Cullen, 175; "person unused": Wood, 42; cookbooks, magazines: *The Home-Maker* 5, 3 (1890): 267; Leslie, 185; luxury liner: Leng, 15; hotel fare: ibid., 267–68.

"Hotel Life": ibid., 38.

Potato chip: origin: William S. Fox and Mae G. Banner, "Social and Economic Contexts of Folklore Variants: The Case of Potato Chip Legends," *Western Folklore* 42, 2 (1983), 114; Godey's: *Godey's Lady's Book*, July 1865, 79; packaging: John C. Bishop and Manisha Perera, "Potato Chip Industry: Cottage to Factory," *Essays in Economic and Business History* 9 (1990), 183.

Labor-saving devices: Strasser, 33.

Rural houses, kitchens: Illinois: Burlend and Burlend, 47, 49; "a skellit": ibid., 59; Koren's houses: Koren, 100, 102, 187, 227; waterlogged stove: ibid., 240; skillet, Dutch oven: A. Bright, 262–63; rolling pin: ibid., 265.

Urban housing: midcentury New York: Whitman, 99; in 1909: Chapin, 115–16, 132, 273–74; luxury: E. G. Stern, *My Mother and I* (New York, 1918), 64; Muncie: Lynd and Lynd, 97; Homestead: Byington, 53, 56.

Housekeeping burden: Burlend's trial: Burlend and Burlend, 89–92; Koren's friend: Koren, 141; cook, maid, and housekeeper: Svendsen, 28; Garland: Garland, 138–39, 156; Washington settler: WPA, II, 24–25. See also: Bolsterli, 31; Haskell, 93, 96; Lynd and Lynd, 97; Angus McDonald, *Old Mc-Donald Had a Farm* (Boston, 1942), 63; WPA, III, 149, 153.

Men design tools: "obstinate": Mrs. H. W. Beecher, 115; "sinful drudgery": *The Home-Maker* 4, 2 (1890): 139–40.

Stove: patents: Hechtlinger, 39; coal use: Strasser, 41; gains, losses: C. Beecher and Stowe, 59–60; Ruth Schwartz Cowan, *More Work for Mother: The Ironies of Household Technology from the Open Hearth to the Microwave* (New York, 1983), 61–62; Strasser, 36; expense no obstacle: see, for example, Svendsen, 53.

Money for household: Svendsen: Svendsen, 99; journalist's complaint: *The Home-Maker* 4, 2 (1890): 139–41.

"Life sentence of hard labor": q. Lynd and Lynd, 169.

"Don't 'founder' yourselves!": Garland, 102.

Cook's friend: Moxley, 287; potato a standby: Bolsterli, 43, 48; Haskell, 97, 98; in Homestead: Byington, 64.

Americans eating fast: Cobbett: Cobbett, *Year's Residence*, 158; "greatest possible rapidity": F. Trollope, 47; "people eating decently": Gustorf, 114; "dull and languid": Dickens, 158; San Francisco: Borthwick, 77; Indianapolis: McCord, 203.

Americans all business: "vast counting-house": Dickens, 27, 249; "full head of steam": Borthwick, 77; "full speed": Leng, 218–19, 317–18; "bolting of food": ibid., 269.

Garland's harvest lunch: Garland, 150.

"Fifty times better": *The Home-Maker* 2, 3 (1889): 214–15.

French table habits: silence, eating slowly: Baroli, 175; Brékilien, 74; Rey, 20; women stood: Baroli, 175, Bouet and Perrin, 275; Chaleil, 89; Mistral, 19; "knocking off": Octave Uzanne, *Le miroir du monde: notes et sensations de la vie pittoresque* (Paris, 1888), 124; "demands of life": Jean-Paul Aron, *The Art of Eating in France: Manners and Menus in the Nineteenth Century*, trans. Nina Rootes (New York, 1975), q. 73.

Americans "ate like horses": Huard, 153.

"Panic in the theater": Maud Younger,

"The Diary of an Amateur Waitress,"
McClure's 28, 6 (1907), 670, 672.

Chapter Twelve:
The Good Companions

Priestland's thoughts: recollections:
Priestland, 17; party conferences: ibid.,
18; "good companions": ibid., 23.
Towns: J. R. Clynes, *Memoirs* (London,
1937), 28, 43–44.
Potato's role: "It's no dinner": Bell, 95;
Lambeth diet: Reeves, 98; per capita
total: Burnett, *Plenty*, 94.
Fried fish: Soyer: Morris, 36; "gin-
drinking": Mayhew, *London Labour*,
I, 166; smell: ibid.
Fried potato: Jefferson: *Economist*, Oct. 13,
1993; Francatelli: Francatelli, 281;
Acton: Acton, 303; Soyer: Walton, 24.
"Half-boiling grease": Reeves, III.
Oldham's tradition: Walton, 25.
Stoves: Walton, 10; peelers: Priestland,
94–95; Walton, 47.
Peeled potatoes a selling point: Priest-
land, 65.
Fishing industry expansion: Walton,
42–43.
Importance: number of shops: Walton, 5;
raw materials: ibid., 7; Smith's survey:
*Sixth Report of the Medical Officer of the
Privy Council, Appendix No. 6: Report by
Dr. Edward Smith on the Food of the
Labouring Classes, 1863*, 249; coal strike:
Walton, 9.
Working-class diet: York: Rowntree, 44;

steel town: Bell, 63, 94; Lambeth:
Reeves, 94, 99, III.
Ill effects: chronic bad health: Drummond and Wilbraham, 488–89; condensed milk: Mingay, *Rural Life*, 86;
infant deaths: Burnett, *Plenty and
Want*, 88; Rowntree, 206; rejection
rate: Drummond and Wilbraham,
484.
Medical ignorance: vitamins: Burnett,
Plenty and Want, 203; enteric fever:
Walton, 13; praise fish: q. ibid.,
151.
Class issues: oil: Priestland, 73; equip-
ment: Walton, 13; "offensive": ibid.;
ethnicity: ibid., 2; chair leg: ibid., 108;
hours: ibid., 85; sensibility: ibid., 137.
Price of meal: Walton, 154.
Poor as spendthrift: "every way wasteful":
Booth, XVII, 207; rebuttals: Bell, 67;
Reeves, 22; Rowntree, 133; shirk re-
sponsibility: Walton, 13.
Pots and pans versus food: Rowntree, 109.
Fuel expense: cooking or light: Bell, 93;
lacking ovens: Reeves, 59; baby's bandage: ibid., 52.
Extravagance: small quantities: Bell,
94–95; storage: Reeves, 110; no knowledge: Gissing, 266; Rowntree, 105;
millhands' wives: Bell, 92; discour-
aged: Reeves, 56.
Trouble with porridge: Reeves, 58.
Press of time: lunchpail: Bell, 92; "pains":
Rowntree, 105; bathing: Reeves, 56;
"no joy": ibid., 112.
Fish and chips as a standby: Walton,
144–45.

Hot weather and tenements: Bell, 95; Booth, XVII, 172.

Farm production: Burnett, *Plenty and Want*, 100–01.

Scurvy outbreak: Walton, 158.

Chapter Thirteen: Good Breeding

Somerville anecdote: Alexander Somerville, *The Autobiography of a Working Man, "By One Who Has Whistled at the Plough"* (London, 1848), 17, 19.

The French and the English: Thicknesse, II, 165.

William Thomson and Birmingham: W. Thomson, 13.

Railway mileage: Jack Simmons, *The Railway in England and Wales, 1830–1914* (Leicester, 1978), I, 271, 276.

Birmingham fish: Dodd, 119.

Selected Bibliography

Acton, Eliza. *Modern Cookery*. 5th ed. London, 1846.

Agulhon, Maurice, Gabriel Désert, and Robert Specklin, *Apogée et crise de la civilisation paysanne, 1789–1914*. Vol. 3 of Duby, George, and Armand Wallon, eds., *Histoire de la France rurale*. Paris, 1976.

Aikin, John. *A Description of the Country from Thirty to Forty Miles Round Manchester*. [1795] New York, 1968.

Arch, Joseph. *Joseph Arch: The Story of His Life, Told by Himself*. 2d ed. London, 1898.

Armengaud, André. *La population française au XIXe siècle*. Paris, 1971.

Babeau, A. *La vie rurale dans l'ancienne France*. Paris, 1885.

Baroli, Marc. *La vie quotidienne en Berry au temps de George Sand*. Paris, 1982.

Beames, Michael. *Peasants and Power: The Whiteboy Movements and Their Control in Pre-Famine Ireland*. New York, 1983.

Beecher, Catharine E., and Harriet Beecher Stowe. *The American Woman's Home: Or, Principles of Domestic Science*. . . . [1869] New York, 1971.

Beecher, Mrs. H. W. *All Around the House; or, How to Make Homes Happy*. New York, 1878.

Bell, Florence. *At the Works: A Study of a Manufacturing Town*. London, 1907.

Bennett, William. *Narrative of a Recent Journey of Six Weeks in Ireland*. London, 1847.

Benoiston de Châteauneuf, Louis François de. *Recherches sur les consommations de tout genre de la ville de Paris en 1817 comparées à ce qu'elles étaient en 1789*. Paris, 1820.

Berkeley, M. J. "Observations, Botanical and Physiological, on the Potato Murrain." [1846] *Phytopathological Classics*, no. 8. East Lansing, MI, 1948.

Bicheno, J. E. *Ireland and Its Economy*. London, 1830.

Billings, John D. *Hardtack and Coffee: The Unwritten Story of Army Life*. [1887] Edited by Richard Harwell. Chicago, 1960.

Bingham, Hiram. *Inca Land: Explorations in the Highlands of Peru*. Boston, 1922.

Block, Maurice. *Statistique de la France comparée avec les divers pays de l'Europe*. 2nd ed. Paris, 1875.

Bolsterli, Margaret Jones, ed. *Vinegar Pie and Chicken Bread: A Woman's Diary of*

Life in the Rural South, 1890–1891.
Fayetteville, AR, 1982.

Bonnefons, Nicolas. *The French Gardiner;
Instructing How to Cultivate....* Translated
by John Evelin. London, 1691.

Boorde, Andrew. *The Fyrst Boke of the
Introduction of Knowledge Made by
Andrew Borde, of Physycke Doctor.* [1549]
Edited by F. J. Furnivall. London, 1870.

Booth, Charles, ed. *Life and Labour of the
People in London.* Vols. 9 and 17. London and New York, 1897 and 1902.

Borthwick, J. D. *The Gold Hunters: A First-
Hand Picture of Life in California Mining
Camps in the Early Fifties.* [1857] Edited
by Horace Kephart. New York, 1917.

Bouet, Alexandre, and Olivier Perrin.
*Breiz-Izel; ou vie des Bretons de l'Ar-
morique.* [1844] Paris, 1970.

Bourke, Austin. *"The Visitation of God"?:
The Potato and the Great Irish Famine.*
Edited by Jacqueline Hill and Cormac
Ó Gráda. Dublin, 1993.

Braudel, Fernand. *The Identity of France.*
Vol. 2, *People and Production.* Translated by Siân Reynolds. New York,
1990.

Brékilien, Yann. Vie quotidienne des
paysans bretons au XIXe siècle. Paris,
1976.

Bright, Abbie. "Roughing It on Her
Kansas Claim: The Diary of Abbie
Bright, 1870-1871." Edited by Joseph
W. Snell. *Kansas Historical Quarterly* 37,
3 (1971): 233-68; 37, 4 (1971): 394-428.

Bright, John. *The Diaries of John Bright.*

Edited by R. A. J. Walling. New York,
1931.

Burke, Edmund. *Thoughts and Details on
Scarcity, ...* In Paul Langford, ed., *The
Writings and Speeches of Edmund Burke,*
vol. 9, edited by R. B. McDowell. Oxford, 1991.

Burlend, Rebecca, and Edward Burlend. *A
True Picture of Emigration.* [1848] Edited
by Milo Milton Quaife. New York, 1968.

Burnett, John, ed. *Annals of Labour: Auto-
biographies of British Working-Class People
1820–1920.* Bloomington, Indiana, and
London, 1974.

——. "The Country Diet." In *The Victorian
Countryside,* edited by G. E. Mingay.
Vol. 2. London, 1981.

——. *Plenty and Want: A Social History of
Diet in England from 1815 to the Present
Day.* London, 1966.

Burton, John. "Introduction of the
Potato in Ireland and England."
Health Education Journal 21 (1963):
71–78.

Byington, Margaret F. *Homestead: The
Households of a Mill Town.* [1910] New
York, 1969.

Caird, James. *English Agriculture in 1850–51.*
2nd ed. Edited by G. E. Mingay. London, 1968.

Carlyle, Thomas. *Reminiscences of My Irish
Journey in 1849.* London, 1882.

Chadwick, Edwin. *Report on the Sanitary
Condition of the Labouring Population of
Great Britain.* [1842] Edited by M. W.
Flinn. Edinburgh, 1965.

Chandlee, Benjamin. "Two Letters of Benjamin Chandlee." Edited by Olive Goodbody. *Quaker History* 64 (Autumn 1975): 110–15.

Chapin, Robert Coit. *The Standard of Living among Workingmen's Families in New York City*. New York, 1909.

Chaleil, Leonce. *La mémoire du village: souvenirs recueillis par Max Chaleil*. Paris, 1977.

Chalon, Marie-Thérèse. *Une vie comme un jour*. Paris, 1976.

Chambers, J. D., and G. E. Mingay. *The Agricultural Revolution 1750–1850*. London, 1966.

Chevalier, Michel. *La vie humaine dans les Pyrénées ariègeoises*. Paris, 1956.

Cieza de Leon, Pedro de. *The Incas of Pedro de Cieza de Leon*. Translated by Harriet de Onis. Edited by Victor Wolfgang von Hagen. Norman, OK, 1959.

Cobbett, James Paul. *A Ride of Eight Hundred Miles in France*. 2d ed. London, 1824.

Cobbett, William. *Cobbett's Cottage Economy*. 19th ed. London, n.d.

——. *Rural Rides*. [1832]. 2 vols. [1853] London, 1957.

——. *A Year's Residence in America*. [1818] London, n.d.

Cobo, Bernabe. *History of the Inca Empire*. [1653] Translated and edited by Roland Hamilton. Austin, TX, 1979.

——. *Inca Religion and Customs*. [1653] Translated and edited by Roland Hamilton. Austin, TX, 1990.

Coles, William. *The Art of Simpling; an Introduction to the Knowledge and Gathering of Plants . . .* [1657] Milford, CT, 1938.

Connell, K. H. *The Population of Ireland 1750–1845*. London, 1950.

Copeland, John. *Roads and Their Traffic 1750–1850*. Newton Abbot, England, 1968.

Corbin, Alain. *Archaisme et modernité en Limousin au XIXe siècle, 1845–1880*. 2 vols. Paris, 1975.

Cormany, Samuel E., and Rachel Cormany. *The Cormany Diaries: A Northern Family in the Civil War*. Edited by James C. Mohr and Richard E. Winslow III. Pittsburgh, 1982.

Crawford, E. Margaret, ed. *Famine: The Irish Experience 900–1900*. Edinburgh, 1989.

Cressot, Joseph. *Le pain au lièvre*. [1943] Paris, 1973.

Cullen, L. M. *The Emergence of Modern Ireland 1600–1900*. London, 1981.

Culpeper, Nicholas. *The Complete Herbal; To Which Is Now Added, Upwards of One Hundred Additional Herbs, with a Display of the Medicinal and Occult Qualities*. [1653] London, 1805 [?].

Cummings, Richard Osborn. *The American and His Food: A History of Food Habits in the United States*. rev. ed. Chicago, 1941.

Cuvier, Georges. *Recueil des éloges historiques*. Vol 2. Paris, 1819.

Davis, James W., and Nikki Balch Stilwell. *Aristocrat in Burlap: A History of the Potato in Idaho*. Boise, ID, 1977.

De Beaumont, Gustave. *Ireland: Social, Political, and Religious.* Edited by W. C. Taylor. 2 vols. London, 1839.

Deffontaines, Pierre. *L'Homme et la forêt.* Paris, 1933.

Defoe, Daniel. *A Tour Thro' Great Britain 1742.* Edited by Samuel Richardson. 4 vols. New York and London, 1975.

Desnoues, Lucienne. *Toute la pomme de terre.* Malesherbes, 1978.

Dickens, Charles. *American Notes and Pictures from Italy.* [1842] [1867] London, 1957.

Dodd, George. *The Food of London.* London, 1856.

Drummond, J.C., and Anne Wilbraham. *The Englishman's Food.* London, 1939.

Edwards, R. Dudley, and T. Desmond Williams, eds. *The Great Famine: Studies in Irish History 1845–52.* New York, 1957.

Engels, Friedrich. *The Condition of the Working-Class in England in 1844.* Translated by Florence Kelley Wischnewetzky. London, 1892.

Fenton, Alexander, and Eszter Kisban, eds. *Food in Change: Eating Habits from the Middle Ages to the Present Day.* Edinburgh, 1986.

Filkin, Francis. *Account Book of a Country Store Keeper in the 18th Century at Poughkeepsie.* Poughkeepsie, 1911.

Foster, R. F. *Modern Ireland: 1600–1972.* London, 1988.

Francatelli, Charles Elmé. *Francatelli's The Modern Cook.* [1846] Edited by Daniel V. Thompson. New York, 1973.

France, Ministère de l'Instruction Publique. *La commission des subsistances de l'an II, procès-verbaux et actes. Collection de documents inédits sur l'histoire économique de la révolution française.* Paris, 1924.

Gailey, Alan, and Alexander Fenton, eds. *The Spade in Northern and Atlantic Europe.* Belfast, 1970.

Garavel, J. *Les paysans de Morette: un siècle de vie rurale dans une commune du Dauphiné.* Paris, 1948.

Garland, Hamlin. *A Son of the Middle Border.* New York, 1919.

Garnier, Russell. *Annals of the British Peasantry.* London, 1895.

——. *History of the English Landed Interest.* Vol. 2. London, 1893.

Gascar, Pierre. *Terres de mémoire.* Paris, 1980.

Gissing, George. *The Nether World.* [1889] New York, 1929.

Glasse, Hannah. *The Art of Cooking Made Plain and Easy.* [1796] Wakefield, England, 1971.

Goldstrom, J. M., and L. A. Clarkson, eds. *Irish Population, Economy, and Society: Essays in Honour of the Late K. H. Connell.* Oxford, 1981.

Goodrich, Chauncey E. "The Potato—Its Diseases—With Incidental Remarks on its Soils and Culture." *Transactions of the New York State Agricultural Society* 23 (1863): 103–34.

Gottschalk, Alfred. *Histoire de l'alimentation et de la gastronomie, depuis la préhistoire jusqu'à nos jours.* 2 vols. Paris, 1948.

Goubert, Pierre. *La vie quotidienne des*

paysans français au XVIIe siècle. Paris, 1982.

Grafteux, Serge. *Mémé Santerre*. Paris, 1975.

Graham, Thomas John. *Sure Methods of Improving Health and Prolonging Life*. 3d ed. London, 1831.

Grenadou, Ephraim, and Alain Prevost. *Grenadou, paysan français*. Paris, 1966.

Griffith, D., Jr. *Two Years in the New Settlements of Ohio*. [1835] Ann Arbor, MI, 1966.

Grigg, David. *Population Growth and Agrarian Change: An Historical Perspective*. Cambridge, 1980.

Guérin, André. *La vie quotidienne en normandie au temps de Madame Bovary*. Paris, 1975.

Guillaumin, Emile. *The Life of a Simple Man*. Edited by Eugen Weber. Revised translation by Margaret Crosland. Hanover, NH, 1983.

Gustorf, Frederick Julius. *The Uncorrupted Heart: Journal and Letters of Frederick Julius Gustorf 1800–1845*. Edited by Fred Gustorf. Translated by Fred Gustorf and Gisela Gustorf. Columbia, MO, 1969.

Harrison, William. *Elizabethan England: From "A Description of England" by William Harrison (in Holinshed's "Chronicles")*. [1577–87] Edited by Lothrop Withington. London, 1889.

Hartwell, R. M., ed. *The Causes of the Industrial Revolution in England*. London, 1967.

Haskell, Rachel. "A Literate Woman in the Mines: The Diary of Rachel Haskell." Edited by Richard G. Lillard.

Mississippi Valley Historical Review 31 (1944–45): 81–98.

Hawker, James. *James Hawker's Journal: A Victorian Poacher*. Edited by Garth Christian. London and New York, 1961.

Hawkes, J. G. *The Potato: Evolution, Biodiversity, and Genetic Resources*. London, 1990.

Hawkes, J. G., and J. Francisco-Ortega. "The Potato in Spain During the Late 16th Century." *Economic Botany* 46, 1 (1992): 86–97.

Hechtlinger, Adelaide. *The Seasonal Hearth: The Woman at Home in Early America*. Woodstock, NY, 1977.

Holyoake, George Jacob. *Sixty Years of an Agitator's Life*. 2 vols. London, 1909.

Houssel, Jean-Pierre, Jean-Charles Bonnet, S. Dontenwill, R. Estier, and P. Goujon. *Histoire des paysans français du XVIIIe siècle à nos jours*. Roanne, 1976.

Huard, Charles. *New York comme je l'ai vu*. Paris, 1906.

Hulbert, Archer Butler, ed. *Historic Highways of America*, Vol. 12. *Pioneer Roads and Experiences of Travelers*. Vol. 2. Cleveland, 1904.

Inglis, Henry D. *Ireland in 1834: A Journey Throughout Ireland, During the Spring, Summer, and Autumn of 1834*. London, 1834.

Johnston, James P. *A Hundred Years Eating*. London, 1977.

Jones, Louis C., ed. *Growing Up in the Cooper Country: Boyhood Recollections of the New York Frontier*. Syracuse, 1965.

Jones, William Bence. *The Life's Work in*

Ireland of a Landlord Who Tried to Do His Duty. London, 1880.

Kalm, Pehr. *Kalm's Account of His Visit to England: On His Way to America in 1748.* Translated by Joseph Lucas. [1753] London and New York, 1892.

Kay-Shuttleworth, J. P. *The Moral and Physical Condition of the Working Classes Employed in the Cotton Manufacture in Manchester.* 2nd ed. [1832] London, 1970.

Kinealy, Christine. *This Great Calamity: The Irish Famine 1845–52.* Boulder, CO, 1995.

Kitchiner, William. *The Art of Invigorating and Prolonging Life, by Food, Clothes, Air, Exercise, Wine, Sleep, &c.* London, 1824.

Kohl, J. G. *Ireland.* London, 1843.

Koren, Elisabeth. *The Diary of Elisabeth Koren, 1853–1855.* Translated and edited by David T. Nelson. New York, 1979.

Labbé, Max. *Cette étonnante pomme de terre.* Paris, 1988.

Lane, Samuel. *A Journal for the Years 1739–1803.* Edited by Charles Lane Hanson. Concord, NH, 1937.

Langer, W. L. "American Foods and Europe's Population Growth 1750–1850." *Journal of Social History* (Winter 1975): 51–66.

La Rochefoucauld, François de. *A Frenchman in England, 1784.* Translated by S. C. Roberts. Cambridge, 1933.

Large, E. C. *The Advance of the Fungi.* rev. ed. New York, 1962.

La Tocnaye, de Bougrenet de. *A Frenchman's Walk Through Ireland, 1796–7.*

Translated by John Stevenson. Belfast, 1918.

Leng, John. *America in 1876: Pencillings During a Tour in the Centennial Year.* Dundee, 1877.

Leslie, Eliza. *Directions for Cookery in Its Various Branches.* 35th ed. Philadelphia, 1850.

Lovell, Robert. *A Compleat Herball.* Oxford, 1665.

Luckombe, Philip. *A Tour Through Ireland; Wherein the Present State of That Kingdom Is Considered.* London, 1780.

Lynd, Robert S., and Helen Merrell Lynd. *Middletown: A Study in American Culture.* New York, 1929.

McKay, Robert, ed. *An Anthology of the Potato.* Dublin, 1961.

Mair, John. "The Journal of John Mair, 1791." *The American Historical Review* 12, 1 (1906): 77–94.

Malthus, Thomas R. *Occasional Papers of T. R. Malthus on Ireland, Population, and Political Economy.* Edited by Bernard Semmel. New York, 1963.

Markham, Gervase. *The English Housewife.* [1631] Edited by Michael R. Best. Kingston and Montreal, Canada, 1986.

Marshall, William. *Marshall's Rural Economy of the West of England.* [1796] 2 vols. New York, 1970.

Mayaud, Jean-Luc. *Les paysans du Doubs au temps de Courbet.* Paris, 1979.

Mayhew, Henry. *London Labour and the London Poor.* [1851] Vol 1. London, 1967.

———. *The Morning Chronicle Survey of Labour and the Poor: The Metropolitan*

Districts. Vols. 1 and 2. Sussex, England, 1980, 1981.

McCord, Shirley, comp. *Travel Accounts of Indiana 1679–1961. Indiana Historical Collections*. Vol. 47. Indianapolis, 1970.

McCulloch, J. R. *A Descriptive and Statistical Account of the British Empire: Exhibiting Its Extent, Physical Capacities, Population, Industry, and Civil and Religious Institutions*. 3d ed. 2 vols. London, 1847.

McIntosh, Thomas P. *The Potato: Its History, Varieties, Culture and Diseases*. London, 1927.

McKeown, Thomas. *The Modern Rise of Population*. New York, 1976.

Mennell, Stephen. *All Manners of Food: Eating and Taste in England and France from the Middle Ages to the Present*. New York, 1985.

Mingay, G. E. *Rural Life in Victorian England*. London, 1976.

———, ed. *The Victorian Countryside*. Vol. 2. London, 1981.

Mistral, Frederic. *Mes origines: mémoires et récits*. Paris, 1906.

Mitchell, B. R. *British Historical Statistics*. Cambridge, 1988.

———. *European Historical Statistics, 1750–1988*. 3d ed. London, 1992.

Mokyr, Joel. *Why Ireland Starved: A Quantitative and Analytical History of the Irish Economy 1800–1850*. London, 1983.

Mokyr, Joel, and Cormac Ó Gráda. "New Developments in Irish Population History, 1700–1850." *Economic History Review*, 2nd ser., 37, 4 (November 1984): 473–88.

Morris, Helen. *Portrait of a Chef: The Life of Alexis Soyer*. Cambridge, 1938.

Moxley, Lydia. "Times Hard But Grit Good: Lydia Moxley's 1877 Diary." Edited by James Sanders. *Annals of Iowa* 47, 3 (1984): 270–90.

M'Robert, Patrick. "Patrick M'Robert's Tour Through Part of the North Provinces of America." Edited by Carl Bridenbaugh. *Pennsylvania Magazine of History and Biography* 59, 2 (1935): 134–80.

Nadaud, Martin. *Les mémoires de Léonard, ancien garçon maçon*. Paris, 1912.

Nicholls, George. *A History of the Irish Poor Law, in Connection with the Condition of the People*. London, 1856.

Nicholson, Asenath. *Ireland's Welcome to the Stranger; or, An Excursion Through Ireland in 1844 & 1845*. New York, 1847.

Ó Gráda, Cormac. *Ireland: A New Economic History, 1780–1939*. Oxford, 1994.

Osborne, Sidney Godolphin. *Gleanings in the West of Ireland*. London, 1850.

O'Sullivan, Humphrey. *The Diary of Humphrey O'Sullivan, 1827–1835*. Translated by Tomas de Baldraithe. Dublin, 1979.

Parkinson, John. *Paradisi in Sole Paradisus Terrestris, Or, a Choice Garden of All Sorts of Rarest Flowers. . . .* 2nd ed. London, 1656.

———. *Theatrum Botanicum: The Theater of Plants, Or an Herball of a Large Extent*. London, 1640.

Parmentier, Antoine Augustin. *Traité sur*

la culture et les usages des pommes de terres, de la patate, et du topinambour. Paris, 1789.

Pawson, Eric. *Transport and Economy: The Turnpike Roads of Eighteenth Century Britain.* London and New York, 1977.

Pierrard, Pierre. *La vie ouvrière à Lille sous le Second Empire.* Paris, 1965.

——. *La vie quotidienne dans le Nord au XIXe siècle.* Paris, 1974.

Pim, Jonathan. *The Condition and Prospects of Ireland and the Evils Arising from the Present Distribution of Landed Property: With Suggestions for a Remedy.* Dublin, 1848.

Plumtre, Anne. *Narrative of a Residence in Ireland During the Summer of 1814, and That of 1815.* London, 1817.

Pococke, Richard. *Pococke's Tour in Ireland in 1752.* Edited by George T. Stokes. Dublin, 1891.

Poitou, Christian. *Paysans de Sologne dans la France ancienne.* Le Coteau, 1985.

Priestland, Gerald. *Frying Tonight: The Saga of Fish and Chips.* London, 1972.

Reeves, Maud Pember. *Round About a Pound a Week.* 2d ed. London, 1914.

Reid, Thomas. *Travels in Ireland in the Year 1822.* London, 1823.

Rey, Raymonde Anna. *Augustine Rouvière, Cévenole.* 3d ed. Paris, 1977.

Rowntree, B. Seebohm. *Poverty: A Study of Town Life.* 2d ed. London, 1902.

Royle, Stephen A. "Irish Famine Relief in the Early Nineteenth Century: The 1822 Famine on the Aran Islands." *Irish Economic and Social History* 11 (1984): 44–59.

Roze, Ernest. *Histoire de la pomme de terre.* Paris, 1898.

Rule, John. *The Experience of Labour in Eighteenth-Century Industry.* London, 1981.

Safford, William Edwin. "The Potato of Romance and Reality." From the *Smithsonian Report for 1925*, pp. 509–32. Washington, D.C., 1926.

Salaman, R. N. *The History and Social Influence of the Potato.* rev. ed. Cambridge, 1985.

Salmon, William. *Botanologia, The English Herbal; Or, History of Plants.* London, 1710.

Senior, Nassau William. *Journals, Conversations and Essays Relating to Ireland.* 2 vols. London, 1868.

Sherrill, Charles H. *French Memories of Eighteenth-Century America.* New York, 1971.

Simmons, Amelia. *American Cookery.* 1796. Edited by Mary Tolford Wilson. New York, 1958.

Sion, Jules. *Les paysans de la Normandie orientale.* Brionne, 1909.

Smee, Alfred. *The Potatoe Plant, Its Uses and Properties: Together with the Cause of the Present Malady.* London, 1846.

Smith, Elizabeth. *The Irish Diaries of Elizabeth Smith 1840–1850.* Edited by David Thomson and Moyra McGusty. Oxford, 1980.

Smollett, Tobias. *Travels Through France and Italy*. [1766] London and New York, 1907.

Society of Friends, Central Relief Committee. *Transactions of the Central Relief Committee of the Society of Friends During the Famine in Ireland, 1846 and 1847*. Dublin, 1852.

Stern, Walter M. "The Bread Crisis in Britain, 1795–96." *Economica* N.S. 31, 122 (May 1964): 168–87.

Strasser, Susan. *Never Done: A History of American Housework*. New York, 1972.

Sutherland, Daniel E. *The Expansion of Everyday Life, 1860–1876*. New York, 1989.

Svendsen, Gro. *Frontier Mother: The Letters of Gro Svendsen*. Translated and edited by Pauline Farseth and Theodore G. Blegen. New York, 1979.

Sylvère, Antoine. *Toinou: le cri d'un enfant auvergnat, pays d'Ambert*. Paris, 1980.

Swift, Jonathan. "A Modest Proposal for Preventing the Children of Poor People in Ireland from Being a Burden. . . ." [1729] In M. H. Abrams, ed., *The Norton Anthology of English Literature*. 3d. ed. Vol. 1. New York, 1974.

Tardieu, Suzanne. *La vie domestique dans le Mâconnais rural preindustriel. Travaux et mémoires de l'Institut d'ethnologie 69*. Paris, 1964.

Thabault, Roger. *Mon village: ses hommes, ses routes, son école*. Paris, 1944.

Thackeray, William Makepeace. *The Irish Sketch Book: Notes of a Journey from Corn Hill to Grand Cairo*. [1843] *The Works of William Makepeace Thackeray*. Vol. 14. London, 1869.

Thicknesse, Philip. *A Year's Journey Through France, and Part of Spain*. Bath, 1777.

Thompson, Flora. *Lark Rise*. London, 1939.

Thomson, William. *A Tour in England and Scotland in 1785, By an English Gentleman*. London, 1788.

Thouvenot, Claude. *Le pain d'autrefois: chroniques d'alimentaires d'un monde qui s'en va*. Paris, 1977.

Thuillier, André. *Économie et société nivernaise au debut du XIXe siècle*. Paris, 1974.

Thuillier, Guy. *Aspects de l'économie nivernaise au XIXe siècle*. Paris, 1966.

Trench, William Steuart. *Realities of Irish Life*. New York, n.d.

[Trevelyan, Charles E.] "The Irish Crisis: Explanatory of the Measures Adopted by Her Majesty's Government for the Relief of Distress Arising from the Failure of the Potato Crop in Ireland." *Edinburgh Review* 87 (1848): 229–320.

Trollope, Frances. *Domestic Manners of the Americans*. [1832] Edited by Donald Smalley. New York, 1949.

Tryon, Thomas. *The Way to Health, Long Life and Happiness, Or a Discourse of Temperance*. 2nd ed. London, 1691.

[Unsigned.] "Reflections on the State of Ireland in the Nineteenth Century." *Edinburgh Review* 73 (June 1822).

Vasquez de Espinosa, Antonio. *Compendium and Description of the West Indies.* 1628. Translated by Charles Upson Clark. *Smithsonian Miscellaneous Collections.* Vol. 102. Washington, D.C., 1942.

Vidal de la Blache, Paul. *Tableau de la géographie de la France.* Vol. 1 of Ernest Lavisse, *Histoire de la France illustrée depuis les origines jusqu'à la Révolution.* Paris, 1911.

Vincenot, Henri. *La vie quotidienne des paysans bourguignons au temps de Lamartine.* Paris, 1976.

Wakefield, Edward. *An Account of Ireland, Statistical and Political.* 2 vols., London, 1812.

Walton, John K. *Fish and Chips and the British Working Class, 1870–1940.* Leicester, England, 1992.

Weber, Eugen. *A Modern History of Europe.* New York, 1971.

———. *Peasants into Frenchmen: The Modernization of Rural France 1870–1914.* Stanford, CA, 1976.

Westmacott, William. *Historia vegetabilium sacra; Or, a Scripture Herbal.* London, 1695.

Wells, Roger. *Wretched Faces: Famine in Wartime England 1793–1801.* Gloucester, England, and New York, 1988.

Whitman, Walt. *New York Dissected: A Sheaf of Recently Discovered Newpaper Articles by the Author of "Leaves of Grass."* Edited by Emory Holloway and Ralph Adimari. New York, 1936.

Wilde, Sir William. *Irish Popular Superstitions.* [1852] Dublin, 1979.

Wilson, Mary Tolford. "Americans Learn to Grow the Irish Potato," *New England Quarterly* 32, 3 (1959): 333–50.

[Wood, Mrs. Henry.] *Letters from the Irish Highlands of Cunnemarra.* 2d ed. London, 1825.

Woodham-Smith, Cecil. *The Great Hunger.* 2d ed. New York, 1989.

Woods, Robert, and John Woodward, eds. *Urban Disease and Mortality in Nineteenth-Century England.* London and New York, 1984.

Woolley, Hannah. *The Queen-like Closet, Or Rich Cabinet Stored with All Manner of Rare Receipts for Preserving, Candying, and Cooking.* 4th ed. London, 1681.

Works Project Administration. *Told by the Pioneers: Tales of Frontier Life As Told by Those Who Remember the Days of the Territory and Early Statehood of Washington.* 3 vols. Olympia, WA, 1937, 1938.

Young, Arthur. *Arthur Young's Tour in Ireland, 1776–1779.* Edited by Arthur Wollaston Hutton. 2 vols. London, 1892.

———. *Travels in France During the Years 1787, 1788 & 1789.* Edited by Constantia Maxwell. Cambridge, 1950.